Corporate Wrongdoing on Film

Corporate Wrongdoing on Film: The "Public Be Damned" provides a unique and groundbreaking analysis of corporate wrongdoing depictions, identifying, describing, and categorizing harms perpetrated by corporations.

The book provides a history of corporate wrongdoing in film, from the silent film to the present day. Early films are summarized and discussed within the historical, social, and political contexts in which they were released. Examining films produced after 1979, the book classifies them by corporate harms to the environment, workers, consumers, and the economy. The book includes a discussion of well over 100 films, from obscure television movies to Hollywood blockbusters. Finally, the book concludes with a narrative analysis exploring the depiction of the protagonists, antagonists, and victims within the corporate wrongdoing film.

Detailed and accessible, *Corporate Wrongdoing on Film: The "Public Be Damned"* will be of great interest to scholars and students of Criminology and Film and Media Studies.

Kenneth Dowler is Associate Professor in the Department of Criminology at Wilfrid Laurier University, Canada. He enjoys teaching courses on Crime, Deviance, and Sport and has developed and taught several groundbreaking courses at Laurier's Brantford campus, such as Mean Justice, Outlaw Bikers, International Organized Crime, and Gangsters, Goodfellas, and Wiseguys.

Daniel Antonowicz is Associate Professor in the Department of Criminology at Wilfrid Laurier University, Canada. Prior to joining Laurier, he was Assistant Professor in the Department of Criminology at the University of Ottawa. The main focus of his research is Corporate Crime.

Routledge Studies in Crime, Media and Popular Culture

Routledge Studies in Crime, Media and Popular Culture offers the very best in research that seeks to understand crime through the context of culture, cultural processes and media.

The series welcomes monographs and edited volumes from across the globe, and across a variety of disciplines. Books will offer fresh insights on a range of topics, including news reporting of crime; moral panics and trial by media; media and the police; crime in film; crime in fiction; crime in TV; crime and music; 'reality' crime shows; the impact of new media including mobile, Internet and digital technologies, and social networking sites; the ways media portrayals of crime influence government policy and lawmaking; the theoretical, conceptual and methodological underpinnings of cultural criminology.

Books in the series will be essential reading for those researching and studying criminology, media studies, cultural studies and sociology.

Corporate Wrongdoing on Film
The 'Public Be Damned'
Kenneth Dowler and Daniel Antonowicz

Criminologists in the Media
A Study of Newsmaking
Mark A Wood, Imogen Richards and Mary Iliadis

Corporate Wrongdoing on Film
The 'Public Be Damned'

Kenneth Dowler and Daniel Antonowicz

LONDON AND NEW YORK

First published 2022
by Routledge
4 Park Square, Milton Park, Abingdon, Oxon OX14 4RN

and by Routledge
605 Third Avenue, New York, NY 10158

Routledge is an imprint of the Taylor & Francis Group, an informa business

© 2022 Kenneth Dowler and Daniel Antonowicz

The right of Kenneth Dowler and Daniel Antonowicz to be identified as authors of this work has been asserted in accordance with sections 77 and 78 of the Copyright, Designs and Patents Act 1988.

All rights reserved. No part of this book may be reprinted or reproduced or utilised in any form or by any electronic, mechanical, or other means, now known or hereafter invented, including photocopying and recording, or in any information storage or retrieval system, without permission in writing from the publishers.

Trademark notice: Product or corporate names may be trademarks or registered trademarks, and are used only for identification and explanation without intent to infringe.

British Library Cataloguing-in-Publication Data
A catalogue record for this book is available from the British Library

Library of Congress Cataloging-in-Publication Data
Names: Dowler, Kenneth, author. | Antonowicz, Daniel H., author.
Title: Corporate wrongdoing on film : the 'public be damned' / Kenneth Dowler and Daniel Antonowicz.
Description: Abingdon, Oxon ; New York, NY : Routledge, 2022.
| Series: Routledge studies in crime, culture and media | Includes bibliographical references and index.
Identifiers: LCCN 2021055451 (print) | LCCN 2021055452 (ebook) | ISBN 9780367757526 (hardback) | ISBN 9780367757540 (paperback) | ISBN 9781003163855 (ebook)
Subjects: LCSH: Corporations--Corrupt practices. | Business ethics in motion pictures.
Classification: LCC HV6768 .D69 2022 (print) | LCC HV6768 (ebook) | DDC 364.16/8--dc23/eng/20220204
LC record available at https://lccn.loc.gov/2021055451
LC ebook record available at https://lccn.loc.gov/2021055452

ISBN: 978-0-367-75752-6 (hbk)
ISBN: 978-0-367-75754-0 (pbk)
ISBN: 978-1-003-16385-5 (ebk)

DOI: 10.4324/9781003163855

Typeset in Times New Roman
by Deanta Global Publishing Services, Chennai, India

To my wife, Laura, and my children Jennifer, Brayden, and Audrey. Thanks for letting me indulge in one of my favorite pastimes, watching movies. Now you can watch the television!

Contents

1 An Introduction   1

2 History of Corporate Harm on Film, 1930s to 1970s   22

3 Harm to the Environment   59

4 Harm to Workers   83

5 Harm to Consumers   106

6 Harm to the Economy   137

7 The Social Construction of Corporate Harms   171

Index   193

1 An Introduction

> *Everyone in this country is a victim of corporate crime by the time they finish breakfast.*
>
> FBI Special Agent Brian Shepard (Scott Bakula), *The Informant* (2009)

Crime is a national obsession. It dominates the collective consciousness, regularly appears in news cycles, is politicized by legislators, and is a dominant narrative in film and television. Filmmakers cater to the public's insatiable desire by producing thousands of movies that feature crime as a central plotline. The crime genre includes the documentary, gangster, prison, heist, police procedural, vigilante, serial killer, and mystery. That said, the depiction of corporate wrongdoing or criminality is a relatively rare occurrence in popular Hollywood features. The absence is curious, as large publicly traded corporations have a long and extensive history of harm. The corporation's role in society is particularly powerful, as these global entities exert tremendous influence over social, economic, and political life. Corporate executives, shareholders, and managers are held in the highest regard and embody the crème de la crème of our society. Conversely, those who engage in conventional "crime" fill our prisons and occupy the most marginalized positions within society. Although there is a level of absurdity in minimizing the harm that corporate wrongdoing has on society, one can assume that the film industry, which by no coincidence is itself a corporation, plays a role in decreasing corporate culpability by ignoring or downplaying corporate harms. However, corporate wrongdoing is not entirely absent in the history of film. From the silent era to the present day, numerous movies depict the harms that corporations or industry inflict on society. As such, the purpose of this book is to provide an exhaustive and extensive analysis of films that depict corporate wrongdoing while also considering the broader social, political, and historical contexts.

What Is Corporate Wrongdoing?

The concept of corporate wrongdoing can be traced to the larger notion of white-collar crime. The term "white-collar crime" was first introduced in 1939 by

Sociologist Edwin Sutherland during his presidential address to the American Sociological Association. In his landmark speech, Sutherland insisted that scholars pay attention to crimes committed by the higher classes. Sutherland argued that while "crime in the streets" captured the newspaper headlines, "crime in the suites" continued unnoticed and unpunished. He noted that white-collar crime was far more costly than street crime, with most cases handled as civil or administrative violations rather than sanctioned under criminal law. Nevertheless, the study of corporate crime has European roots, most notably Dutch Criminologist Willem Bonger, who argued that capitalism had a damaging influence on society and can create criminal behavior and allow it to flourish (Braithwaite, 1985; Hebberecht, 2015). In his *Criminality and Economic Conditions* (1916), Bonger theorized that the bourgeoisie class engage in greedy, corrupt and unethical business practices. Also predating Sutherland's presidential address, in 1907, sociologist E.A. Ross developed the term "the criminaloid," which referred to individuals that prospered from criminal activities through their occupation but were not publicly labeled as criminals. The dismal conditions imposed on the working class through exploitative capitalism allow criminal attitudes and behaviors to ferment. At the same time, parallel criminal attitudes thrive among the criminaloid including corrupt corporate executives, bankers, judges, and labor leaders engaged in such schemes as bribery and kickbacks. The primary element of the criminaloid was their inclination to victimize an anonymous public and make financial restitution when caught (Friedrichs, 2009). Ross further argued that the criminaloid "counterfeits the good citizen" by engaging in unethical behavior in the civic and commercial spheres while demonstrating high virtues in family and religious matters. Simply stated, the criminaloid is not anti-social but enjoys a double standard of morality (Geis, 2015:10).

Aside from scholarly writing, the early part of the century also featured several reform-minded journalists and novelists, labeled as muckrakers. These muckrakers exposed occupational safety abuses, disregard for consumer health, corporate bribery, and many other wrongdoings of big business. Some of the most prominent included Ray Stannard Baker's *The Right to Work* (1903), which exposed the coal mining industry; Ida Tarbell's *The History of Standard Oil* (1904), which uncovered corruption within the oil industry; Samuel Hopkins Adams' *The Great American Fraud* (1905), which examined the fraudulent claims of patent medicines; John Spargo's *The Bigger Cry of Children*, an uncovering of child labor practices; and Upton Sinclair's *The Jungle* (1906), a novel that exposed the harsh conditions and exploited lives of immigrants in the meatpacking industry. The novel revealed the unsanitary practices that plagued the meatpacking industry, helping usher in reforms such as the Meat Inspection Act and the Pure Food and Drug Act of 1906. The precursor to investigative journalism, the muckraker's work led to a massive public outcry, leading to governmental intervention and policy changes. For example, the presidency of Woodrow Wilson, from 1913 to 1917, was highlighted with a series of progressive legislation and reform-minded bills, including the creation of child labor laws, governmental agencies tasked with watchdog functions, and electoral reforms (Filler, 1993).

However, criminologists' focus was primarily on the lower classes, not the crimes of big business and the elites within society. Early criminologists attempted to explain why the poor were seemingly engaged in more criminal activity than the rest of society. The assumption was that poverty caused crime, which effectually neglected the pervasive and damaging nature of the crimes of the powerful. That changed when Edwin Sutherland gave his Presidential Address to the American Sociological Association in 1939. The talk entitled "The White-Collar Criminal" criticized traditional theories that attributed poverty, broken homes, mental illness, and immigrant status to criminal behavior. Ten years later, Sutherland wrote *White Collar Crime* (1949), a shocking account of the crimes perpetrated by the 70 largest private companies and 15 utility corporations in the United States. Of note, the publisher, Dryden, did not allow the names of the companies to be used for fear of libel suits. It took another 34 years before the unabridged version was fully published. Despite the title, the book focused almost exclusively on corporate crime, including false advertising, patent abuse, wartime trade violations, price-fixing, fraud, or intended manufacturing and sale of faulty goods. Sutherland became the so-called founding father of white-collar and corporate crime scholarship, defining white-collar crime as "a crime committed by a person of respectability and high social status in the course of his (sic) occupation" (Sutherland, 1983:7). The definition itself is problematic as the terms are vague and atheoretical in nature. That said, Sutherland's call for action influenced future scholars to study crimes of the powerful, reimagining the study of criminology and white-collar crime. For instance, Geis and Goff (1983: p. ix) claim that Sutherland "altered the study of crime throughout the world in fundamental ways by focusing attention upon a form of lawbreaking that had previously been ignored by criminological scholars."

In spite of Sutherland's call for action, the study of crimes of the powerful was limited, with only a handful of scholars engaged in theoretical discussions of corporate wrongdoing. Heavily influenced by Sutherland, Marshall Clinard was notable in shaping the study of white-collar crime. Clinard (1952) applied differential association theory to the corporate environment, revealing it as a major cause of white-collar crime. In 1980, Clinard and Peter Yeager published *Corporate Crime,* which replicated Sutherland's *White Collar Crime* by examining the wrongdoings of 477 of the largest publicly owned manufacturing corporations in the United States during 1975 and 1976. They found that 60 percent of the companies had at least one action instigated, with an average of 2.7 violations. Most disturbing, 8 percent of the corporations accounted for 52 percent of all the infractions with an average of 23.5 violations (Clinard & Yeager, 1980, p. 116). That said, the pair recognized that many illegal acts were not detected by the methods they used. Aside from the shocking numbers, the enduring legacy of their work was their examination of the "culture of the corporation," in which they considered how corporate organizations facilitated lawlessness and rationalized immoral or unethical behavior (Clinard & Yeager, 1980:58). At the same time, John Braithwaite researched the unethical and criminal behaviors of the pharmaceutical and coal mining industries (Braithwaite, 1984, 1985). He argued that reintegrative shaming could be applied to white-collar criminality, claiming that illegal activities of corporate actors involve little shaming, which allows the criminal culture to persist without sanctions. Braithwaite further suggested that attempts to shame or control corporate wrongdoing have unforeseen consequences of strengthening business ethos rather than lessening.

Some criminologists contend that the study of corporate crime is a branch or sub-type of white-collar crime. These criminologists further assert that white-collar crime should be categorized into two distinct types: (1) occupational crime, which is an illegal activity that is committed during a legitimate occupation for the sole benefit of the transgressor, and (2) corporate crime, in which the goal is to financially benefit the company or its shareholders, not to enrich the transgressor personally. For instance, John Braithwaite defines corporate crime as "the conduct of corporation or employees acting on behalf of a corporation, which is prescribed and punishable by law." However, the term "corporate crime" has been criticized as not an accurate account of corporate behavior. The term refers to a narrow set of activities that violate criminal law. In reality, corporations are investigated by regulatory agencies and rarely face criminal sanctions. Moreover, corporations that engage in illegal activities are more likely to violate administrative or civil law, which is resolved through consent decrees, settlements, judgment against the firm, and fines (Mokhiber, 1988). As such, the term "corporate wrongdoing" offers a broader and more profound interpretation of the range of harms that corporations inflict on society. The terminology is especially relevant in identifying corporate harms in film, as many of the actions of corporations are not technically criminal or even illegal, but certainly morally and ethically dubious.

The Costs of Corporate Wrongdoing

It is well established that the effects of corporate wrongdoing are more harmful than street crime, with costs that injure the public economically, physically, socially, and environmentally. According to consumer advocate Ralph Nader (2000), "business wrongdoing inflicts far more preventable violence and economic damage on society than all street crimes combined." Corporations neglect workplace safety, place toxic chemicals into our environment, and knowingly sell unsafe goods to unsuspecting consumers – actions that injure, maim, sicken, and kill thousands of people. In terms of death, injury, and dollars lost, corporate wrongdoing dwarfs street crime. Although difficult to quantify, it is estimated that corporate crime can cost $200 billion per year, while burglary and robbery are estimated at just $3.8 billion (Clinard et al., 2017). For example, the most famous case involved the energy giant Enron, which engaged in accounting and corporate fraud, costing shareholders $74 billion and causing thousands of employees to lose their jobs and pension plans.

Annually, approximately 24,000 Americans are murdered, continually propelling the violent crime narrative in the mainstream media. Violent crime invokes a tremendous amount of fear and concern among many Americans. However, corporate wrongdoing is even more dangerous. In 2019, 5,333 workers perished on the job from traumatic injuries, while estimates suggest that 95,000 die from occupational diseases such as black lung and asbestos-related illnesses (AFL-CIO, 2021). There are also tens of thousands of Americans who die because of contaminated foods, hazardous consumer products, and hospital malpractice. This "silent epidemic" is normalized as part of American society, as accidental and unavoidable "bad luck," but most cases result from criminal recklessness. They are preventable and unnecessary deaths that could be avoided with humane, enforceable, and strict government intervention and regulation.

Despite the staggering and long-lasting impacts of corporate wrongdoing, perpetrators are rarely held accountable, much less punished. Corporate wrongdoing is most often dealt with by regulatory bodies or civil/administrative law, with consequences that include fines and regulatory oversight. Unfortunately, it is business as usual for corporations, as corporations and their shareholders enjoy substantial profits while experiencing little to no shame for their wrongdoing. For example, the world's largest health care company, Johnson & Johnson, marketed and sold several products that have had adverse effects on consumers. The seemingly "respected" company has been embroiled in several lawsuits, including one in which 24,000 women sued after suffering severe complications following a vaginal mesh implant procedure. In July 2017, 22 women and their families were awarded $4.7 billion in damages after finding that asbestos in Johnson & Johnson talcum powder caused their ovarian cancer. Moreover, in 1980, the Ford Motor Company was criminally charged after three teenage girls who perished after their Ford Pinto was rear-ended in northern Indiana. It was alleged that Ford knew that the Pinto was a defective product, knowingly covering up that the gas tank would explode when rear-ended, causing the unnecessary deaths of consumers. As per the corporate playbook, Ford's skilled defense lawyers manipulated the judge, jury, and evidence, securing a not-guilty verdict (Cullen et al., 2014). Within this environment, corporate crime thrives, as Ralph Nader (2013) wrote:

> Corporate crime wave has long swept our nation, draining people's hard-earned savings and severely harming the health and safety of millions more. The pin-stripe-suit wearing perpetrators of this spree are, far more often than not, getting away scot-free. Ironically, it's many of the same politicians who say they are "tough on crime" that are collecting millions of dollars in campaign money from the biggest crooks in America.

The Distortion of Reality

Influential sociologist C. Wright Mills (1963) once wrote that "corporate crime creates higher immorality" within society. Corporate wrongdoing reveals a disregard for humanity, deeply embedded in bourgeois culture and attitudes. This indifference toward humanity is cultivated by business interests, in which crimes of the powerful are most often dealt with by regulatory bodies rather than criminal courts. In this way, it is not seen as a "real" crime, even though the social, financial, and health costs are enormous. Moreover, corporate wrongdoing is associated with the higher classes of society, with perpetrators that are wealthy, powerful, respected, and even celebrated or admired. As such, many individual actors rationalize or justify their illegal behavior and view their actions as a normal part of doing business in corporate America. In this respect, the image of the corporate criminal is in stark contrast to the "typical" street criminal. The corporate criminal operates within the milieu of respectable society and is perceived as successful purveyors of the American Dream. Indeed, these individuals do not believe their activities are criminal, nor do they believe they are criminals. This belief is the ultimate paradox, as corporate crime wreaks far more damage on society than all street crime combined.

In 1979, philosopher Jeffrey Reiman authored his influential book *The Rich Get Richer and the Poor Get Prison*. Not only did the book reveal the inequities of the Criminal Justice System, but Reiman exposed corporate harms in a powerfully written chapter entitled "A Crime by Any Other Name." In this chapter, Reiman revealed how corporate practices endanger the health of workers and the public. He used a "carnival mirror" analogy to argue that crimes of corporations are distorted and not treated as "real" crimes, despite the harms being much greater than street crime. In a similar vein, British Criminologist Stephen Box published *Power, Crime and Mystification* in 1983. The book was a condemnation of the justice system, in which crimes of the powerful (the state and corporations) are ignored. In contrast, the crimes of the powerless are exaggerated and publicized. Box (1983: 16) argued that "corporate crime is rendered invisible by its complex and sophisticated planning and execution, non-existent or weak law enforcement and prosecution, and by lenient legal and social sanctions which fail to reaffirm or reinforce collective sentiments on moral boundaries."

Likewise, the mainstream media contributes to the invisibility of corporate wrongdoing by ignoring, minimizing, and even rationalizing the misdeeds of corporations. Meanwhile, film studios churn out movies that predominately depict street crime and crimes of violence, reinforcing stereotypical images of criminality that suggest either a dangerous underclass or mentally deranged perpetrators, ala Hannibal Lector. This is not surprising as the film industry is a capitalistic enterprise with corporate sensibilities and directives. Film executives are a homogenous group that occupies the highest strata of society, with wealth, power, and prestige. Hollywood producers and writers construct narratives with specific goals: to gain an audience and to generate revenue. This business model impedes the production of socially relevant films, as the goal is profit-maximization, not social justice or betterment. However, there are outliers, films pushing the boundaries and breaking free from standard Hollywood tropes and clichés. Some filmmakers challenge restrictive stereotypes and normative assumptions that are embedded within popular culture.

The Importance of Film

Film can be a powerful tool that continuously alters the way humans experience and perceive the world around them. Some scholars argue that popular cultural narratives can influence public attitudes and shift governmental policy. In particular, documentary films have often called attention to social issues and problems. Notable film critic and theorist Bill Nichols (2017) argues that documentary film enhances our aesthetic awareness and social consciousness. Documentaries can incite conversations around important topics and act as a catalyst for social change by engaging viewers in critical and emotional ways to tell the film's story. Documentaries have explored social issues such as gun control, wrongful convictions, animal rights, pollution, genocide, and racism. For instance, Frederick Wiseman's *Titicut Follies* (1967) depicted the abuse and maltreatment of patients at Massachusetts's Bridgewater State hospital for the criminally insane. Although banned between 1967 and 1991, the film spurred the closure and reform of several psychiatric hospitals. Errol Morris's *The Thin Blue Line* (1988) helped exonerate Randal Dale Adams, who was accused of murdering a police officer. Michael Moore's *Bowling for Columbine* (2002) expose of gun violence resulted in K-Mart prohibiting the sale of bullets in their stores. *An Inconvenient Truth* (2009) helped spur discussion of global warming, while *Blackfish* (2013) led to SeaWorld ending its orca breeding program and modifying all orca performances so that whales would be treated more ethically. Finally, *The Cove* (2009) is credited with a vast reduction in the hunting of dolphins. Furthermore, several documentaries vividly depict corporate wrongdoing. Directed by Barbara Kopple, *Harlan County, USA* (1976) and *American Dream* (1990) highlighted the exploitation of workers in the coal mining and meatpacking industry, respectively. Directed by Josh Fox, *Gasland* (2010) helped mobilize the anti-fracking movement, with film critics comparing it to Rachel Carson's book *Silent Spring*. Charles Ferguson's *Inside Job* (2010) won an Oscar for depicting the 2008 global financial meltdown that plunged the United States into a recession, causing millions of Americans to lose their jobs, homes, and retirement savings.

Despite the informative nature of the documentary, cynics argue that documentaries have little impact on social issues and policy. Social justice documentaries mobilize like-minded audience members to support a cause with limited appeal to much larger audiences. Generally, most documentaries have smaller audiences and revenues than scripted films and television series. Reality television shows, primarily silly and mindless, garner larger audience shares than socially relevant documentaries. The Kardashians are household names, while *The Apprentice* helped propel Donald Trump to the White House, transforming a failing real estate mogul into a mythical business figure that appealed to Americans' notion of the American Dream (Keefe, 2019). The public is more aware of the "Tiger King" than Monsanto's nefarious and harmful activities. In this way, the scripted film may have increased power to marshal change by exposing social causes or issues to much wider audiences. History has shown that film is a powerful tool for propaganda, which can sway public opinion and values. The scripted film can be protest cinema, highlighting social injustices such as racism, police brutality, homophobia, sexism, and corporate wrongdoing. Although the overwhelming majority of films provide escapist entertainment – a diversion from everyday problems – some noteworthy films educate

8 An Introduction

audiences about social ills while also advocating for social reform. In terms of corporate or industry wrongdoing, the film as a mode of reform had a powerful beginning during the silent film era.

The Beginnings: The Silent Film Era (1894–1929)

Like today, early films relied heavily on conventions. Film producers employed stock characters, plots, and settings drawn from vaudeville; popular melodrama; Wild West shows; comic strips; and other types of late-19th-century popular entertainment. The narratives were employed to amuse and entertain audiences, who marveled at this new form of recreation by flocking to movie houses. Producing movies became big business, with 20 Hollywood studios and numerous smaller studios competing for the seemingly insatiable demand for films. Major studios released an estimated 10,000 features from 1895 to 1929. Unfortunately, many of these films are unavailable as early motion pictures were released on nitrate film, which is dangerously inflammable and susceptible to decay. It is estimated that only 14 percent of these films remain today (Pierce, 2013). As such, it is difficult to categorize or develop film genres and certainly impossible to identify all films with themes of corporate wrongdoing. That said, several silent films dealt with prevailing social issues of the day. Film historians argue that silent film was born in the age of reform. The subject matter of films reflected the major social and moral issues of the Progressive era, including birth control, child labor, divorce, immigration, political corruption, prisons, prostitution, women's suffrage, race, and poverty (Brownlow, 1990). The mood conveyed in these films varied considerably. Some were realistic and straightforward, while others involved melodrama, sentimentality, and even humor.

Notably, many films in the era were based in working-class settings. This was not surprising, as the lower classes flocked to movie houses to enjoy the moving pictures. The upper class would deride the medium as a "poor man's theater." However, social critique of industry was limited, with very few films that challenged the capitalist ethos. Films that featured business wrongdoing blamed the grafting politician or a selfish mill owner. In even more films, the superintendents or foremen were the real villains, as noble owners were unaware of the horrendous work conditions. *The Blacklist* (1916) featured the superintendents as the villains, the owner unaware of the deplorable conditions. The owner, Warren Harcourt is alerted to the poor working conditions by Vera Maroff. Vera is a local schoolteacher and daughter of a miner and Russian anarchist. The workers' strike, and against the specific orders of Harcourt, several workers are killed by armed guards. In a melodramatic twist, Vera is tasked with killing Warren, but she is torn, as the pair have fallen in love. In a failed assassination attempt, Vera only superficially wounds Harcourt. In a happy ending, the benevolent president accedes to the workers' demands and co-runs the mine with the help of his new love, Vera. The film was described as a socialistic drama, but Upton Sinclair was not impressed, critiquing the premise that an owner would help workers. Sinclair wrote,

An Introduction 9

> if he [owner] made terms with the union which didn't please the coal miner's association, he would be blacklisted and have his credit cut off. Then he would find he couldn't get coal cars, and before he knew it, he would be out of business.
>
> (as cited in Brownlow, 1990: 445)

Sinclair was disillusioned with the film industry, believing that his work was being exploited to appease "feeble-minded audiences," which required happy endings. Sinclair had also been swindled by several Hollywood producers, who used his name to sell tickets to productions with nothing to do with his work. For example, *The Moneychangers* (1920) was supposedly based on Sinclair's book of the same title published in 1908. In the book, Sinclair detailed corruption in Wall Street that led to the Panic of 1907, which almost caused the collapse of the banking industry. Notable financier J.P. Morgan was hailed as a hero for using his own money and convincing other wealthy Americans to step in to save several banks and brokerage firms. However, Sinclair and other progressives alleged that it was a ploy that enabled Morgan to become even richer, as he could buy underpriced assets while monopolizing the nation's financial investments. However, the film version inexplicably featured a plot involving drug traffic in Chinatown. In a particularly damning indictment of the medium, Sinclair argued that

> the moving pictures furnish the principal intellectual food of the workers at the present time and the supplying of this food is entirely in the hands of the capitalist class, and the food supplied is poisoned ... the whole industry is so completely controlled by big business that there is practically no chance of breaking in with a true idea.
>
> (as cited in Brownlow, 1990: 435)

That said, there were some exceptions. The decidedly socialist film *Why?* (1913) explored the harsh consequences of capitalism, including child labor, gambling, fatal train accidents, animal cruelty, and poor working conditions. The plot featured a wealthy hero dreaming that he travels the world, where he experiences the hardship and injustice of labor. The film showed horrible working conditions, low pay, and the capitalist class enjoying the benefits of laborers' suffering. In a compelling scene, a child laborer is shot and transformed into a gold bag, illustrating that it is impossible to kill capital. In yet another segment, the protagonist is invited to an opulent feast, but the gorging is disrupted by working men, who demand a seat at the table. The industrialists call for military intervention, and the workers are shot. Similarly, *Money* (1914) also features a scene in which starving workers storm a banquet, an allegory for the rich oppressing the poor, feasting on the fruits of their labor. Even Sinclair himself had some success with film when his classic expose of the meatpacking industry was adapted to film, with the debut of *The Jungle* (1914). Set in the fictional Packingtown, the film was the most anti-capitalist film of the period and began with a panoramic view of the Chicago stockyards. The protagonist is

Jurgis Radkus, a newly arrived Lithuanian immigrant who works in the stockyards, marries, buys a house, and becomes debt-ridden. The villain, stockyard owner John Durham, mercilessly orders a considerable reduction in wages for the workers, which leads to a strike. The melodramatic story features an abundance of personal tragedies, including eviction, industrial poisoning, rape, sexual exploitation, and death. Jurgis seeks revenge for the injustice served on his family and kills a villainous foreman by throwing him into a cattle pen. Jurgis is imprisoned and, upon release, attends a Socialist party rally and dedicates his life to the establishment of a "cooperative commonwealth." The film was screened at socialist meetings serving as a rallying cry for socialism – even Sinclair himself appeared in the prologue.

By highlighting inequality, the socialistic film depicted the struggle of the poor against the rich. Indirectly, these films established a powerful critique of inequities embedded within the capitalist system (Jacobs, 2002; Robinson, 1997). Notable film historian Kevin Brownlow (1990) claimed that the silent screen offered vivid glimpses of urban tenements and ethnic ghettos, gangsters, loan sharks, drug addicts, and panderers. Some of the most poignant depictions of poverty occurred in the silent film era. Charlie Chaplin's Tramp became an iconic figure in the representation of poverty. Although based on slapstick humor, the Tramp films provided social commentary about the dismal reality of poverty and the ills of capitalism. While Chaplin films were lighthearted, other silent films were bleaker, with heart-wrenching depictions of the consequences of poverty, child labor, and poor working conditions.

Poverty

Poverty afflicted approximately 15–20 million people during the era, with some estimates suggesting that almost a quarter of the population experienced poverty. As such, depictions of poverty were widespread in the silent film era, especially from 1911 to 1915, when the issue was a national concern (Brownlow, 1990). These films attempted to depict the plight of the poor in slum settings – with portrayals of hunger, tuberculosis, loansharking, malevolent landlords, and inequities within the justice system. Directed by Cecil B. DeMille, *Kindling* (1915) graphically depicts a filthy slum with disturbing scenes of a malnourished baby dying surrounded by flies. There was also a poignant scene in which children fight over scraps of food from the garbage. After 1915, films featuring poverty became rarer, as the compassion of the Reform era was supplanted with hatred of the "Huns." When the Great War ended, the evils of Bolshevism became popular, launching the so-called red scare era. Paralleling 1950s McCarthyism, the "Red Scare" impeded the production of any film that had a hint of socialist sentiment, social justice doctrine, or depiction of the evils of capitalism. For instance, there were nearly a dozen red scare films produced from 1919 to 1920. Film producers had to consult David Niles, the head of the motion picture section of the US Department of Labor. Movies that featured socialism or labor unrest were summarily cancelled under threats of censorship, a clear antecedent to the Production

Code. Moreover, the economy in the 1920s was booming, and going to the theater became a more luxurious experience, with orchestras and elegant surroundings, hardly the setting for a film about the bleakness of poverty.

Child Labor

At the turn of the 20th century, almost 2 million child laborers were in the United States. Although most states had enacted legislation that provided some regulation, the laws did not have enough power to be effectively enforced. The industrialists argued that ending child labor was a plot derived by Bolshevists, Communists, and Socialists to destroy the capitalist spirit. The issue was further compounded as many parents relied on their children's wages (Brownlow, 1990). However, several films explored industry exploitation of child labor. Produced in conjunction with the National Child Labor Committee, *Children Who Labor* (1912) opened with the title "The appeal of the child laborers," with a visual of Uncle Sam hovering over lines of children entering a factory. The word "GREED" ominously appeared in the sky. The film's plot is simple: a greedy and ruthless owner has an epiphany and stops employing children. Similarly, *The Cry of Children* (1912) featured the death of a young girl, forced to work in a mill after her mother became ill. *The Cry of Children* was successfully used as political propaganda during the 1912 presidential election. The democratic candidate Woodrow Wilson seized on the message of the film by claiming that the film was "the boldest, most timely, and most effective appeal for stamping out the cruelest of all social abuses" (as cited in Brownlow, 1990:429). *The Blood of Children* (1915) featured an attempt by two mill owners to bribe a Senator to vote against a child labor bill. Through a series of flashbacks, the Senator tells the pair about his days as a factory employee and later mill owner. The film educated audiences about the number of men, women, and children seriously injured or who had died in the workplace. The mill owners are convinced and decide to fund the passage of the legislation. Similarly, *The Woman that God Sent* (1920) depicted the exploits of a young woman and a Senator attempting to enact a law forbidding child labor in factories.

Poor Working Conditions

Several films explored the plight of adult workers, including lack of safety measures, low or unfair wages, and poor working/living conditions. Although these critical issues were highlighted, the films did not squarely blame the owners. The lack of safety measures in factories and sweatshops killed an estimated 15,000 people, while over half a million were seriously injured or disabled per year (Brownlow, 1990). The issue was highlighted after the devastating fire at the Triangle Shirtwaist Company in New York on March 25, 1911. Forever known as the Triangle Fire, 146 perished, with some jumping to their death out the windows. The factory was overcrowded, poorly ventilated, and the floor was littered with combustible material. Worse yet, the owner bolted the door to the stairway to prevent the employees from using restrooms and interrupting their work. Despite the tragic events, the building owners were acquitted after "proving" that the deaths of the garment workers were the result of worker carelessness. The Triangle Fire loosely inspired several films. Although set in a mill rather than a garment factor, *The Crime of Carelessness* (1912) equally placed the burden of a tragic fire on a worker and the mill owner. After being reprimanded for smoking, Tom, the protagonist, retreats to light up a cigarette in the cellar. He recklessly throws the match on some garbage, and the mill is set ablaze. Panic ensues, and Tom's fiancé, Hilda, is trapped inside due to a locked door. Tom races through the fire to rescue Hilda, who survives but is permanently disabled. Tom is fired and is unable to find work. Becoming destitute, Tom lives with guilt and considers suicide. Hilda visits the mill owner and accuses him of wrongdoing, shouting, "It's your fault I have crutches." The bewildered mill owner realizes his negligence, writes a letter to Tom, admits his culpability, and offers Tom a job. The acclaimed *The Locked Door* (1914) was produced in collaboration with the New York Fire Department. The film juxtaposed the safety measures of two companies that worked in the same building. The Atlas Waist Syndicate Loft had women working at sewing machines closely together, scraps of material covering the aisles, a chain-smoking foreman, no fire extinguishers, and locked doors. Conversely, one flight up, the Century Suit Company took safety precautions very seriously, with containers for scrap material, fire extinguishers, and sprinkler pipes. The film ends with an Atlas foreman carelessly discarding a cigarette that kills a worker, the foreman, and the Atlas owner. As a result of proper safety measures, the Century Suit Company is spared the devasting effects of the fire. Finally, *The Children of Eve* (1915) and *The High Road* (1915) climaxed with deadly fires, panic, and locked doors. Regrettably, these films overlooked the culpability of factory and mill owners, many of which stubbornly ignored union demands for improved safety conditions.

The depiction of hazardous working conditions in factories was also the subject of several silent films. In *Dust* (1916), a muckraking author, Frank Kenyon, attempts to expose the deplorable conditions in a factory owned by John D. Moore, the father of his fiancé, Marion. After the tragic death of a young girl, Frank makes an impromptu speech at a charitable event that Marion had organized. The speech propels him into the state legislature, advocating for safety reform in factories. Marion breaks their engagement, but her father ironically dies after perishing in a factory fire. As a result, Marion now understands the necessity for reform, renews her engagement to Frank, and vows to fight against dangerous working conditions in factories. Similarly, *Fires of Youth* (1917) was a redemptive story about industrial capitalist Peter Pemberton. A steel magnate, Pemberton, was dubbed "Iron Heart" because of his relentless pursuit of wealth at the expense of his workers. In his waning years, he realizes that he has squandered his life in the pursuit of profit and returns to his hometown to recapture his youth. Pemberton befriends Billy and Rose, the son and daughter of a mill worker. Taking the alias Peter Brown, he begins to work in the mill, where he learns first-hand of the unsafe conditions of the factory and the discontent of the workers. In an intense moment, an explosion injures Billy, who has replaced Peter in the mill. The text reads, "if he dies, it's Pemberton who has killed him—with proper safety equipment, this couldn't have happened." Several workers decide that Pemberton must die for his transgressions. The workers draw straws to determine who will commit the murder, with Brown (aka Pemberton) unluckily winning the task. Pemberton decides to go to the woods to commit suicide but is stopped by Rose. Peter admits that he is Pemberton and is urged by Rose to bring happiness to the workers. In the end, Pemberton redeems himself after correcting the deplorable conditions of the mill.

Many films attributed the poor working conditions to corrupt supervisors or absentee owners, who are unaware of the horrendous conditions. There was little to no critique of industry or the capitalist system's responsibility in treating workers. An *American in the Making* (1913) is the quintessential film highlighting the lack of corporate responsibility. The film was produced under the direction of the United States Steel Corporation and its Committee of Safety. It follows a Hungarian peasant who emigrates to the United States to achieve the American dream. The character becomes a skilled trade worker, marries, and has a family. The corporation is seen as benevolent and caring, willing to help employees who are ambitious and competent. The overriding narrative – from an industry perspective – is that workers' incompetence caused accidents. Similarly, *The Workman's Lesson* (1912) produced by the National Association of Manufacturers showed an Italian immigrant carelessly leaving a safety device open, causing him to be injured.

Monopolization, Price Fixing, and Unsafe Products

A handful of films mirrored the muckraking journalists of the day with fictional depictions of business wrongdoing. For example, *A Corner in Wheat* (1909) was loosely based on the work of author Frank Norris. Before his death, Norris wrote on an uncompleted trilogy – *The Epic of the Wheat* – about the production, distribution, and consumption of wheat. The central theme was the danger of monopolization in the American economy, with the notion that monopolies were simultaneously creating and destroying the underclass. With the help of screenwriter Frank Woods, famed director D.W. Griffith attempted to merge and condense Norris's work into a feature film. *A Corner in Whea*t featured a greedy tycoon, Frank Powell, who attempts to corner the world market on wheat, destroying the lives of people who can no longer afford to buy bread. The film interweaves images of the poor in bread lines with the lavish and wealthy lifestyle of the "Wheat King." The film was an anti-monopoly social commentary, but it had difficulty explaining the novels' financial intricacies. Griffith reduced society's problems to heroes and villains, a standard trope used in Hollywood films. Technological advancements allowed for a remake, with director Maurice Tourneur's *The Pit* (1915) depicting a full-size replica of the Chicago Board of Trade. At the same time, *The Corner* (1915) was a reworking of the film, with a millionaire's attempt to corner the food supply – the monopoly results in the protagonist losing his job and his life savings. The protagonist steals a loaf of bread to feed his starving children – is caught and is sent to a workhouse. His wife is forced to prostitute herself to feed her children. When released, the protagonist seeks revenge by tying up the millionaire in a warehouse surrounded by food. Ironically, the food baron starves to death.

Several films mirrored the concern over the high cost of food. *The Merchant Mayor* (1912) featured a crusading mayor who was so enraged by the high prices of food that he confronted the city's merchants by buying potatoes, poultry, and other food products and selling them at cost. The greedy merchants were now forced to sell their outrageously priced goods at a fair price, alleviating the pressure on the poor in the city. After the United States entered the Great War, food prices escalated, leading to food riots in poorer districts in the big cities. Several films accused speculators of driving up food prices and advocated for state control to end profiteering by middlemen. *The Public Be Damned* (1917) squarely blamed food barons bilking the public of millions of dollars every day. The story featured the struggle of a farmer's compassionate, socially aware wife against the Food Trust, which was buying the farmer's produce at an absurdly small price and selling it at an exorbitant rate to consumers, causing the poor to starve. The film received positive reviews, with Variety describing it as

> showing the machinations of trust, their methods of stifling competition, their control of legislation, and the ultimate winning over of the food baron through his love for a woman [farmer's wife] and his realization of the iniquitous methods of doing business.
>
> (as cited by Brownlow, 1990: 289)

Similarly, *The Food Gamblers* (1917) depicted widespread starvation in the tenements because of food speculation. The protagonist, a female reporter, exposes a food baron who is profiting from price gouging. In a melodramatic twist, the food baron falls in love with the reporter and dedicates himself to reforming and dismantling the corporation he controls.

Like the gouging of food prices, tuberculosis was also a national concern. The so-called "White plague" swept through the tenements killing thousands of people each year. The public health crisis was brought to the moving pictures to educate audiences about prevention and cures. Several films highlighted the predominance of fake cures and unsafe medicine. For example, *The Price of Human Lives* (1913) and *The Toll of Mammon* (1914) were stinging indictments of "quack" patent medicines. *The White Terror* (1915) attacked patent medicine merchants who were peddling unsafe medicine. The film also contained powerful critiques on child labor, inadequate housing and factory conditions, corrupt politicians, and the overindulgences of the idle rich. The plot features a romance between a wealthy young man and the daughter of a patent medicine manufacturer. The young man buys a newspaper company to expose the poor conditions within the magnate's factory and the lethality of the medicine, which contained opium and arsenic. The daughter contracts tuberculosis but is spared from her father's medicine after a doctor intervenes. The father is relieved and becomes a philanthropist.

In an eerily similar storyline, *The Clarion* (1916) also features a wealthy young man who buys a newspaper company and exposes his father's patent medicine business as fraudulent and unsafe. Absent the tuberculosis angle, *For His Son* (1912) was an extremely rare depiction of unsafe consumer products and false advertising. The film featured a doctor who developed a unique soft drink called Dopokoke, laced with cocaine. The soda is advertised as relief "for that tired feeling." The doctor's primary reason for inventing the drink is to provide financial security for his son, but his son becomes seriously addicted to the product. The film was loosely based on accusations that the Coca-Cola Company and other soft drink manufacturers laced their soda with addictive substances.

The Struggle of Labor in Silent Film

The struggle between capital and labor was exemplified with depictions of the strike. In many industries, the workers were in a state of feudal serfdom, forced to pay high rents to live in poorly constructed shelters provided by the company and buy supplies from the company stores at exorbitantly high prices. The strike could be a messy affair, with big businesses hiring strike-breakers to "bust heads" to prematurely end any talk of better working conditions and pay. Railroad baron Jay Gould once snidely commented, "I can hire one half of the working class to kill the other half" (Lens, 1973: 6). Big business also had the support of politicians, who would call in the police or the National Guard to quell any labor disturbances. The National Guard became a quasi-private army for industrialists' control over the workers.

For the most part, there was little radical flavor or realism in films that featured strikes. In The *Power of Labor* (1908) a brutal mill supervisor cuts wages to make extra cash after losing money in the stock market. A worker leads a revolt but is kidnapped and thrown into a furnace. The absentee owner returns to the steel mill and is made aware of the manager's misdeeds by the worker who somehow managed to survive. Incredulously, the worker is the owner's son. A fight ensues, and the protagonist gets revenge by throwing the crooked manager into a furnace. Even more incredulous, *Out of Darkness* (1915) features a woman with amnesia forced to work for 39 cents a day at a canning factory. The conditions are bad, forcing a strike, which results in the burning down of the building. The chaos causes the woman to regain her memory, and it is revealed that she is the absentee owner of the factory. In the end, she rebuilds the factory and is committed to following the laws of sanitation and humanity.

These films avoided controversy, as poor factory or mill conditions resulted from corrupt managers, not the systemic problems with the industry. This is not surprising, as the film industry and manufacturing industry feared the labor movement. Indeed, some films were blatantly anti-labor. Not to be confused with the 1970 version, *The Molly Maguires* (1908) told a very distorted version of the Irish American coal miners in Pennsylvania. In the film, the Maguires are seen killing innocent bosses, provoking strikes, and murdering foreign miners. The existence of the Molly Maguires remains the source of some controversy, as some historians claim that the stories were fabricated by Alan Pinkerton and his spy James McParlan, to suppress coal workers from unionizing. Nonetheless, some 20 men were convicted of murder and hanged in 1877 and 1878.

Film producers walked a thin line, as much of their audience was working class, so the overall depiction of workers was favorable. The anarchists or Bolsheviks were the villains, agitating industrious, noble, yet naive workers to strike. *Men of Steel* (1926) provides a classic example of the villainy of labor activists in film. The protagonist, Jan Bokak, is a fugitive wrongly accused of murder and takes a job at a steel mill. Unfortunately, he is injured in an accident caused by labor agitators and convalesces at the owner's home. Naturally, he falls in love with the owner's daughter and eventually clears his name after the real murderer confesses in a violent confrontation with the hero. The film was very successful, employing an orchestra to play in packed movie theaters. With so few films supporting labor, in 1910, the American Federation of Labor (AFL) protested and called for the boycotting of movie houses that showed anti-labor films. That said, a handful of films produced by large studios had somewhat favorable depictions of the labor movement. *The Struggle* (1913) offered a damning depiction of the absentee owners of industrial property, who scandalously reap profits while doing nothing for the welfare of their employees. In *Dusk to Dawn* (1913), an employee of an ironworks is fired as a dangerous agitator who protests the dangerous conditions of the mill. After his friend dies in a preventable explosion at the mill, the protagonist successfully runs for governor on a labor ticket. Conversely, *The Strike at Coaldale* (1914) was more muted in its support of labor. The plot featured a strike triggered by poor working conditions in the railroad industry. Strike-breakers are brought in, violence erupts, and the owner's daughter, Edith, is seriously injured. A leading union man, Joe Gregory, rescues Edith by commandeering a train and heroically transports the injured woman to the hospital, despite the tracks being set on fire by the strikers. The strikers repudiate Joe, kidnap the company's president, and threaten to kill him, but Gregory convinces the strikers to spare his life. With the help of Edith, Joe pleads the strikers' cause to the president, who agrees to their demands.

In 1914, the infamous Ludlow Massacre inspired several films to explore strikers and the violence. The Ludlow Massacre was prompted by a strike at the Colorado Fuel and Iron Company owned by John D. Rockefeller Jr. The company was run as a dictatorship. Workers experienced squalid living and working conditions, long hours, and low pay. The company even censored films that the employees were allowed to view. The National Guard was brought in to quell the violence but quickly supported the strike-breakers, accelerating the violence. It is estimated that between 69 and 199 people were killed during the strike, culminating with the tragedy on April 20, 1914. The National Guard entered a makeshift camp of tents, dousing them with kerosene before lighting them on fire. The ensuing mayhem resulted in the death of at least 20 people, with six adults and one child being shot, while eleven children and two pregnant women were burned to death. Historian Howard Zinn (2013) called the massacre "the culminating act of perhaps the most violent struggle between corporate power and laboring men in

American history." The resulting congressional hearings blamed Rockefeller, who became a figure of disgust among the working class and on the silver screen. D.W. Griffith's, *The Mother and the Law* (1914) depicted Rockefeller as the villain, using the pseudonym Jenkins. The film showed strikers being brutally attacked by National Guardsman with rifles and machine guns. The film was re-released during the red scare, with a new intertitle claiming that "The militiamen having used blank cartridges, the workmen fear only the company guards." Similarly, Rockefeller was the villain in *Two News Items* (1916). This time with the alias, John Rockland, a millionaire factory owner who owns several filthy tenements. In the film, Rockland cuts wages by 25 percent, which leads to a strike.

The scarcity of pro-labor films led several progressive organizations to produce and distribute their own films. Under the leadership of Joseph Cannon, The Labor Film Service's mandate was to contest the red scare pictures that distorted socialist ideals and the activities of the labor movement. *The Contrast* (1921) was financed by coal miners in West Virginia, Ohio, and Pennsylvania. The film depicted cave-ins caused by the owner's negligence and attempted to dramatize the contrast between the rich and the poor in the United States. For example, a starving girl sneaks' food from the garbage that a pampered dog had neglected to consume. The film had to be shown in secret, as censors felt it too radical for Americans. The Federal Film Corporation (FFC) was a Seattle-based company operated by radicals and militant trade unionists. The FFC produced *The New Disciple* (1921), which was set in the fictional town of Harmony. The plot features a class struggle precipitated by the leading capitalist of the town becoming a war profiteer. The protagonist returns from the war and leads workers to take back the mill with capital secured from local farmers. Finally, the American Federation of Labor (AFL) produced *Labor's Reward* (1925), in which a young woman named Mary collapsed after working a grueling ten-hour day in the sweatshop. A coworker expresses concern for Mary and is subsequently fired by the foreman. Mary leads a strike for the right to form a union, which results in better conditions, including an eight-hour day. The intertitles demonstrated the benefits of membership in a trade union.

Finally, *The Passaic Textile Strike* (1926) is considered the most notable union film in the silent era. The film was produced to raise public awareness and financial support for the 1926 Passaic Textile Strike, which involved over 16,000 New Jersey textile mill workers and lasted more than a year. The film was part-fictional melodrama and documentary. The prologue depicted fictional Polish worker Stefan Breznac, a recent immigrant who takes a job in a textile mill. Stefan lives the American Dream, marries Kada, and has a daughter named Vera. The villain is the boss of the mill, a German capitalist named Mr. Mulius. The family falls on hard times after Mr. Mulius cuts wages, forcing the 14-year-old Vera to quit school and find employment in the mill. Vera is raped by Mulius and eventually fired, which forces Stefan to work 72 hours a week to make ends meet. Initially reluctant, Stefan now urges his co-workers to form a union only to die just two days later, succumbing to the poor working conditions. His wife, Kada, takes a job working the night shift, ending the prologue. The next part of the film, entitled

"*The Strike*," depicts interspersing dramatic re-enactments with actual footage of the workers and their families. The footage is remarkable, highlighted by the vigorous and violent opposition by mill owners and police authorities. The injured workers are graphically displayed, with broken bones and bandages. There is footage of police using clubs, shotguns, fire hoses, and tear gas against the strikers. The film is a watershed moment in the American labor movement, as it is one of the only early American labor films to have been preserved largely intact.

Science Fiction Films and The Corporation

A silent film, *Metropolis* (1927) is considered one of the most influential films ever produced. The first feature-length science fiction film was a futuristic glimpse of class divisions, with prominent themes of modernity, mass production, automation, fascism, and communism. The film was released during Germany's tumultuous Weimar period, highlighted by staggering poverty, political struggles, and social anxiety. Directed by Fritz Lang, the futuristic landscape overflowed with symbolism and metaphors about class struggles. The film depicts two realms – the bustling, urban space of the decadent Metropolis and the subterranean workers who toil below the city. *Metropolis* uncovers the damaging machinations of capitalism – the laboring class occupies the bottom, while the elite rules the top echelon of society. The film serves as a warning about inequality, conveying that the future will be synonymous with corruption, exploitation, and greed.

Continuing in the tradition of *Metropolis*, the science fiction genre has continued to serve as a vehicle for social commentary, decrying corporate control and greed. The 1970s produced several dystopian films about corporate control over society, including prominent films like *Soylent Green* (1973) and *Rollerball* (1975). Set in 2022, *Soylent Green* presents a dystopian future in which industrial capitalism has left the planet overheated from the greenhouse effect, overpopulated, and undernourished. However, the Soylent Corporation continues to profit by producing the communal food supply – wafers referred to as Soylent red, yellow, or green – for most of the world's population. The corporation is essentially a state-sanctioned monopoly that manufactures and distributes food rations for increasingly hungry citizens. Meanwhile, the wealthy and elite can afford luxurious dwellings, clean water, and natural food. The film serves as a warning of unregulated corporate power, environmental neglect, and social inequality. Similarly, *Rollerball* imagines a future in which corporations control every aspect of life, supplanting nation-states and eroding individual freedoms. Corporations use violent sport – rollerball – as a circus-like diversion to pacify the masses.

The "evil corporation" has emerged as a pop culture trope in the science fiction genre, conveying profound fears of the power of business (Allan, 2016). Numerous popular films depict "evil" corporations that value profit over humane values, including the Weyland-Yutani corporation in the Alien series, Cyberdyne Systems in the Terminator series, and the Umbrella Corporation in the Resident Evil series. Set in "Old Detroit," *Robocop* (1987) features Omni Consumer Products (OCP), a corporation that controls public services, including hospitals, prisons, and the police. In *Looker* (1981), the Digital Matrix corporation develops a sinister technology that hypnotizes consumers into purchasing products they advertise. Similarly, *The Manchurian Candidate* (2004) depicts a corporation employing a nanotechnological implant to brainwash the Vice-President-elect. It is no small coincidence that the "anti-Christ" Damien Thorn is the powerful CEO in the horror film *The Omen 3: The Final Conflict* (1981). Thorn Industries is the largest multinational corporation in the world, producing everything from nuclear warheads to soybeans. *The Omen 2* (1978) features a prophetic scene in which an executive, who is a secret aide to the anti-Christ, advocates for genetically modified foods, arguing that "are profitable future, aside from energy, also lies in famine." Once again, driving the narrative that in the future, corporations will dominate the planet – even the universe – with storylines that feature genetic experimentation, cybernetics, viral weaponry, and the end of civilizations. The trope occupies a special place in Hollywood, and the sci-fi genre can offer a helpful lens to understand corporate narrative in film. That said, this book will not include sci-fi films that feature corporate wrongdoing, as they are worthy of much more profound and richer exploration. Moreover, the book explores the depiction of "actual" harms that corporations inflict on society, not prophetic evils or unrealized technology.

The Paper Gangster: White-Collar Crime on Film

White-collar or occupational criminality is also featured in several films. The line between white-collar crime and corporate wrongdoing is unclear, as sometimes the corporation or business benefits from white-collar transgressions. However, films that depict white-collar criminality feature characters that enrich themselves through criminal frauds such as insider trading and Ponzi schemes. Although the corporation or business may profit, the overarching narrative involves occupational criminality, not corporate wrongdoing.

Many plots feature "corporate raiders" or "boiler rooms." Corporate raiders buy large shares in undervalued businesses and then sell the stock making enormous profits. As veteran muckraker Barbara Ehrenreich (1988) quipped, "they did not sow, neither did they reap, but rather sat around pushing money through their modems in games known as 'corporate takeover' and 'international currency speculation." The boiler room refers to a "pump and dump" scheme, in which salespersons employ unfair and dishonest sales tactics to pressure clients into buying worthless stocks, fraudulently driving up the value of the stock. The brokerage firm sells the stock at a hugely inflated price, making large profits, while the client is left with a worthless portfolio, ultimately losing their investment. Some of the most prominent white-collar crime films include *Trading Places* (1983), *Wall Street* (1987), *Other People's Money* (1991), *Boiler Room* (2000), *The Wolf of Wall Street* (2013), and *The Wizard of Lies* (2017). Of note, *Wall Street* introduced audiences to Gordon Gekko (Michael Douglas). Gekko is a character that represents the corruption and excess of venture capitalism. The film introduced audiences to the iconic phrase, "greed is good," the character idolized by a generation of corporate or big business wannabees. Likewise, *The Wolf of Wall Street* was an entertaining depiction of the excessive greed and debauchery of the financial industry. Jordan Belfort (Leonardo DiCaprio) is an anti-hero, a con artist who swindled millions of dollars pushing worthless penny stocks. Like *Wall Street*, the film glamorized and glorified perpetrators of white-collar crime. Conversely, *The Wizard of Lies* does not glorify white-collar crime, grimly telling the story of Bernie Madoff's (Robert DeNiro) Ponzi scheme, which bilked millions from his unsuspecting clients. Although the films highlight the culture of greed that permeates the corporate and business world, the films will not be discussed in the subsequent chapters. The depiction of occupational crime on film is worthy of a standalone monograph. Moreover, while the line between occupational and corporate crime is sometimes "blurry," the film narratives are essentially different.

Overview of the Book

The primary objective is to provide readers with an extensive review of films that feature corporate wrongdoing. The purpose is to develop typologies or categories of corporate harm on film while also exploring the film's broader cultural, historical, and political contexts. The second chapter will provide a detailed account of corporate or industry wrongdoing in films that debuted from 1930 to 1980. The chapter serves to deliver a deeper understanding of how the corporation or industry has been depicted in scripted Hollywood films. The third chapter will explore the portrayal of corporate harms to the environment, including the poisoning of the public, the oil spill, nuclear accident, and the climate crisis. The fourth chapter examines the depiction of corporate harm to workers, while the fifth chapter considers harm to consumers. The sixth chapter will explore harms to the economy, including the real-estate bubble, uber-capitalism, lobbying, conspiracy-thriller genre, and the robber baron on film. The seventh and final chapter will present an overview of familiar narratives around the protagonist, antagonist, and victim within corporate harm films.

Reference List

AFL-CIO. (2021). *Death on the job: The toll of neglect: A national and state-by-state profile of worker safety and health in the United States* (30th ed.). American Federation of Labor & Congress of Industrial Organizations. https://aflcio.org/sites/default/files/2021-05/DOTJ2021_Final.pdf

Allan, A. (2016, April 25). How the 'evil corporation' became a pop-culture trope. *The Atlantic*. https://www.theatlantic.com/business/archive/2016/04/evil-corporation-trope/479295/

Box, S. (1983). *Power, crime and mystification*. Routledge.

Braithwaite, J. (1984). *Corporate crime in the pharmaceutical industry*. Routledge & Kegan Paul.

Braithwaite, J. (1985). White collar crime. *Annual Review of Sociology, 11*(1), 1–25.

Brownlow, K. (1990). *Behind the mask of innocence*. Alfred a Knopf Incorporated.

Clinard, M.B. (1952). *The black market: A study of white collar crime* (pp. 79–85). Rinehart.
Clinard, M.B., & Yeager, P.C. (1980). *Corporate crime*. Free Press.
Clinard, M.B., Yeager, P.C., & Clinard, R.B. (2017). *Corporate crime*. Routledge.
Cullen, F., Cavender, G., Maakestad, W., & Benson, M. (2014). *Corporate crime under attack: The fight to criminalize business violence*. Routledge.
Ehrenreich, B. (1988). A farewell to work. Mother Jones May, 10.
Filler, L. (1993). *The muckrakers*. Stanford University Press.
Friedrichs, D.O. (2009). *Trusted criminals: White collar crime in contemporary society*. Cengage.
Geis, G. (2015). *White-collar and corporate crime*. Oxford University Press.
Geis, G., & Goff, C. (1983). Introduction. In E.H. Sutherland (Ed.), *White collar crime: The uncut version* (pp. ix–xxxiii). Yale University Press.
Hebberecht, P. (2015). Willem Bonger: The unrecognised European pioneer of the study of white-collar crime. In J. van Erp, G. Vandewalle, & W. Huisman (Eds.), *The Routledge handbook of white-collar and corporate crime in Europe* (pp. 125–32). Routledge
Mills (1963) A diagnosis of moral uneasiness. In I. Horowitz (Ed.), *Power, politics, and people: The Collected Essays of C. Wright Mills* . Oxford University Press.
Jacobs, L. (2002). Experimental cinema in America. Part one: 1921–1941. In E. Smoodin & A. Martin (Eds.), *Hollywood quarterly* (pp. 5–27). University of California Press.
Keefe, P.R. (2019, January 7). *How Mark Burnett resurrected Donald Trump as an icon of American success*. https://www.newyorker.com/magazine/2019/01/07/how-mark-burnett-resurrected-donald-trump-as-an-icon-of-american-success
Mokhiber, R. (1988). *Corporate crime and violence: Big business power and the abuse of the public trust*. Random House (NY).
Lens, S. (1973). *The Labor Wars: From the Molly Maguires to the sitdowns*. Doubleday Books.
Nader, R. (2000, May 5). Corporate crime. *Nader.org*. https://nader.org/2000/05/07/corporate-crime/
Nader, R. (2013, March 3). Getting tough on devastating corporate crime. *HuffPost*. https://www.huffpost.com/entry/corporate-crime_b_2934600
Nichols, B. (2017). *Introduction to documentary*. Indiana University Press.
Pierce, D. (2013, September). *The survival of American silent feature films, 1912–1929*. Council on Library and Information Resources and the Library of Congress.
Robinson, D. (1997). *From peep show to palace: The birth of American film*. Columbia University Press.
Sutherland, E.H. (1983). *White collar crime*. Yale University Press.
Zinn, H. (2013, August 30). Ludlow Massacre. *Howard Zinn Website*. https://www.howardzinn.org/labor-day-history-ludlow-massacre/

2 History of Corporate Harm on Film, 1930s to 1970s

> *There are no nations. There are no peoples ... There is only IBM and ITT and AT&T, and DuPont Dow, Union Carbide and Exxon. Those are the nations of the world today. The world is a college of corporations, inexorably determined by the immutable bylaws of business.*
>
> Arthur Jensen (Ned Beatty), CEO of Communications Corporation of America (*Network*, 1976)

The year 1979 was a pivotal year in the depiction of corporate wrongdoing on film, with the debuts of *The China Syndrome* and *Norma Rae*. *The China Syndrome* featured a "whistleblower" who exposed corruption within the nuclear industry, while *Norma Rae* highlighted a large textile factory's poor working conditions and union-busting activities. These two films launched the issue of corporate wrongdoing into the public consciousness, leading to several popular films such as *Silkwood* (1983), *Class Action* (1991), *A Civil Action* (1998), *The Insider* (1999), *Erin Brockovich* (2000), *The Informant* (2009), *The Big Short* (2015), *Deepwater Horizon* (2016), and *Dark Waters* (2019). Post-1979, most depictions of corporate crime on film can be categorized as either harming the environment, workers, consumers, or the economy. That said, pre-1979, several films integrated themes of corporate wrongdoing and unethical behavior. In this way, individual villains represented the ethos of corporate greed and corruption. Moreover, negative depictions of big business have been muted or sanitized. Hollywood studios were reluctant to provide critiques of capitalism or industry, as they were constrained by the Production Code and McCarthy era witch-hunts. More importantly, Hollywood studios are themselves mega-capitalistic enterprises in the business of profit, not social and economic justice. In scripted films, it is challenging for directors to depict corporate or industry wrongdoing. Instead of a "corporation," most villains were corrupt businessmen, bankers, land barons, railroad tycoons, and oil industry executives. The purpose of this chapter is to furnish a historical overview of films that feature corporate wrongdoing. This will allow for a broader understanding of how the corporation or industry has been depicted in film, from the advent of the "talkie" to the 1980s.

DOI: 10.4324/9781003163855-2

The "Talkie" and the Great Depression, the 1930s

On October 6, 1927, *The Jazz Singer*, starring Al Jolson, premiered at the Warner Brothers theatre in New York. The film was the first feature-length film that utilized recorded sound and dialogue. The debut marked the metaphorical end to the silent film era. By 1929, almost every film that was released employed sound. The use of sound changed the process of filmmaking, further transforming the economic structure of the industry. It hastened in some of the largest mergers in motion-picture history. This process had begun during the 1920s, when Paramount, MGM, and other large studios acquired first-run theatre chains, cornering the market for the films they produced. By 1930, 95 percent of all Hollywood productions were concentrated in only eight studios, with the major studios also controlling exhibition. For example, a handful of studios possessed 2,600 first-run theatres, which represented 16 percent of the national total, but generated 75 percent of the revenue in the film industry (Croce, 2015). The Big Five included MGM, Paramount, Fox, Warner Brothers, and RKO, while "the little three" were United Artists, Universal Pictures, and Columbia. Then there was the so-called "Poverty Row," which consisted of small, independent studios such as Monogram, Republic Pictures, and Grand National. Labeled as B-Movies, the poverty row films were cheaply and quickly made, intended to be shown in double features to counter the Depression-era box-office slump. These studios produced approximately 40–50 movies per year. Although lacking in quality, they served as a training ground for future movie stars, such as John Wayne (Hurst, 2007).

The domination of the studio system allowed the Motion Picture Production Code to flourish. Also known, as the Hays Code (after William Hays), the Production Code was first introduced in 1930 due to several scandals in the motion picture industry and the perceived immorality within film. The Production Code set specific restrictions on language and behavior, specifically regarding sex and crime, which were huge box office draws. The Code prohibited drug use, suggestive dances, sexual innuendo, nudity, graphic violence, criminality, and even the mocking of religion. Criminals were not to be depicted in a positive light and were not allowed to evade punishment. Hays persuaded studios to adopt the code to avoid government intervention. Hays argued that reshooting films to appease state censors was costly. The movie industry was reeling from the stock market crash and the costs of introducing sound to movies. As a cost-cutting measure, the Code was adopted in 1930 but was not strictly enforced, with many producers blatantly ignoring the edicts. From 1930 to 1934, hundreds of films pushed the boundaries of morality, including many with provocative and sexually suggestive storylines (Doherty, 1999). The gangster film became popular with almost 80 films released from 1930 to 1934, including *Little Caesar* (1931), *The Public Enemy* (1931), and *Scarface* (1932). These films shepherded in the anti-hero character, increasing depictions of violence, criminality, and immorality (Croce, 2015; Munby, 2009).

Although tame by today's standards, the salacious nature of pre-code films shocked conservative audiences and religious leaders. After continued pressure from the Catholic church, Hays was prompted to hire Joseph Breen, a strict Catholic, to enforce the Code under the auspices of the Production Code Administration (PCA). The PCA was formally adopted on June 13, 1934, and now had the authorization to review all films and order script changes. Setting July 1, 1934, as a deadline, all films received a certificate of approval from the PCA. More importantly, theatres were subject to a $25,000 fine if they showed a film without the PCA seal of approval. Previously unenforceable, the Code now "had teeth" with Breen proclaiming that "the vulgar, the cheap, and the tawdry is out. There is no room on the screen at any time for pictures which offend against common decency. And these the industry will not allow". Unfortunately, film producers acquiesced and accepted the Code as law, creating films that met Breen's strict moral standards for the next 20 years, with no exceptions (Doherty, 1999). The code was overwhelmingly repressive, but studio executives institutionalized this system of de factor censorship because they believed it to be necessary for the continued success of their enterprise. Already reeling from the Depression and lower box office revenues, the studios feared national boycotts of their films. That said, from 1930 to 1945, studios produced more than 7,500 feature films (Croce, 2015). The popular genres included westerns, musicals, slapstick comedy, biographical pictures, and animation. The large movie studios used repressive contracts to control directors and actors, loaning them out to rival studios with strict rules. Basically a monopoly, there was little competition in the movie industry and coupled with the repressive nature of the Production Code, creativity was stifled. Essentially, it served the interests of the capitalist class.

The Nefarious "Businessman"

Mirroring the latter part of the silent era, film producers refused to make films that provided any social critique of industry or capitalism. However, several films, mainly pre-code, depicted businessmen and industrialists in an unfavorable light. Nicknamed the "King of Pre-Code," William Warren brilliantly depicted a greedy businessman in several films. In *Skyscraper Souls* (1932), Warren played David Dwight, a ruthless and ambitious owner of Manhattan's largest skyscraper, the Seacoast National Bank Building. Dwight is blunt, dishonest, and unscrupulous, in both finance and with personal relationships with women. Although married, he has an affair with a married assistant, lusts after a secretary, and cheats his business partners. The nefarious character was illegally manipulating stock prices to keep control of his beloved building. After triumphing over business rivals, he boasts that business has no ethics or rules, smugly claiming,

> Listen, If I double-crossed anybody for you, I wouldn't be a double-crosser. I'd be a financial genius. You'd profit by it. You'd love it, you'd love me. I'd be your pal, your leader. But I put one over on you, so I'm a double-crosser. It's all in the point of view, gentlemen. But don't despair, there lots of small fry that you can double-cross, just like the good old days before you've gone out of your class.

Warren portrays a similar character in *Employee's Entrance* (1933) when he plays Kurt Anderson, an amoral, conniving, tyrannical general manager of Franklin & Munroe, a large department store with 12,000 employees. Anderson is a compulsive philanderer that sexually harasses women and demeans his employees. His autocratic leadership is brutally efficient, making the business financially successful despite the owner's incompetence. Finally, *The Match King* (1932) features Warren as Paul Kroll, a smooth, charming, yet heartless character that builds a worldwide empire from the manufacture and sale of matches. Kroll lies, cheats, and bribes his way to the top of the business world, using a Ponzi-like scheme to borrow money to acquire assets and expand his business. Eventually, he forms a monopoly, destroying competition and even resorts to kidnapping an eccentric recluse that invented a reusable match, which would threaten his bottom line. In the end, Kroll commits suicide after the stock market crash of 1929 destroyed his monopoly, and he was exposed as a financial fraud. The film was based on Ivar Kreuger, whose Swedish Match Company controlled more than half of the output of matches. Kreuger killed himself in a Paris hotel room in 1932 after his frauds were exposed. The film was rushed into production after his death (Partnoy, 2010).

Produced by Poverty Row's Majestic Pictures, *The World Gone Mad* (1933), aka *The Public Be Damned*, pitted a newly minted District Attorney, Lionel Houston (Neil Hamilton), and his reporter friend, Andy Terrell (Pat O'Brien), against the Cromwell Investment Corporation. The corporate executives manipulate stock to keep their firm from collapsing, defrauding investors and the public. They hire a gangster to arrange the murder of the former District Attorney, Avery Henderson, making it appear as a crime of passion involving a mistress. However, Houston and Terrell join forces to find the real culprits, as they know that Henderson was devoted to his wife and child. In melodramatic fashion, Houston's fiancée is the daughter of Grover Cromwell, the CEO of Cromwell Investment Corporation. Houston meets with his future father-in-law and two corporation executives, telling them that Henderson was set up and not murdered by an alleged mistress.

Lionel Houston: On the very night of Avery Henderson's death, he told me that he was on the verge of uncovering one of the most gigantic corporation lootings in this city's history. Well, wouldn't those men have paid to avoid exposure?
Grover Cromwell: Have you any idea who those men are, Lionel?
Lionel Houston: No. No, but I'm going to find out. The public looks to the law for protection from these leeches, who have chiseled and gouged and swindled them out of their hard-earned dollars—given them nothing but death and misery in return. If I had my way, I'd line up against a wall and shoot em. But as long as the law doesn't permit that, I can at least send them away for as long as the law does permit. That is what Avery Henderson meant to do, and that is what I am going to do.

In yet another noteworthy scene, two executives within the corporation, Gaines and Osborne, discuss their stock fraud

Osborne: I can't get it out of my mind Gaines, we're crooks.

Gaines: [laughing] you talk as if you're just finding that out.

Osborne: If Suburban's [stock] true condition ever comes out. The Cromwell Investment Corporation and every subsidiary it controls will collapse. Our investors …

Gaines [interrupting]: you are thinking of your own skin and the years you'll spend in prison if it does blow up.

Osborne: I am thinking about the public too! The thousands of people …

Gaines [angrily interrupting]: Oh, the public be damned! If you must worry. Worry about yourself!

In the end, it is revealed that the CEO of the corporation is not aware of the misdeeds of his executives and commits a murder-suicide so that his daughter and investors will be paid out through his life insurance policy. The film blurred the lines between corporate executives and gangsters, strongly hinting that the harms of financial fraud had dangerous consequences for the public.

Another poverty row film, *Beggars in Ermine* (1934), was a melodramatic story of retribution and greed. John "Flint" Dawson is the owner of a steel mill that loves and is loved by his workers. He even has lunches with the men. Out of concern for his employees, Flint refused a corporate merger that would net him millions of dollars. He claimed that bankers and promoters would pocket $15–20 million while the workers who hold stock in the company would be left behind. His second-in-command, Mr. Marley, orchestrates a workplace accident that confines Dawson in a wheelchair. Dawson's unfaithful wife has power of attorney, and she sells the company, running off with all the funds, leaving Dawson penniless. Dawson is now destitute and resorts to panhandling. Incredulously, he regains his fortune by forming a union of disabled panhandlers and beggars, helping them find employment with health and retirement plans. Marley plays the classic evil boss, firing workers that were too old, callously telling the board of directors that you "can't put new wine, in old bottles" and that the corporation was "not a charitable institution." Marley then devises a scheme to get more control by manipulating the stock so that the price will devalue, and he can repurchase it at a lower rate. He even resorts to selling the stock that the workers legally own. However, the beggars start buying the artificially low stock, increasing the value and thwarting Marley's plan. After a confrontation with Dawson, Marley commits suicide, while Dawson returns as the rightful owner, much to the delight of the workers who get their stock back.

Apart from *Beggars of Ermine* (1934), the above films were a rather savage depiction of survival-era capitalism playing out in real-time during the height of the Depression. These films fueled the deep cynicism that many Americans had toward business and speculative capitalism during the height of the Depression (Schindler, 2005). They were somewhat muted, focused on individual transgressors, and did not focus on the structural problems with capitalism and business ethics.

Transforming Society: The New Deal in Film

The Depression hit Americans hard. Unemployment peaked at almost 25 percent, with millions of poverty-stricken and hungry Americans flocking to breadlines. The homeless formed shantytowns, known as "Hoovervilles," and many desperate farmers migrated to California. Banks had heavily invested depositor's savings in the stock market, losing billions of dollars after the Wall Street Crash of 1929. The banking collapse caused depositors to "rush" to withdraw their savings before it was too late. These "runs" forced many banks out of business, with 4,000 banks failing by 1933 and depositors losing $140 billion. The film industry also suffered. The record profits generated from the talkies disappeared. By 1931, box office returns had dropped 10–35 percent in most theaters, and by mid-1932, one-third of the nearly 20,000 movie theaters had closed as attendance had dropped by 33 percent from 1930 to 1933 (Croce, 2015).

Despite the societal upheaval, most films were escapist, with few that depicted the suffering and pain of the Great Depression. There were exceptions, including Charlie Chaplin's *City Lights* (1931), and *Modern Times* (1936), both of which, ironically, were silent films. *City Lights* reminded audiences about the staggering social inequality between the working and upper classes. The contrast between the rich and poor is highlighted by a poor, blind flower girl and an alcoholic millionaire that the Tramp befriends. Nevertheless, most viewers were unlikely to make that observation, as they focused on the slapstick rather than the more serious undertones in Chaplin's work. Conversely, *Modern Times* depicts the Tramp struggling to survive in the modern, industrialized world. The Tramp works on a factory conveyor belt at the Electro Steel Corporation, where he suffers a nervous breakdown after experiencing several mishaps, including a hilarious scene in which he is forced to volunteer to demonstrate the efficiency of a feeding machine. The machine was invented so that workers could continue to work during their lunch breaks. The film is a social commentary on the dire employment and financial conditions of the Great Depression. The comedy incorporates challenging issues such as strikes, riots, unemployment, poverty, and the tyranny of automation.

Similarly, the quickly plotted, *Heroes For Sale* (1933) delves into drug addiction, stolen valor, communism, poverty, unemployment, police brutality, automation, and unethical business practices. It was one of the few films that acknowledged the Depression and the desperation that many Americans felt. The film was produced by First National, a subsidiary of Warner Brothers. At that time, Warner Brothers had a reputation as the most socially conscious of the "Big Five" studios. Their films catered to the working class and dealt with socially relevant themes in such movies as *I Am a Fugitive from a Chain Gang* (1932) and *Wild Boys of the Road* (1933). The story begins as Tom Holmes (Richard Barthelmess) courageously captures a German officer before being seriously injured and taken prisoner by the Germans during the Great War. His immediate superior, Roger, cowardly hid in the trench, only to be given credit for Tom's heroic deed. After the War ends, Tom is reunited with Roger, who admits that he took credit for Tom's heroism. Feeling guilty, Roger helps Tom acquire a job at the bank that his father owns. Unfortunately, Tom is addicted to morphine and is fired by the banker, who discounts Tom's military service and heroism, as Roger remains silent about the stolen valor. Tom overcomes his addiction, ends up at a flophouse in Chicago, befriending the owner, Mary. He also meets his future wife, Ruby and Max, an eccentric inventor who is an outspoken communist. Tom starts work at a laundromat, where he is praised for his industriousness and ingenuity. He is quickly promoted and soon has a son with Ruby. Tom invests in the laundry-processing machine that Max has invented, convincing both the workers and owner to utilize the labor-saving device. The owner agrees not to cut jobs, but he dies of a heart attack, and the new owners callously use the invention to fire three-quarters of the workers. The jobless are enraged and start a riot where Tom's wife is killed. Tom is falsely imprisoned for starting the riot and spends five years in prison. He is released at the height of the Great Depression and introduced to the misery of the times. In a particularly compelling scene, a hungry crowd is grimly peering through the diner's window. At that moment, Tom decides to use his fortune from the invention to feed the hungry, telling Mary (the owner of the flophouse/diner) to spare no expense.

Max: This is ghastly. With my brains, my intellect, my imagination, I make you rich. And now you throw that good money away on those lazy mooches.
Mary: Well, they're nothing of the sort. They are honest, hardworking people out of jobs. They ate here and paid for it when they could afford it.
Tom: They can afford it now. Every last one of them.
Max: Oh, charity, it is like a snowball running down the hill. It gets bigger, bigger and bigger. The poor, the needy, cancer on civilization. If I was running the world, I would kill everybody that needed it. Needed anything.
Mary [snidely]: If you were running the world.

However, Tom is struck with misfortune once again, as he is falsely labeled a "Red" by the Red Squad, a group of thugs paid by big business to thwart any attempt at communism or social unrest. He is forced to leave Chicago, where he takes up with a group of unemployed and destitute men that wander throughout the country. Tom meets up with Roger, who is also homeless, after being released from prison for embezzlement. The pair discuss the past, with Roger admitting that he and his father used the bank depositor's money to play the stock market, losing everything after it crashed. They then discuss the future in a thinly veiled metaphor of America under the Roosevelt administration.

Roger: The country can't go on this way. It's the end of America.
Tom: Nah, maybe the end of us, but it is not the end of America. In a few years, it will go on bigger and stronger than ever.
Roger: You know you're the last guy in the world that I ever expect to find was an optimist.

Tom: That's not optimism, just common horse sense. You read President Roosevelt's inaugural address?
Roger: Yeah.
Tom: He's right. You know it takes more than one sock on the jaw to lick 120 million people.

The film was undoubtedly a critique of capitalism, prominently displaying the greed and dishonesty of bankers and the callousness of businessmen that used innovation to displace the working class. The protagonist also gave away all his wealth to help the poor, an overly transparent message to endorse New Deal principles. Yet, the film also made light of communist ideals, revealing the self-avowed communist Max Brinker as an unequivocable hypocrite, a hardcore Marxist that becomes a Social Darwinist. The hypocrisy is comically displayed in a scene where Max attempts to get funding for a patent from Tom.

Tom: Now wait a minute, I thought you hated all employers and capitalists?
Max: I despise them. I spit on them [pretends to spit]. But I am willing to get rich with them.

After Max becomes wealthy from his laundry invention, he visits Tom in prison, asking him what he wants to do with his share of the money earned from the invention.

Max: There is only one thing important in the world. To have money. Without it, you are just garbage. With it, you are a king.
Tom: You used to hate the capitalists.
Max: Naturally, that is before I had money.

Some might argue that the Max character was actually a capitalist, who was masquerading as a communist, a wolf in sheep's clothing, so to speak. However, despite the ridiculousness of the Max character, the capitalist class was roundly critiqued in this film, highlighting their lack of compassion, corruption, and greed. This was contrasted with the heroism of Tom, who had a humanely socialist viewpoint, couched within a uniquely American entrepreneurial spirit. This is evident, as the film ends with Mary telling Tom's son, "He lives for everyone but himself. He has given everything and taken nothing."

In a similar vein, *Our Daily Bread* (1934) explored alternatives to free enterprise and laissez-faire economics by advocating for collectivism over American individualism. Arguably, the only genuinely socialist picture of the era, *Our Daily Bread*, was directed by King Vidor as a follow-up to his silent drama, *The Crowd* (1928). *The Crowd* depicted the struggles of average Americans within the alienating machinery of the city. *Our Daily Bread* featured a down-and-out couple who cannot pay their rent and decide to move to the country after an uncle offers the couple an old farm. The problem is that the couple knows nothing about farming and starts a commune, where depression sufferers work together to build a sustainable and thriving community. The climax involves the community desperately digging a canal to irrigate their failing crops. The movie was overly optimistic and advocated for returning to the "Back to Land" movement that prevailed in the 1930s. This included a collection of relief and reform projects seeking agrarian solutions to the decade's social and economic crises, whereby unused lands would be open to a new class of small producers. Under FDR's New Deal, public and private initiatives attempted to resettle and retrain families for small production on individual and collective small farms. Most were state or municipal initiatives to use open lands as a means to reduce urban overcrowding and unemployment. An artifact of the times, *Our Daily Bread* was a groundbreaking depiction of the Depression. That said, given the socialist theme of communal farming, Vidor received no studio backing and had to finance the film with his funds.

The film was produced under the banner "Viking Productions" and distributed by United Artists with the help of Charlie Chaplin. It was also one of the first films to comply with the production code, ensuring clean dialogue and sexual morality. In California, where *Our Daily Bread* was made, hundreds of cooperative communes had formed to tackle the crisis, just like in the film. The story's theme of collectivization, its distrust of cigar-chewing banker types, and its assertion of a working-class identity over racial and national identities lent it a communist flavor. However, Vidor was a conservative who later joined the anti-communist group called Motion Picture Alliance for the Preservation of American Ideals. The idea of self-sufficient people building a community was a very American notion. Conservative studio heads believed that the film might boost the campaign of Democratic candidate Upton Sinclair, who was running for the governor of California. The devout socialist Sinclair had pledged to End Poverty in California (EPIC) with a radical set of collectivist measures that alarmed studio elites. The head of United Artists delayed the film's release by several months, and other studio heads actively funded the Republican candidate. MGM even commissioned fake newsreels about bums pouring into California to sponge off the state (Neve, 2016).

Conversely, *Make a Million* (1935) was a screwball comedy produced by Poverty's row, Monogram Studios. The film starred Charles Starrett as a radical college professor, Reginald Q. Jones. Jones espouses that the wealthy are nincompoops and that there should be a 90 percent inheritance tax. One of the students is a banker's daughter who mocks the professor and arrogantly blames the poor for their predicament. After failing the daughter, the banker, accuses the professor of being in league with Russian communists and has the Dean place Jones on an unpaid leave of absence. To get his position back, Jones must prove his economic theories by making a million dollars. Jones meets up with a panhandler and devises a plan to ask the public for support by sending him one dollar to the World Improvement League. He receives a sympathetic reaction from the public and receives many donations. The villainous banker attempts to seize his newfound wealth, and the hobos form a board of directors for the imaginary "World Improvement League" to prove that it exists. In the end, the banker's daughter falls in love with the professor and each donor is given an article worth up to three dollars, while the suppliers get rid of surplus goods at cost, which ensures that they can pay off their creditors. The film was a thinly veiled attempt to boost support for New Deal economic policy, with redistribution of wealth as a key to creating jobs and putting money back into the economy, which would spur economic recovery. It also played to Depression-era audiences, as the upper-class banker was depicted as a greedy crook.

The Struggle between Labor and Capital

The struggle between capital and labor was rare and, when shown, usually had a muted message that ensured that socialist leanings were limited. The specter of the red scare continued, with the capitalist class afraid that the Depression could trigger labor movements, or worse yet, communism. The 1930s also featured labor troubles within Hollywood, limiting the executives' appeal to make films that supported unions. However, the decade featured some films that depicted the struggle between labor and capital, notably *Cabin in the Cotton* (1932) and *Black Fury* (1935). Directed by Michael Curtiz, *The Cabin in the Cotton* contrasted the poor cotton tenant farmers and their wealthy landlords. Another of Warner Brother's socially conscious films, the film had a muted pro-labor rights message, critiquing the mistreatment of the sharecroppers, known as "peckerwoods," by the plantation owners. That said, the film proclaimed a middle ground between exploitative capitalism and the tyranny of communism. In the forward, the producers pronounce their neutrality, claiming:

> In many parts of the South today, there exists an endless dispute between the rich landowners, known as planters and the poor cotton pickers, known as tenants or "peckerwoods". The planters supply the tenants with the simple requirement of everyday life, and in return, the tenants work the land year in and year out. A hundred volumes could be written on the rights and wrongs of both parties, but it is not the object of the producers of "The Cabin in the Cotton" to take sides. We are only concerned with an effort to picturize these conditions.

The film starred Richard Barthelmess as Marvin Blake, a poor sharecropper's son. Marvin attempted to better his class situation by focusing on school, despite the objection of the plantation owner, Lane Norwood. After Marvin's father dies, Norwood has a change of heart, sending Marvin to school and providing him with a store clerk and bookkeeper position. Norwood then asks Marvin to spy on the sharecroppers, who are stealing cotton. Marvin is caught in the middle of two worlds, the sharecroppers and his wealthy benefactor. Marvin is sympathetic toward the sharecroppers, knowing that they have been mistreated for years. The local district attorney summarizes the injustice in a conversation, "Same old system. Thirty, forty percent interest, and carrying charges. A devil of a situation. The big fish and little fish. The weak and the strong. And what's to be done about it." The sharecroppers even ask Marvin to use his expertise and connections to help sell the stolen cotton. The sharecroppers, led by Uncle Joe, even try to blackmail the hesitant Marvin into their scheme, making them appear as ruthless and immoral as the landowners. However, after a brutal lynching of a sharecropper, Marvin becomes more concerned with the system's brutality. Marvin learns that his father was cheated, telling Norwood, "My father worked for you for 15 years. One year like another. And the money that might have brought him a little happiness you took away. He's dead ... and you worked him to death." The film climaxes with Marvin giving an impassioned speech about the injustices that the sharecroppers face, contrasting the wealth of landowners with the tenants' poverty. Railing against the system, Marvin argues:

> All day long out there in the cotton fields in the hot sun and dust. The gin blowing its whistle out yonder in the hot baked land, work. Work and for what? Nothing. Nothing but the long summer. The long winter. And in the end, the grave. When settling time comes, they got nothing left, when advances are paid, and interest is taken out, nothing for a year's sweat. A man and his whole family. You can't blame the tenant for standing up and asking where does he come in? And the answer is that he don't come in. He's got nothing left. He has a little old shack down there in the cotton patch to live in. The stores let him have some sow-belly meat, and some compound lard and molasses, and corn meal all the year. Some cheap shoes and no account dress stuff. Charging four or five prices for it. He's used all his credit, and he's in debt. No wonder he gets sore and tries to settle matters some other way. Steal if necessary. How can you blame him? Lately, I have been living where things are different. Where folks talk about buying a new car because the old one's a little scratched. Where money is spent like water. Four hundred dollars for a jazz band! And that money was sweated out of the blood of my people!

Norwood rebukes Marvin, claiming that the cooperative scheme will not work. He claims that the sharecroppers are lazy and unwilling to better themselves, an age-old argument that the wealthy lord over the poor. Indifferent, Norwood is reluctant to agree until Marvin threatens to expose the fraudulent books and the lynching of the sharecropper. This marks the end of the film, where there is a reconciliation between the landowners and tenants. Although the filmmakers attempt to be "neutral" in their presentation, the film is pro-labor, with Norwood revealing his greed and heartless nature.

Also directed by Michael Curtiz, *Black Fury* (1935) featured Paul Muni as Joe Radak, a good-natured immigrant coal miner who dreams of owning a pig farm and marrying Anna. The film depicts the bleak conditions of the "company" town, a shantytown far more unsavory than the idyllic Welsh village in *How Green Was My Valley* (1941). The mine is equally unpleasant. It is dark, grim, and claustrophobic. The miners receive unfair wages, being paid only for the coal they haul out each day, with much of their labor being "dead work," in which they are not paid. The film is sympathetic to the workers. However, it is not anti-industry, as the primary villain is a manpower company who relies on labor unrest for profits. They plant newcomer Steve Croner, an agent provocateur, to stir up grievances with the men, prompting them to strike. The company president unwittingly meets with the manpower company leaders, who promise to supply temporary workers to serve as strikebreakers and enforcers. In a compelling scene, a bunch of thugs are hired by the McGee Coal and Iron Police, with one of the nefarious characters saying, "first side I've ever been on the right side of copper's badge." The Coal and Iron police are seen brutalizing the strikers and gleefully evicting families from their homes.

In a pivotal moment, Radek's best friend is killed by a company cop, with Radek seriously injured in his attempt to save his friend. The murder was inspired by the real-life death of coal-miner John Barcoski, who was killed by the Coal and Iron Police. While recovering, Radek learns that the strike has settled, with the workers receiving less than before. He decides to stage his solo underground protest, blowing up the entrances and hiding in the mine. The resulting media interest, which draws attention to injustice against the miners, results in the mining and union officials to agree to the original pre-strike agreement. Most importantly, the federal government is depicted as justice seekers who expose the manpower company and their illegal tactics, punish wrongdoers, and uphold the union's rights. The portrayal aligns with New Deal policies that showed that labor and capital could reconcile, free of outside agitation. Not coincidently, 1935 marked the Wagner Relations Act's passing, arguably the most important labor legislation enacted in the 20th century. It established the legal right of workers (excepting agricultural and domestic workers) to organize, join labor unions, and collectively bargain with employers. *Black Fury* (1935) was banned in several mining towns for promoting social conflict. While in 1935, Andre David Sennwald Jr. of the *New York Times* called the film "the most notable experiment in social drama since "*Our Daily Bread*" (as cited in Schindler, 2005:192).

The War Years, the 1940s

Some film scholars argue that 1939 was the greatest year in film, the so-called peak of Hollywood's Golden Age. The year featured 365 releases, with notable releases including *Wuthering Heights, Gone with the Wind, The Wizard of Oz, Stagecoach, The Hunchback of Notre Dame,* and *Mr. Smith Goes to Washington*. Although the big studios continued to dominate the film industry, the end came with multiple lawsuits alleging studio monopolization over the film industry. The system of "vertical integration" was expensive to maintain but very lucrative. The studios had exclusive contracts with actors, directors, and owned theatres where their movies were shown. Some studios even owned the companies that process the film. By the end of the 1940s, the studio system would collapse after the Supreme Court ruled that studios had violated antitrust laws on May 4, 1948 (Croce, 2015). As in the 1930s, the depiction of corporate or business wrongdoing was minimal during the 1940s. This was even more so due to the advent of World War II. Film studios undertook a concerted effort to support the government's war-aims information campaign. The federal government established the Bureau of Motion Picture Affairs to organize films with patriotic, morale-boosting themes and missives about the duty to enlist, the bravery of the soldiers, evils of the enemy, and civilian responsibility on the home front (Koppes & Black, 1990).

Industry was essential to the war effort, and labor trouble was viewed as unpatriotic. *Pittsburgh* (1942) best illustrated the self-aggrandizing and smarminess of a typical war propaganda film. The film featured an all-star cast, including John Wayne as Pittsburgh Markham, Randolph Scott as Cash Evans and Marlene Dietrich as Josie "Hunky" Winters. The film embodied the American entrepreneurial spirit with a heavy dose of patriotism. The story begins during World War II, with industrialist Cash Evans giving a very patriotic speech to workers about the need to continue to support the war effort. Afterwards, the old friends reminisce about the old days and their humble beginnings, and the film flashbacks to Cash and Pittsburgh happily working in the coal mines. Markham is very ambitious, manipulating financial backing (through a forgery) to become a wealthy tycoon. Glossing over the apparent fraud, the narrator claimed that "hard work meant happiness and success." Pittsburgh cheats, swindles, and connives his way to the top, becoming an owner of a coal mine and a steel mill. His partner, Cash, serves as his moral conscious, only agreeing to Markham's unscrupulous methods because he believes that workers will be treated more fairly under their management. The daughter of a coal miner, the glamorous Josie served as the love interest of the pair, with both men vying for her attention, with Pittsburgh winning, but eventually losing her love with his philandering ways, marrying a steel tycoon's daughter for increased social standing. Gradually, Pittsburgh becomes a twisted and greedy industrialist, even saying, "in my book, every time that clock strikes, it ought to ring like a cash register." Markham ruthlessly breaks promises of safety shafts, higher wages, free healthcare, and schools for the miner's children. The coal miners revolt, with Markham, in typical John Wayne fashion, going down the coal mine to confront the agitators. A dramatic fight between Pittsburgh and Cash ensues, as Cash is disillusioned with Markham's tyranny and greed. Josie also descends into the mine but is seriously hurt because a safety device was not installed.

Now fully aware of his past transgressions, Pittsburgh has an epiphany and decides to give back to workers, providing better housing and hospitals. However, he is still despised, unable to find redemption for his past sins and double-crossing. Markham is now alone, abandoned by his wife, his friends, and eventually loses his fortune. After seeing a poster for the war effort, "what are you doing," he starts to work as a coalminer, using the alias Charles Ellis. With ingenuity and hard work, Ellis is recommended for the position of production manager. However, after finding out that Ellis is Pittsburgh, Cash angrily refuses to give Ellis the position, until Josie (now married to Cash) intervenes with a patriotic speech about "devotion to our country," telling both men that "your country needs you, what are you going to do about it?" Both men agree and work together to increase the productivity of the company for the war effort. The film's last ten minutes essentially serve as unashamed propaganda for the war effort, urging workers that the greater good is more important than individual wealth and that capital and labor must coexist for the nation's good.

Audiences must have found a strong resemblance between *Pittsburgh* and *Boomtown* (1940), which came out two years prior. While Pittsburgh was set in the coal and steel sector, the backdrop of *Boomtown* was the oil industry. However, except for the wartime propaganda, Boomtown had the same plotline as Pittsburgh, two friends who strike it rich, become enemies, engage in a fistfight, and in the end, regain their friendship. Like *Pittsburgh*, there was also a messy love triangle in which the friends vie for the same woman. The film also starred two Hollywood heavyweights, Clark Gable as "Big John" McMasters and Spencer Tracy as "Square" John Sand. The characters are wildcatters that strike it rich in the oil business. The pair lie, cheat and scheme, and lose and gain their fortunes throughout the film. The film is extremely pro-business, an ode to laissez-faire capitalism and the glorification of the American dream. The film's pro-business stance and negative depiction of antitrust laws were predictable as MGM studio head Louis B. Mayer was one of the film industry's staunchest conservatives. His studio, along with the others, was subject to years of lawsuits alleging monopolization. *Boomtown* expounds that dishonesty, deception, and stealing are as acceptable as exploiting others and ruining their businesses by fair or foul means. The film culminates with McMasters on trial for Sherman Antitrust violations. In patented Spencer Tracy style, John Sand makes a heartfelt – yet nauseatingly pro-business – speech defending his former friend, arguing that antitrust legislation was un-American.

John Sand: Well, as I get it. McMasters is on the hook because he broke the antitrust laws. He signed up a bunch of oil operators and formed a monopoly in restraint of trade, whatever you call it. I know he signed them up to make more money ... but after all, he's not exactly original with that. A lot of us have got those ideas. But what he was doing although he didn't know it ... in a way, he was working for these here United States too. Am I out of line yet, Judge?

Judge: Proceed, Mr. Sand

John Sand: He wanted these guys to produce less oil ... so that their wells would flow years longer and not ruin the fields. That way, they'd get all the oil there was to get out of the well. Don't you get the idea? He was for conservation. How can a guy be breaking the laws when he's trying to save the natural resources of the country? He didn't know that he was doing anything that you might call noble ... but being one of the best oil men there is, he's got the right hunch about oil. He knows that it took billions of years to put it here ... and if we keep taking it out at the rate were going, before long, there won't be any oil left in the good old U.S.A. Won't be any left for him or men like him ... to break up into lube and fuel and gasoline ... so that people can get their stuff moved around in trucks ... and so that you can light furnaces and homes and schoolhouses. If that time ever comes, what'll be the good of American schoolhouses, anyway? What'll be the good of you two oceans? What are you gonna run airplanes and battleships on? Tomato soup? I only got a couple more words, okay, Judge?

Judge: Proceed, Mr. Sand.

John Sand: Well, it is just this ... McMasters is a wildcatter. If it wasn't for automobiles, he'd be driving a covered wagon. It's always been his breed that has opened up the country ... and made it what it is. So now I'm wondering ... is it getting out of line, in these United States, for a man like him to make a million dollars with his brains and hands? If that's true, we'd better rewrite this land-of-opportunity stuff. I admit that he's ornery and he's mean ... but he's an oil man with the right idea of what to do with our oil. And he's always met the payroll, and you can put his word in the bank. Now, that's all I got to say. Now you talk.

In the end, both McMasters and Sand have lost their wealth, reconciled, and started again, wildcatting in Kettleman Hills, California. The film ends with a scene depicting production at a massive oil field, implying that the pair, once again, become incredibly wealthy.

Conversely, the *Grapes of Wrath* (1940), which debuted in the same year as *Boomtown*, was a powerful depiction of Depression-era poverty and the struggles of honest sharecroppers to eke out mere subsistence. The film was directed by John Ford and was based on John Steinbeck's novel of the same title, published in 1939. The film centers on the Joads, a poor family of tenant farmers forced from their Oklahoma home by drought, economic hardship, agricultural industry changes, and bank foreclosures. The hopeless family heads West to California, where thousands of "Okies" sought farm labor. The film depicted blinding poverty, with authentic characters that suffer and die. They were not capitalist caricatures that espouse the myth of the American Dream, where the characters get rich quickly due to their hard work and ingenuity, ala *Boomtown* and *Pittsburgh*.

The film references communal living and the brutality of the landowning class, who have the police in their back pocket. Although not as powerful as the book, the film critiques capitalism, revealing how the free market, wage labor, and private-business model can lead to homelessness and extreme poverty. A memorable scene depicts how the capitalist system devalues humanity, with farmer Muley Graves questioning who was to blame for his eviction:

Agent: The fact of the matter, Muley, after what them dusters done to the land, the tenant system don't work no more. You don't even break even, much less show a profit. Why, one man and a tractor can handle twelve or fourteen of these places. You just pay him a wage and take all the crop.

Muley: Yeah, but uh, we couldn't do on any less than what our share is now. Why, the children ain't gettin' enough to eat as it is, and they're so ragged. We'd be ashamed if everybody else's children wasn't the same way.

Agent: I can't help that. All I know is, I got my orders. They told me to tell you to get off, and that's what I'm tellin' ya.

Muley: You mean get off of my own land?

Agent: Now don't go to blamin' me! It ain't my fault.
Muley's son: Who's fault is it?
Agent: You know who owns the land. The Shawnee Land and Cattle Company.
Muley: And who's the Shawnee Land and Cattle Company?
Agent: It ain't nobody. It's a company.
Muley's son: They got a President, ain't they? They got somebody who knows what a shotgun's for, ain't they?
Agent: Oh son, it ain't his fault because the bank tells him what to do.
Muley's son: All right, where's the bank?
Agent: Tulsa. What's the use of pickin' on him? He ain't nothin' but the manager. And he's half-crazy hisself tryin' to keep up with his orders from the East.
Muley: Then who do we shoot?
Agent: Brother, I don't know. If I did, I'd tell ya. I just don't know who's to blame.
Muley: I'm right here to tell you, mister, there ain't nobody gonna push me off my land! My grandpaw took up this land seventy years ago. My paw was born here. We was all born on it. An' some of us was killed on it. An' some of us died on it. That's what makes it arn. Bein' born on it and workin' on it and dyin', dyin' on it. An' not no piece of paper with writin' on it.

Nevertheless, the controversial social and political messages that thrive in the book did not translate on the screen. The socialist message that was omnipresent in the book was sanitized in favor of a sentimental human drama. The film even featured a happy ending, where the Joad family finds optimism in a clean camp run by the Department of Agriculture. Considering that the film was produced by a Hollywood mega-studio (20th Century Fox), and during the code era, it was still a very remarkable production.

Also directed by John Ford, *How Green Was My Valley* (1941) was a sentimental tale of the Morgans, a hardworking Welsh coal-mining family. The story was told through the eyes of Huw (Roddy McDowall), the youngest of the six Morgan brothers. The setting was a quaint village during the late-Victorian era. The film depicts the family saving their meager earnings, sharing hearty meals, and happily singing. The narrator, an elderly Huw, contrasts the past and present, transforming the valley from green to black.

> There is no fence nor hedge around time that is gone. You can go back and have what you like of it, if you can remember. So I can close my eyes on my valley as it is today, and it is gone, and I see it as it was when I was a boy. Green it was and possessed of the plenty of the Earth. In all Wales, there was none so beautiful. Everything I ever learned as a small boy came from my father, and I never found anything he ever told me to be wrong or worthless. The simple lessons he taught me are as sharp and clear in my mind as if I had heard them only yesterday. In those days, the black slag, the waste of the coal pits, had only begun to cover the sides of our hill. Not yet enough to mar the countryside, nor blacken the beauty of our village, for the colliery had only begun to poke its skinny black fingers through the green.

Certainly, the film's beginning was a romantic vision of coal mining far from the realities that many workers confronted. Despite the idyllic surroundings, the story provides a glimpse of miners' experiences, including wage reductions, hunger, family separation, dangerous working conditions, illness, and death. The mine owners cut wages, forcing the men to contemplate striking. The family patriarch, Gwilym (Donald Crisp), is against the strike, which causes his sons to leave the family's homestead. As the strike lingers on, Gwilym is scorned by the workers who are upset with his views on the strike. The ostracism leads to a powerful scene in which his wife Beth defiantly defends her husband in front of the miners. The confrontation leads the boys back to the homestead, recognizing that the family is more important than labor strife. However, despite the mixed messages, the film was decidedly pro-union, with the local minister, Mr. Gruffydd (Walter Pidgeon), telling the men, "First, have your union. You need it. Alone you are weak. Together you are strong."

After the strike is settled, the heartlessness of industry is revealed, as two of his sons are not retained, forced to seek new lives in America. The sentimental drama had several poignant scenes, including the death of the eldest son, Ivor, in a mine accident the same day his wife Bronwyn gives birth. There is also a scene in which children are sent down the mine shaft, including young Huw, who uses his meager earnings to help the widow, Bronwyn. The film culminates with a tragic mine accident that kills several coal miners, including the family patriarch, Gwilym. The final scene has Huw reminiscing, once again seeing his entire family sitting at the dinner table. The film was undoubtedly sentimental, an idealistic vision of life intermingled with tragedy and injustice in a mining village. Still, the film was not overly pessimistic or anti-capitalist.

Conversely, *Citizen Kane* (1941) is considered by some film historians as an anti-capitalist masterpiece. The story is centered on Charles Foster Kane's life, a character based on press baron William Randolph Hearst. The film was directed by Orson Welles and used a complex flashback structure to reveal pathetic insecurity and emptiness in the main character. The film depicts a wealthy and powerful businessman as sinister and tortured, not as a figure of romance and sentiment. Kane's motives are driven by a massive ego nourished by his incredible wealth. Kane utilizes his wealth and power to oppress those around him. He lifts the restraints in return for love, expecting them to be grateful for his magnanimous gesture. The notion parallels modern capitalism, in which corporations exploit workers, consumers, and the political system but will then give back to society, in obvious public relations exercises to drive profits further. Kane's college friend, the ethical, Jed Leland, tells Kane:

> Remember the working man ... he's turning into something called organized labor. You're not gonna like that one little bit when you find out it means that your working man expects something as his right not your gift ... when your precious underprivileged really get together, that's gonna add up to something bigger than your privilege and I -don't know what you'll do.

Hearst was enraged by the film, banning his newspaper from running advertisements and promotional material for the film. Hearst's newspapers targeted Welles as a communist sympathizer and questioned his patriotism. Louis B. Mayer of MGM studios even offered RKO studio President George Schaefer $842,000 to destroy the negative and all prints of Citizen Kane. After refusing to distribute the film, Schaefer threatened to sue Fox, Paramount, and Loew's theatre chains. In the end, the chains conceded and permitted a few showings, allowing the film to break even financially. Despite the difficulties, the film was nominated for nine Oscars, winning only one for best screenplay, with Welles being roundly booed during the ceremony (Mulvey, 2017).

Post-War Hollywood

From 1942 to 1945, Hollywood had experienced the most steady and profitable years in its history, peaking in 1946, when two-thirds of the American population went to the movies at least once a week. That soon changed as inflation and labor unrest lifted domestic production costs. The industry was severely diminished in 1948 when a federal antitrust against the five major and three minor studios ended in the "Paramount decrees," which compelled the studios to strip themselves of their theatre chains and required competition in the exhibition sector for the first time in 30 years. Lastly, the introduction of network television broadcasting in the 1940s gave Hollywood its first real competition for Americans' leisure time by offering entertainment at home (Croce, 2015; Schatz, 1999).

Post-war pictures continued a trend of depicting bankers in an unfavorable light. The Oscar-winning, *The Best Years of Our Lives* (1946) was a timely depiction of World War II vets' struggles acclimating to society. In a particularly poignant speech at a banquet for the Cornbelt Savings and Loan, the inebriated Al Stephenson derides the banking system and the lack of compassion for returning vets, with a cynical speech:

> I love the Cornbelt Loan and Trust Company. There are some who say that the old bank is suffering from hardening of the arteries and of the heart. I refuse to listen to such radical talk. I say that our bank is alive, it's, it's generous, it's, it's human, and we're going to have such a line of customers seeking and getting small loans that people will think we're gambling with the depositors' money. And we will be. We'll be gambling on the future of this country. I thank you

The same year, audiences were introduced to Mr. Potter (Lionel Barrymore), arguably the most famous banker in film history. A Christmas staple, *It's a Wonderful Life* (1946), was directed by Frank Capra and starred James Stewart as George Bailey, the reluctant owner of Bailey Building and Loan. Set in Bedford Falls, the story pits George against Mr. Potter, a cruel, greedy, and unfeeling banker.

> *Mr. Potter*: George, I am an old man, and most people hate me. But I don't like them either, so that makes it all even. You know just as well as I do that I run practically everything in this town but the Bailey Building and Loan. You know, also, that for a number of years I've been trying to get control of it. Or kill it. But I haven't been able to do it. You have been stopping me. In fact, you have beaten me, George, and as anyone in this county can tell you, that takes some doing. Now take during the Depression, for instance. You and I were the only ones that kept our heads. You saved the Building and Loan, I saved all the rest.
>
> *George Bailey*: Yes, well, most people say you stole all the rest.
>
> *Mr. Potter*: The envious ones say that, George. The suckers.

As Potter was offset by James Stewart's depiction of George Bailey, a quintessential American, a small businessman with a heart of gold, the film was not anti-capitalist. However, Bailey advocated for the socialistic notion of affordable housing and objected to monopolization. George attempts to stop a "run" on the Bailey Building & Loan, with George telling customers:

> If Potter gets hold of this Building and Loan, there'll never be another decent house built in this town … He wants to keep you living in his slums and paying the kind of rent he decides. Joe, you had one of those Potter houses, didn't you? Well, have you forgotten? Have you forgotten what he charged you for that broken-down shack? Here, Ed. You know, you remember last year when things weren't going so well, and you couldn't make your payments? You didn't lose your house, did you? Do you think Potter would have let you keep it? Can't you understand what's happening here? Don't you see what's happening? Potter isn't selling. Potter's buying! And why? Because we're panicking, and he's not. That's why. He's picking up some bargains. Now, we can get through this thing all right. We've got to stick together, though. We've got to have faith in each other.

It's a Wonderful Life was loosely inspired by Charles Dickens, *A Christmas Carol,* which has been adapted in several films and is also a staple at Christmas time. Dickens novels were a harsh indictment of industrial capitalism and the greed that pervades the upper classes. Nevertheless, Dicken's work was not purely socialistic, as it did not advocate for revolution, instead opting for a system in which the wealthy give back to communities through charitable actions (Owen, 2017). This narrative continues in contemporary society. The belief that capitalism can happily coexist with altruism, transforming billionaires into charitable philanthropists. These so-called virtuous capitalists now utilize their excessive, grotesque wealth for good, justifying the dishonest tactics that helped them acquire their fortunes.

It's a Wonderful Life is quintessential Americana, a classic film that is beloved by generations. However, the FBI had the film placed on a list of suspected communist propaganda, keeping it there until 1956. An FBI memo (dated May 26, 1947) stated that

With regard to the picture *It's a Wonderful Life*, [redacted] stated in substance that the film represented rather obvious attempts to discredit bankers by casting Lionel Barrymore as a "scrooge-type" so that he would be the most hated man in the picture ... This, according to these sources, is a common trick used by Communists.

In 1947, the House Un-American Activities Committee even had a hearing on *It's a Wonderful Life*, with critic John Charles Moffitt defending the picture, "I think Mr. Capra's picture, though it had a banker as villain, could not be properly called a Communist picture. It showed that the power of money can be used oppressively, and it can be used benevolently" (Noakes, 1998).

McCarthyism Lands in Hollywood, the 1950s

Film content was strongly affected by the fear of communism that permeated in the late 1940s and early 1950s. The witch-hunts began in 1947 when the House of Un-American Activities Committee (HUAC) investigated communist influences in the movies. Over 100 witnesses, including some of Hollywood's most prominent actors, directors, screenwriters, and producers testified at the hearings. A group of eight screenwriters and two directors, best known as the Hollywood Ten, were sentenced to prison for refusing to testify. The Association for Motion Picture Producers, comprised mainly of studio heads, published the so-called Waldorf Declaration, articulating their support of HUAC and firing the Hollywood Ten. So began an unofficial policy of blacklisting or denying employment to any person suspected of having communist associations or leanings. Filmmakers abstained from producing films that were left-leaning or controversial. As such, the 1950s continued the trend of non-critical depictions of the corporate or business elite. Socially conscious films could be deemed communist and subject to draconian censorship. Worse yet, producers and screenwriters would be blacklisted for any perceived attack on capitalism or the business class. In 1952, films were granted free speech rights under the First Amendment, foreshadowing the end of the Production Code. The Code was officially abandoned in 1968 and replaced by a system of age-based ratings that exist to this day. Film noir became a dominant genre in the late 1940s and 1950s. Film noirs, which translates to "black cinema," is a stylized film marked by pessimism, fatalism, and cynicism. Nevertheless, most studios continued to focus on traditional fares, such as westerns, musicals, and comedies that were safe and sanitized (Croce, 2015).

Corporate Culture on Film: The Beginnings

The decade featured several films that explored corporate culture, including *Executive Suite* (1954), *Woman's World* (1954), *The Man in the Gray Flannel Suit* (1956), and *Patterns* (1956). That said, these films were not the first films to negatively portray corporate politics and practices. *Oil for the Lamps of China* (1935) featured Stephen Chase (Pat O'Brien), an enterprising, albeit naïve young man that works for the Atlantis Oil company. Chase puts the corporation first, relocating to China and neglecting his pregnant wife. Despite his faith in the corporation, a ruthless new manager puts considerable pressure on him to quit, giving his position to a subordinate and assigning Stephen menial tasks. True to the Production Code, the film had a happy ending, as Chase is reinstated by the President of Atlantis, restoring Stephen's faith in the company. *Executive Suite* is a gripping tale of the backroom deals by executive staff at the Tredway Company, a large furniture manufacturing business. The story begins in New York City, as Avery Bullock leaves a meeting with investment bankers to return to his company's headquarters in Pennsylvania. After he arranges a meeting with his executives, he dies while waiting for a cab. The death causes a commotion, where George Caswell, an external board member of Tredway, looks out the window to observe Bullock's dead body being taken away by authorities. Like a vulture, Caswell immediately phones his stockbroker, instructing him to sell short on Tredway stock. Caswell believes that the stock will plummet when the death becomes public knowledge, and he will make a substantial profit repurchasing the stock at a discount. Caswell's scheme takes an unexpected turn, as Bullock's body is not readily identified. The panicked Caswell phones the police, tipping them off about the dead man's identity, whom the newspapers had labeled as John Doe, with only the monogram, AB on his suit. In the meantime, the story turns to the company headquarters in Pennsylvania, where the viewer is introduced to vice presidents, each with equal standing in the company: VP and Treasurer, Fred Alderson (Walter Pidgeon); VP Manufacturing, Jesse Grimm (Dean Jagger); VP and Controller, Loren P. Shaw (Fredric March); VP for Sales, J. Walter Dudley (Paul Douglas); and VP Design and Development, McDonald "Mac" Walling (William Holding). The vice presidents anxiously await the return of Bullock, surprised the usually prompt Bullock is not in attendance of the meeting he just called. With the help of Caswell's insider tip, Bullock's death is announced, which propels the plot into the struggle for control of the company.

The story is a fascinating glimpse into each man's motivations and the tangled backstories that impede their promotion to the top position. Fred Alderson is the logical successor but is quickly undermined by the ambitious Loren Shaw, who callously arranges the funeral so that employees would not get the day off work. In the end, it comes down to two men, Loren P. Shaw, the company controller, who is more concerned with profit over quality and MacDonald Walling, the design chief, who wants to streamline designs and bring back quality products. Shaw is the quintessential corporate villain, focused on profits and shareholder dividends. Shaw is shrewd and calculating, orchestrating a scheme to take control of the company. He sets a board meeting, knowing that he needs four votes out of seven board members to gain the presidency. Shaw blackmails the VP of Sales, who was having an affair with his secretary and makes a deal with Caswell, promising to cover his short sale if Caswell votes for Shaw as president. He also manipulates Julia Tredway, a major shareholder and receives her proxy vote. In contrast, McDonald Walling is devoted to quality craftsmanship and is very concerned about the company's future if a "bean counter" like Shaw is elected president.

Unlike Shaw, Walling is concerned for the workers, and the town, which depends on the company as a major source of employment.

Shaw smugly awaits the vote in the culminating scene, knowing he has the votes to win the presidency. Shaw confidently argues for his cold and calculated approach to business, claiming that the primary emphasis should be on return on investment. Shaw arguing that the business should be "a financial institution yielding the highest and safest return on investment." Shaw believes that the emphasis must be on the financial aspects of the corporation, not on manufacturing and selling. He decries the notion that "efficiency" should be seen as a dirty word. In response, Walling delivers a heartfelt speech, advocating for superior product quality and growth. Walling condemns the quality of the product, going as far as to break a piece of furniture that was of substandard quality. Walling believes that they have a bigger obligation, to use profits to ensure the company's growth, not to appease shareholders. Walling vociferously argues that "you can't make men work for money alone—you starve their souls when you try it, and you can starve a company to death the same way." In typical Hollywood fashion, the good guy wins, with Walling assuming the presidency of the company. The film certainly renewed faith in the business world, as the new leader is depicted as having ethics and is motivated to serve the customers' best interests. Unfortunately, this is not a reality in the current corporate environment, as financial considerations often precede consumer happiness, employee rights, and business ethics.

Corporate succession was also a central plotline in *Woman's World*, a drama mixed with comedic elements. The film featured a trio of executives competing for the top position at Gifford Motor Company. The owner decides to interview the contenders' wives as part of the selection process. In melodramatic fashion, the weaknesses or strengths of marriage are explored, with a dramatic ending. The winning executive jettisons his predatory wife, realizing that she is manipulative and insincere. Similarly, *The Man in the Gray Flannel Suit* is set in the corporate world, depicting an ever-increasing corporate organization of society, reducing white-collar workers or "gray-suited men" to "yes men." The film depicts a world in which the collective demands of the corporation clashes with individualism, including the traditional roles of spouse and parent. In the end, the protagonist, Tom Rath (Gregory Peck), decides that family is more important than the corporation, turning down a promotion, as he wants to "work 9 to 5 and spend the rest of the time with my family." In a similar vein, the romantic-comedy *Desk Set* (1957) featured employees at a large media corporation who worry that they are being replaced by a computer, a clash involving automation, efficiency, and cost-cutting in the corporate world. These corporate culture films reveal how the democratic tenets of fair play ultimately triumph in the corporate setting, thus propelling a mythological narrative within corporate culture, in which ethics win out over unscrupulousness. Excepting the poor-quality products depicted in *Executive Suite*, corporate wrongdoing was not fundamental to the storylines.

Alternatively, corporate cruelty and malice were brilliantly depicted in *Patterns*. The story is highlighted by the aggressive and harsh management style of Walter Ramsey (Everett Sloane), a cold, manipulative, and ruthless CEO of the

Ramsey Corporation. Ramsey seeks to replace his longtime second in command, Bill Briggs (Ed Begley), with his new hire, industrial engineer Fred Staples (Van Heflin). Briggs is affable and humane, and Ramsey does not believe he is suitable for the modern corporate world based on efficiency and cold-heartedness. However, Staples forms a quick friendship with the like-minded Briggs, creating a moral dilemma for the new hire. Ramsey plans to create an untenable environment for Briggs, forcing him into retirement. Under stress, Briggs has a massive heart attack and tragically perishes. Unfortunately, the ending corresponds with the notion that good guys can win in the corporate world, with Staples taking the position with the mission to ensure that Ramsey is held in check and held accountable for his actions. The film provides viewers with mixed messages, which are ultimately contingent on points of view. The pro-business crowd may view the film as pro-capitalist, revealing that the dog-eat-dog ethos is necessary for the corporate environment, with men like Ramsey essential for economic survival. In contrast, anti-capitalists view the heartlessness of Ramsey as indicative of the entire problem with corporations and corporate structure – the lack of humanity.

While Patterns was a thought-provoking drama about the inner workings of a corporation, the comedy *Solid Gold Cadillac* (1956) was a light and fluffy depiction of corporate wrongdoing. The film features unethical corporate executives that are not accountable to shareholders. These overpaid executives utilize insider information, and resort to cronyism to try to manipulate government contracts. The story begins at a shareholders meeting of an International Projects, a large publicly traded corporation, where the company's founder and CEO is resigning to work for the federal government. Laura Partridge (Judy Holliday) is a minority shareholder who only owns ten shares of the company but is resolute in asking difficult questions about the decisions being made by the board of directors, asking the men how they justify such large salaries. She proves quite burdensome for the self-serving executives. They decide to give her a made-up position of director of shareholder relations, to keep her occupied and distracted from their sordid business dealings. There is nothing to do, so she writes the shareholders, gaining a following in the process. Laura uncovers several crooked ventures, insider trading, political cronyism and attempts to secure government contracts. The film culminates at a board meeting, where Laura replaces the entire board of directors with the help of smaller investors through proxy votes. In typical Hollywood fashion, good triumphs over evil, as the American corporation rids itself of unethical and corrupt business practices. The villains are reduced to cartoonish caricatures, not reflective of the reality of corporate wrongdoing or corruption. Still, the film was a good satire on corporate greed, exposing the ethics and machinations of corporate boards.

Conversely, the ugliness of corporate greed was on full display in the French-language film *Wages of Fear* (1953). The film was primarily a thriller that incorporates psychological drama with suspenseful action. The masterful film was decidedly anti-American, with a not-so-subtle message about industry exploitation of developing countries. The setting was in the fictional village of Las Piedras, in an unspecified Latin American country. The plot features four down-on-their-luck

European men hired to transport the highly explosive nitroglycerine over treacherous mountain roads to extinguish a fire at an oil well. The fictional Southern Oil Company (SOC) dominates the local economy, exploiting local workers and the environment. In a very compelling scene, a woman addresses a crowd of villagers, decrying the corporation's treatment of the residents,

> They came around with their money. "To make you rich," they said. No! To ruin our lives! To send our boys to their death. And yesterday, a catastrophe happened. It's not fair. We're always the ones to suffer. We're always the ones to die! The gringos never die! They kill my father or your brother. They give you a handful of money, and that's that!

The scene cuts to Bill O'Brien, an American that works for the company. On the phone, he tells an underling that the safety commission is coming, telling them to "give a good meal, and plenty of liquor, put all the blame on the victims." He callously tells managers that the one dead American will be the scapegoat for the accident. He further details the plan of bypassing the union to hire "tramps" to drive the trucks through the rugged and dangerous terrain. In 1955, the film was released in the United States, but only after anti-American scenes, totaling 35 minutes, were cut from the original version. Even without editing, the anti-corporate message was lost on most audiences, as the focus was on the gripping drama that ensued from the terrifying drive through the rough terrain. An American version of the film *Violent Road* (aka *Hell's Highway*) was released in 1958, and naturally, the anti-corporate and anti-American message was eliminated. The oil company was replaced with a rocket development plant. In 1977, William Friedkin produced and directed, *Sorcerer*, loosely based on the original French novel, *Le Salaire da la peur* (*The Salary of Fear*). The exploitation of the land and workers remained in this version.

Labor on Film, 1950s Style

In 1952, the famed director, Elia Kazan, "named names" during testimony before the House of Un-American Activities Committee (HUAC), identifying eight others who had been Communist Party members with him during the 1930s. As a result, Kazan became a traitor in some Hollywood circles. Many writers and actors who refused to "name names" were blacklisted, and their careers in Hollywood destroyed (Navasky, 2003). Released in 1954, *On the Waterfront* was Kazan's justification for his snitching on his friends and colleagues. The classic film depicts union corruption and violence on the waterfronts of Hoboken, New Jersey. Terry Malloy (Marlon Brando) becomes an informant, testifying in court against union-sponsored corruption and murder. The film helped propagate the theme that unions were corrupt, toiling at the behest of the mob. This image is played repeatedly in several movies. Aside from the corrupt union angle, only a few films attempted to depict the plight of workers pitted against corporate greed. A comedy/musical, *The Pajama Game* (1957) starred Doris Day as Babe Williams, a member of the union's grievance committee. The light-hearted film was an artifact of the times, a non-threatening depiction of workers' demands and rights. The workers at a pajama factory are threatening to strike. The workers demand a raise of seven-and-a-half cents, highlighted by several musical numbers such as "Racing with the clock," which underscores their plight. In the end, it is revealed that the crooked manager had instituted a raise a month earlier and was greedily pocketing the money for himself. The labor strife ends, with the workers given their rightful wage.

In sharp contrast, *The Salt of the Earth* (1954) was a grim portrait of the exploitation of salt mine workers in New Mexico. It was a far cry from comedies such as *The Solid Gold Cadillac*, *Desk Set*, and *The Pajama Game* and very distant from the board rooms in *Executive Suite* and *Patterns*. Independently produced, the film was sponsored by the International Union of Mine, Mill and Smelter Workers and featured the efforts of blacklisted Hollywood writers, directors, and actors. The screenplay was written by Michael Wilson, who had been blacklisted after the HUAC hearings. The film was produced by Paul Jarrico and directed by Herbert Biberman, who were also blacklisted. Finally, Will Greer, a noted blacklisted actor and labor activist, also appeared as the Sheriff. The film was based on the 1951 Empire Zinc strike in Grant County, New Mexico. The film only included five professional actors, with several local union members rounding out the cast of characters. For instance, the protagonist Ramon Quintero was played by Juan Chacón, the real-life union local president involved in the strike. Mexican actress Rosaura Revueltas depicted his wife, Esperanza, as a struggling mother of three who yearned for equality within her home over her domineering yet loving husband. The film was decidedly pro-union, with the mineworkers going on strike over the dangerous working conditions at the fictional Delaware Mining company. The company utilizes the Taft-Hartley Act to prevent the men from picketing outside the mine. Circumventing the injunction, the wives replace the men on the strike line, with Esperanza joining the picket lines while carrying her newborn baby. In a poignant scene, the company resorts to evicting the Quintero family from their home, only to meet with resistance from a mass of workers and their families, who successfully protest and prevent the eviction. In the end, the company decides to settle, with Esperanza triumphantly ending the story, saying "then I knew we had won something they could never take away, something that I could leave for my children, and they the salt of the earth would inherit it." The film was condemned as "subversive" and encountered obstacles in its production and distribution (Lorence, 1999). The United States House of Representatives accused *Salt of the Earth* of having communist sympathies, the FBI investigated the film's financing, and the American Legion asked for a nationwide boycott. It opened in New York City but sunk to obscurity, as only 12 theatres allowed it to be screened. The film was revived in the 1970s, as labor activists, feminists, and film scholars rediscovered the film's important message surrounding the dismantling of race, class, and gender barriers. Fundamentally, the groundbreaking, historically significant film is a powerful expose of the ruthlessness of corporations, with vivid depictions of dangerous working conditions, poor pay, and racism that permeated the mining industry.

Cash McCall Meet Ralph Nader, 1960s

Business and corporate ethics, or lack thereof, were important elements within the storylines of romantic comedies, *The Apartment* (1960) and *Cash McCall* (1960). Directed by Billy Wilder, *The Apartment* starred Jack Lemmon as C.C. "Bud" Baxter, a lowly employee of an insurance corporation in New York City. Baxter desperately wants to climb the corporate ladder and garners favor by allowing his company managers to use his Upper West Side apartment to carry on extramarital dalliances. The film subtly roasts corporate culture by highlighting executives who reward employees with promotions for covering up their immoral behaviors. An American classic, the picture won the Academy Award and is considered one of the best comedies of all time. Conversely, *Cash McCall* is a pedestrian film that has largely been forgotten. The film was based on a Cameron Hawley novel and starred James Garner as the titular character. McCall is a corporate vulture who buys struggling businesses and disassembles them for profit. Cash is initially depicted as a scoundrel that abandons and forsakes the workers and communities that depended on the companies. The opening scene features McCall's lawyer, Winston Conway (E.G. Marshall), discussing Cash's dubious transactions.

Winston Conway: All of his [Cash McCall's] actions in reference to Mr. Tompkins and the Tompkins land company have been one-hundred percent legal.
Reporter: There is a difference between legal and moral.
Winston Conway: I'm not a moralist. I am a lawyer.

Given that it was a romantic comedy, the protagonist softens considerably during the film, becoming a full-fledged business humanitarian that puts communities first and foremost, producing the typical happy ending. The film was a light and fluffy depiction of unethical financial practices. It did not illustrate the dangers of unrestrained capitalism, where merger mania can lead to unfair trade practices, layoffs of employees, and the cheating of consumers. Similarly, *How to Succeed in Business Without Really Trying* (1967) depicted corporate betrayal, corruption, and nepotism. A musical, the film follows the rising career of a young window cleaner to the board chairman. The film was a precursor to several 1980s comedies about rising through the business world, such as *The Secret to My Success* (1987) and *Working Girl* (1988).

The 1960s also introduced Ralph Nader to the business, political, and social landscape. Nader is a prominent consumer activist who works tirelessly to promote progressive ideas. His work has enhanced public awareness and heightened public knowledge, and increased government and corporate accountability. Like the early muckrakers, his advocacy inspired an entire generation of consumer advocates, citizen activists, and public interest lawyers who have formed their own grassroots organizations throughout the country and abroad. A lawyer, Nader's most famous treatise was his pioneering book *Unsafe at Any Speed*, which was a blistering condemnation of the auto industry's safety record. The book revealed that the auto industry knowingly neglected safety to focus on the comfort and marketability of their products. The book precipitated several congressional hearings and the establishment of automobile safety laws in 1966. In 1968, Ralph Nader founded the Center for the Study of Responsive Law, a public advocacy group that included seven law student volunteers, popularly known as "Nader's Raiders." Initially, the organization investigated the Federal Trade Commission (FTC), which protected consumers from faulty products, fraudulent business practices, and deceptive advertising. They discovered the FTC was utterly ineffective, with rampant cronyism and overly incompetent bureaucracy that allowed corporate America free access to reap enormous profits at the expense of consumers. As a result of their report, the American Bar Association commenced a probe, which led President Nixon to revitalize the agency and pass stricter anti-trust legislation. Since 1969, the Center has actively worked in air and water pollution, food, nuclear energy, auto and occupational safety, pensions, Freedom of Information, government corruption, and corporate welfare.

Ralph Nader was also instrumental in developing and expanding federal consumer protection laws, including the motor vehicle safety laws, the Safe Drinking Water Act, the Pure Food and Drug Act, the Clean Air Act, and the landmark Freedom of Information Act. His work contributed to the introduction of federal regulatory agencies such as the Occupational Safety and Health Administration (OSHA), the Environmental Protection Agency (EPA), and the Consumer Product Safety Commission (CPSC). Nader's activism led him to be cited as one of the 100 most influential figures in American history (Bollier, 2021). In the early 1980s, under the banner, New Citizen Productions, Nader and his associates were in discussions to bring several movie projects to the American public. After the success of *Norma Rae* (1979) and *The China Syndrome* (1979), there was optimism that a Ralph Nader Production might have some traction with moviegoers. Mark Litwak, the President of the fledgling New Citizen Productions, believed that the success of *The China Syndrome* would inspire more stories that focused on critical social issues (Hamilton, 1980). The Nader-inspired films were never developed. Years later, Nader and his supporters pitched a script based on *Unsafe at Any Speed*. In the mid-1990s, HBO was interested in producing the script, hiring three different scriptwriters and spending over $500,000 on the process. However, after Production President Bob Cooper left HBO, the plans were quietly abandoned. Nader was not even told that the option for the book was not being renewed, learning about it through a second-hand conversation. Nader wrote a letter to Time-Warner asking if external factors or advertiser concerns impacted the reversal of interest, believing that HBO parent company Time Warner did not want to upset corporate interests. Nader alleged that Ted Turner, vice chairman of Time-Warner, told him that G.M. was one of their biggest advertisers. They could not insult them again, back-peddling by telling Nader that it was an old story and they were producing safer cars. Former HBO executive, Bob Cooper who had championed the Ralph Nader vs. General Motors script, claimed that the change of direction is just the inner workings of Hollywood, which can be fickle and unpredictable (Eller, 2000). Ironically, Hollywood has produced several biopics that celebrate business giants, such as Howard Hughes, Bill Gates, and Steve Jobs.

Hollywood likes the "David vs. Goliath" story, where the underdog takes on seemingly insurmountable odds, a manifestation of Nader versus giant corporations. Even so, the likelihood of a Nader biopic has been considerably reduced after the 2000 election. Many establishment Democrats unjustly blamed him for the defeat of Al Gore at the hands of Republican George W. Bush. Corporate America likely salivated after the so-called "limousine liberals" blamed Nader rather than an ineffective political system rife with corporate donations, corruption, and gerrymandering. Nader ran an idealistic campaign to highlight the problems within the political establishment. He ran afoul of the Democratic political machine, with his rightful criticism of Democrats' reliance on corporate donations and their growing attachment to corporate interests. For example, under the Clinton presidency, Wall Street was deregulated, which ended Glass-Steagall protections, precipitating increased bank mergers and financial speculation. The Clinton administration further promoted a corporate globalist agenda with the promotion and passage of NAFTA. As a Green Party candidate, Nader campaigned to end the drug war, promoted workers' rights and fair trade, established free education and universal health care, and abolished corporate control over the political process (Shor, 2016).

While Nader was making his mark fighting for consumer rights, in the latter part of the 1960s, Hollywood was experiencing a renaissance of sorts. The so-called New Hollywood was a film movement that roughly started in 1967 and ended in 1976. The movement was led by a handful of film students heavily influenced by foreign films and a desire to challenge the status quo. Also known as Hollywood New Wave, notable filmmakers such as George Lucas, Steven Spielberg, Martin Scorsese, Peter Bogdanovich, Brian De Palma, and Francis Ford Coppola brought independent and radical perspectives to mainstream filmmaking, which had grown stale and stagnant (Croce, 2015). However, the new wave of young filmmakers did not turn their attention to corporate America, with only a handful of films that critiqued contemporary corporations or industry. In 1969, independent filmmaker Robert Downey Sr. wrote and directed *Putney Swope*, an avant-garde satire of the advertising industry that incorporated themes of racism with corporate and political corruption. The film starred Arnold Johnson as the titular character, Putney Swope. The avant-garde film had a successful run as an "arthouse picture," depicting advertising as a parasitical industry that targets consumers with deceptive tactics and pushes harmful products.

The film is set in New York's Madison Avenue, best known as the advertising capital of the world. The movie opens at an agency board meeting, where the executives argue about advertising. One executive claimed that "our job is to manipulate the consumer by arousing his desires, and then we satisfy those desires for a fixed price." The "token" African American, Putney Swope, serves as the music director who urges the board to drop the toy guns account, as it promotes violence. He is quickly dismissed, and the CEO arrives to pitch a groundbreaking advertising idea. The CEO starts to stutter and stammer, dying from a stroke before finishing his thoughts. The executives hold an immediate election for a replacement, with the deceased CEO still lying on the table. Board rules prohibit members from voting for themselves, so in a secret ballot, each executive picks Swope, believing that he is the least likely to be voted the new CEO. In an accidental twist, Swope is unanimously voted in as the chairman, and he promptly fires all but one of the white executives. Swope replaces the board with militant black power activists and changes the firm's name to "Truth and Soul, Inc." He prohibits the firm from producing advertisements for liquor, cigarettes, or toy guns. He revolutionizes the ad agency and seeks out new ideas that do not cater to the establishment. Surprisingly, the firm becomes very profitable with money bags symbolically deposited in a large glass structure. The film is shot in black and white, while the commercials are seen in color. The president of the United States is a drug-addled little person controlled by corporate executives and interests. The president persuades Putney to advertise the Borman Six roadster, an unsafe automobile that features "defects, pollution, velvet safety belts, strobe headlights, [and] fiberglass windshields." As the film progresses, Putney loses his values, becoming an autocrat who hires and fires employees, steals ideas, and creates obscene commercials. At the movie's end, he "cops out" and asks his executive team to develop ideas for liquor, cigarettes, and toy guns. Initially, his executives resist, and Putney tells his bodyguard that he is pleased, as it was a test to see if his executives would "cop" out. However, soon after, the executives decided that working with the harmful corporations was acceptable, greedily accepting the bags of money from the glass enclosure – the former militants succumbing to the allure of big money. In the final scene, the glass tower case is set afire, a metaphor for the greed of capitalism and the downfall of morality and idealism.

We're Mad as Hell and We Are Not Going to Take It Anymore, the 1970s

As America entered the 1970s, a new generation of young filmmakers thrived in Hollywood. They radically absconded from outdated filmmaking standards and traditional values to create films that were more pessimistic and cynical, with such films as *Midnight Cowboy* (1969), *Five Easy Pieces* (1970), *Mean Streets* (1973), and *Taxi Driver* (1976). The collective trauma of Vietnam was mirrored in these films, with a fundamental sense of powerlessness and disorientation, which was set in a corrupt and exploitative system (Cook, 2002). The theme of paranoia was submerged within conspiratorial depictions of government and corporations. The growing distrust of corporations, government, and authority peaked after the Vietnam War, Watergate, the release of the Pentagon Papers, and revelations of crimes committed by the CIA. The decade also introduced the "whistleblower" to audiences, including *Serpico* (1973) and *All the President's Men* (1976), both based on true stories. *Serpico* starred Al Pacino as the titular character, who doggedly exposed corruption within the NYPD. In comparison, *All the President's Men* featured the exploits of Robert Woodward (Robert

Redford) and Carl Bernstein (Dustin Hoffman), *Washington Times* reporters who uncovered Watergate.

While the "whistleblower" emerged as a protagonist, the corporation became a symbol of distrust, with murky depictions that implied that big business exerted much power, controlling the highest levels of government, and was capable of murder to achieve complete control of society. For example, *The Parallax View* (1974) depicts a nebulous vision of a corporation, which recruits assassins to murder for corporate and business interests. Although the specific reason for the murders is never fully revealed, the corporation motivations are solely profit-oriented, in the form of a "finders fee." The film commences with the assassination of a prominent politician at the Space Needle in Seattle, Washington. A governmental commission reports that the murder was committed by a sole perpetrator, who had died after falling off the space needle. However, the audience sees two shooters at the scene of the crime. Three years later, television reporter Lee Carter visits her former boyfriend, investigative journalist Joe Frady (Warren Beatty), telling him that they are in danger as she witnessed the assassination. Clearly paranoid, she tells him that she is afraid for her life, as she has uncovered that six of the witnesses have mysteriously died. The unsympathetic Frady dismisses her concerns, telling her that he no longer believes others were involved in the murder. However, after Lee turns up dead, in an apparent overdose, Frady begins to probe her theory and soon uncovers documents that reveal that the Parallax Corporation is recruiting political assassins. The film is a complex thriller that follows Frady's investigation into the mysterious corporation. In a non-traditional Hollywood ending, Frady is framed for the assassination of a politician and subsequently murdered by a hitman hired by the corporation. Mirroring the beginning, a governmental committee reports that Frady was the sole perpetrator, who killed the politician out of paranoia and misguided patriotism.

The Conversation (1974) also featured a shadowy corporate entity that was unclear in nature. The film starred Gene Hackman as Harry Caul, a surveillance expert who appears to work for business or corporate interests. Caul is aware that his recordings may be used for nefarious purposes, even murder. However, after taping the conversation of Ann and Mark, he is no longer able to maintain his professional distance or apathy. He believes that his client, "the director" of what is presumed to be a large corporation, may have the young lovers murdered. In a moment of moral clarity, Caul refuses to hand over the tapes, fearing that the conversation on the tapes may precipitate the murder of the couple. However, Caul misunderstood the conversation, mistakenly believing that the couple was in danger when it was the couple plotting to kill "the director." The viewer learns that Ann is the director's wife and is having an affair with Mark, another employee at the corporation. They murder the director, which leads Harry to question reality. The viewer questions whether the murder occurred or whether it was a figment of Caul's deteriorating mental state and paranoia. Regardless, the film depicts corporations as an increasingly complex and bureaucratic power structure that is impenetrable, ambiguous, and mysterious.

Paranoia was a central feature in *Coma* (1978), a conspiratorial thriller that stoked distrust within the medical establishment. The film provided a glimpse into the bureaucratic machinations of a large organization. This time in a hospital that held a disturbing secret where healthy and young patients were mysteriously going into comas after surgery. Dr. Susan Wheeler (Genevieve Bujold), a surgical resident, starts a personal investigation into unexplained comas. She uncovers a wicked plot involving the Jefferson Institute, a shadowy corporate entity that profits from the sale of organs. The cadavers become commodities to be sold on the black market for a substantial profit. The climatic ending reveals that the Chief of Surgery, Dr. George Harris (Richard Widmark), was the ringleader for a conspiracy carried out by the shadowy corporation.

Film noir resurfaced in Roman Polanksi's *Chinatown* (1974). The film was a complex and vivid depiction of political and economic corruption involving a water conspiracy in 1930s' Los Angeles. The film starred Jack Nicholson as Jake Gittes, a meddlesome private detective involved in a tangled plot of deception, double-crossing, and greed. Gittes provides evidence of extramarital affairs, and he is hired by a woman who claims to be the wife of Hollis Mulwray, the head of the Water and Power Department. Jake collects the evidence of infidelity, which Jake is surprised to find in the newspaper. Jake is confronted by Hollis's real wife, Evelyn Mulwray (Faye Dunaway), who threatens to sue Jake for ruining her husband's reputation. Soon afterwards, Hollis's drowned body is discovered in the Oak Pass Reservoir, which leads Jake to question the finding of suicide, determined to find answers to the death. Jake discovers Hollis was murdered because he was about to expose a massive corruption scheme involving the city's water supply. The rich and powerful Noah Cross (John Huston) was at the center of the scheme, which involved a collection of wealthy and influential members of the Albacore Club, a private association of the elite of Los Angeles society. He is part of a more extensive corrupt system in which exploitation and dishonesty reach the highest levels in business and government.

The nefarious plot involved triggering an artificial drought for the entire city of Los Angeles, duping the citizens into building an unnecessary and dangerous dam, poisoning the wells in the Northwest Valley to force farmers to sell their orange groves at artificially low prices, and using residents of a retirement home as straw men for massive land purchases in the valley. Noah Cross is the archetype of American entrepreneurism and a self-made man who rises from rags to riches. In this way, he represents the robber barons of the past, a wealthy and influential businessman that achieved the American Dream. The film highlights the myth of America built on self-made men that have superior qualities that enable them to rise to the top. Instead, it reveals a shallow façade underlying the American Dream, in which there are monstrous levels of greed and even perversion. For instance, Cross is involved in an incestuous relationship with his daughter, with whom he bore a child. Noah Cross is the personification of an evil character, yet he maintains his power and agency throughout the film. Even in the end, he is not held to account for his horrible crimes. In New Hollywood, happy endings were not the norm, reflecting the pessimism and cynicism of the 1970s. The conspiracy that governs the plot is based on an actual scandal in Los Angeles in 1904. A consortium of investors illegally acquired knowledge of a proposal to build an aqueduct in the city. The conspirators bought masses of cheap land in the San Fernando Valley, knowing that the property would become fertile and increase in value. A central figure in the plot, Water Commissioner William Mulholland, is celebrated with plaques in the city. The film had a bleak view of America's founding "fathers" exposing them as purveyors of fraud. Essentially, *Chinatown* is a metaphor for the unstable values and ingrained corruption embedded within the psyche of 1970s' America (Thomson, 2004).

The Struggle of Labor, 1970s Style

In the 1970s, there were a handful of films that depicted the labor movement. Loosely based on a true story, *The Molly Maguires* (1970) depicted the labor wars of Pennsylvania in the 1870s. The meandering film shows the dangerous working conditions and low pay that were associated with the coal industry. The miners were subject to deductions, including the cost of explosives and shovels. The film starred Richard Harris as James McParlan, a notorious labor spy for the Pinkerton Detective agency. Taking the name McKenna, he investigates the Molly Maguires, a radical group of laborers who destroy company property, flood mines, and assault supervisors. The Molly Maguires were a secret group of Irish American miners alleged to have committed a series of violent assaults, arsons, and murders from 1861 to 1875 in Schuykill County, Pennsylvania. In the film, the ringleader is "Black Jack" Kehoe (Sean Connery), who initially suspects McKenna is a spy until they slowly become friends. In the end, McKenna's true identity is revealed with Kehoe and his accomplices sentenced to death for their crimes. As McParlen visits Kehoe in his cell, the story ends dramatically, with Kehoe telling him that "You'll never be free. There is no punishment this side of hell that can free you from what you did." McParlen cleverly retorts, "see you in hell". In real life, McParlan's testimony led to the execution of 20 men, with ten executed on June 21, 1877, better known as Black Thursday. Many historians debate the very existence of the Maguires. However, most agree that the trial and executions were a blight on the criminal justice system. In fact, John Kehoe, the "King" of the Molly Maguires, was given a full posthumous pardon in 1979 (Kenney, 1998).

Conversely, *Which Way Is Up?* (1977) was a comedy that starred Richard Pryor in three roles, a fruit picker named LeRoy, his grouchy, oversexed father, and a shady preacher. After inadvertently getting caught up with a labor protest, union-busting thugs force him from his cramped home. Without his wife and kids, Leroy moves to Los Angeles, where he has an affair (and son) with a labor organizer, Vanetta. After witnessing an attempted murder of an American Farm Workers United (AFWU) leader, he becomes a corporate pawn, becoming an executive with an agricultural conglomerate, AGRICO FOODS. Leroy relocates back home, where he attempts to balance two wives and families. However, he is transformed from a simple orange picker to a heartless manager who suppresses the plant's labor movement and safety issues. His former friends turn on him, with one friend yelling at him, "You don't care about us man, or the union. All you care about is your goddamn quota. Well, what about us?" In the end, Leroy loses his friends, his two wives, and decides to quit his position. The film was essentially a vehicle for the comedic stylings of Richard Pryor, but it did draw attention to management's efforts to stifle labor organizing. Pryor also starred in *Blue Collar* (1978), which depicted the working-class in the Rust Belt and corrupt union practices. The film was primarily a crime drama that had nominal amounts of patented Pryor humor. The plot featured three auto workers who steal from the union, only to find incriminating information linking the union to organized crime. The film features corruption, murder, and conflicts between the former friends. *Blue Collar* was a gritty drama that showed the consequences of union corruption on the plight of the worker.

Similarly, *F.I.S.T.* (1978) was a crime drama that highlighted union corruption. The film starred Sylvester Stallone as Johnny Kovak, a labor organizer in Cleveland, Ohio, and was a thinly veiled attempt to fictionalize the rise and fall of Jimmy Hoffa. Set in the 1930s, the movie illustrated the unfair working conditions that dockworkers faced, with no overtime pay, unreasonable cutting of pay for damaged products, and unwarranted dismissals. Kovak starts to work as a recruiter at the Federation of Inter-State Truckers (F.I.S.T.), where he rises to a leadership role. The movie features crooked industry leaders, strike-breakers, violence, collusion with the local mob, and unethical union practices. In the end, Kovak is killed and made to disappear, with the bumper sticker "Where's Johnny?" appearing on the back of an 18-wheeler, mimicking the story of Hoffa. In the end, the labor collusion with the mafia becomes the overarching theme, mitigating the noble telling of unfair labor practices.

The Hollywood "Renaissance"

The so-called Hollywood "renaissance" featured a new generation of groundbreaking film directors that challenged audiences and diverged from standard filmmaking norms. However, the 1970s also featured many films bereft of social meaning and imbued with sheer escapist themes with the sole purpose of profit. For example, the 1970s introduced the concept of the summer blockbuster, with the release of *Jaws* (1975), which became the first film to earn $100 million at the box office (Croce, 2015). Moreover, the so-called disaster film became a prominent genre in the decade. The disaster film featured spectacular "catastrophes" that threatened an all-star cast of characters. The first "disaster" film was *Airport* (1970), which was followed by three sequels (1975, 1977, and 1979) of diminishing value and inspired the *Airplane* (1980 and 1982) parodies. The genre also included *The Andromeda Strain* (1971), *The Poseidon Adventure* (1972), *Earthquake* (1974), *The Cassandra Crossing* (1976), *Rollercoaster* (1977), *The Swarm* (1978), *Meteor* (1979), and *City on Fire* (1979). Most of these films were cheesy attempts to capitalize on the popularity of the genre. However, some films included elements of corporate wrongdoing, whereby a corporation ignored obvious safety issues or was complicit in their disaster. For example, *The Towering Inferno* (1974) featured payoffs and kickbacks, resulting in improper installation of safety equipment. In *City of Fire,* a corrupt mayor allows an oil refinery to be built in the city's center. The result was a fire engulfing the city, threatening a shoddily built hospital that lacked safety features. Although the genre is worth noting, these films fall on the periphery of corporate wrongdoing depictions. The primary theme is not corporate wrongdoing but the cataclysmic event that encapsulates the plot.

Conversely, huge conglomerates were a prominent element of the storyline for *Network* (1975), a brilliant and somewhat prophetic glimpse at corporate control of media. The film was set in the orifices of the United Broadcasters System (UBS), a fictional television network controlled by the Communications Corporation of America (CCA). In an Oscar-winning role, Peter Finch starred as Howard Beale, a mentally deranged news anchor for UBS who was experiencing dwindling ratings. The film begins with Max Schumacher (William Holden), the president of the news division, telling his old friend, Howard, that he is about to be fired and has two weeks left on the air. The next night, on live television, Beale announces

> I would like at this moment to announce that I will be retiring from this program in two weeks' time because of poor ratings. Since this show is the only thing I had going for me in my life, I've decided to kill myself. I'm going to blow my brains out right on this program a week from today. So tune in next Tuesday. That should give the public relations people a week to promote the show. You ought to get a hell of a rating out of that. Fifty share, easy.

Beale is immediately taken off the air and fired. However, Schumacher allows him one last broadcast to have a dignified farewell and apologize to viewers. On the next broadcast, Beale has another eruption, informing the audience that "I just ran out of bullshit," continuing to rant about his philosophy of life. Surprisingly, the ratings increased, which prompted Diana Christensen (Faye Dunaway), the head of Programming to encourage CCA executive Frank Hackett (Robert Duvall) to allow Beale to stay on the air as an "angry prophet denouncing the hypocrisies of our time." In a classic moment in film history, Beale rouses the audience by persuading viewers to "get up out of your chairs, open the window, stick your head out, and yell, and say it: I'M AS MAD AS HELL, AND I'M NOT GOING TO TAKE THIS ANYMORE!"

Schumacher is terminated due to corporate restructuring, and Christensen revamps it as the Network News Hours, with Sybil the Soothsayer, Mati Hari and her Skeletons in the closet, and the mad prophet of the airwaves, Howard Beale. He preaches his angry message on a nightly basis but runs afoul of the corporation after revealing ties between the CCA and business interests in Saudi Arabia. He rails on mega-corporate mergers, telling viewers to send telegrams to the White House to stop the merger between CCA and Saudi interests. Beale's tirade angers Arthur Jensen (Ned Beatty), the CCA chairman and primary stockholder, who meets with Beale to explain his position.

Arthur Jensen: You have meddled with the primal forces of nature, Mr. Beale, and I won't have it! Is that clear? You think you've merely stopped a business deal. That is not the case! The Arabs have taken billions of dollars out of this country, and now they must put it back! It is ebb and flow, tidal gravity! It is ecological balance! You are an old man who thinks in terms of nations and peoples. There are no nations. There are no peoples. There are no Russians. There are no Arabs. There are no third worlds. There is no West. There is only one holistic system of systems, one vast and immane, interwoven, interacting, multivariate, multinational dominion of dollars. Petro-dollars, electro-dollars, multi-dollars, reichmarks, rins, rubles, pounds, and shekels. It is the international system of currency which determines the totality of life on this planet. That is the natural order of things today. That is the atomic and subatomic and galactic structure of things today! And YOU have meddled with the primal forces of nature, and YOU ... WILL ... ATONE! Am I getting through to you, Mr. Beale? You get up on your little twenty-one-inch screen and howl about America and democracy. There is no America. There is no democracy. There is only IBM, and ITT, and AT&T, and DuPont, Dow, Union Carbide, and Exxon. Those are the nations of the world today. What do you think the Russians talk about in their councils of state, Karl Marx? They get out their linear programming charts, statistical decision theories, minimax solutions, and compute the price-cost probabilities of their transactions and investments, just like we do. We no longer live in a world of nations and ideologies, Mr. Beale. The world is a college of corporations, inexorably determined by the immutable bylaws of business. The world is a business, Mr. Beale. It has been since man crawled out of the slime. And our children will live, Mr. Beale, to see that ... perfect world ... in which there's no war or famine, oppression or brutality. One vast and ecumenical holding company, for whom all men will work to serve a common profit, in which all men will hold a share of stock. All necessities provided, all anxieties tranquilized, all boredom amused. And I have chosen you, Mr. Beale, to preach this evangel.

Howard Beale: Why me?

Arthur Jensen: Because you're on television, dummy. Sixty million people watch you every night of the week, Monday through Friday.

Howard Beale: I have seen the face of God.

Arthur Jensen: You just might be right, Mr. Beale.

Narrator: That evening, Howard Beale went on the air to preach the corporate cosmology of Arthur Jensen.

Beale's bleak new message on dying democracy and the dehumanization of society was depressing, and the television ratings started to fall rapidly. Hackett wanted to fire Beale, but the CEO would not permit it. In the end, the network executives decide to hire the Ecumenical Liberation Army (ELA) to assassinate Beale on the air, to end his show.

Concluding Thoughts

Network was a superb film that garnered Paddy Chayefsky an Oscar for best screenplay. It was a prophetic film that predicted the decline and debasement of television programming, the absurdity of reality television, and the deluge of shock-jock "media" personalities who articulate popular rage in the guise of hard news. The film also highlighted the increasing corporate control over the media and society. This is illustrated by Arthur Jensen's remarkable treatise on global capitalism. This rather bleak worldview would become a reality, as big business and conservative governments – exemplified by Ronald Reagan and Margaret Thatcher – would dominate the 1980s and beyond. In the 1980s, several film studios were taken over by multinational conglomerates in mega-mergers, including United Artists, 20th Century Fox, and Columbia Pictures (Croce, 2015). The Hollywood studios have always been "big business," but increasing monopolization further pushed small independent producers to the margins of the entertainment world. Moreover, despite the insistence by right-wing pundits that Hollywood is politically on the left and controlled by liberal and even "socialist" devotees, in truth, Hollywood is predominantly on the left in terms of social issues, but certainly not on the economic front. There are very few negative depictions of corporations or their role in society, even with the enormous harms that corporations inflict within society. In early depictions, the corporation was absent, replaced by an individual conspirator that represented the greed of big business. Moreover, early films generally depicted "industry" rather than a specific corporation, or they shied away from complete condemnation of the wrongdoing within the film. That said, Hollywood has not ignored the malfeasance of large corporations. Beginning in 1979, with the debut of *Norma Rae* and *The China Syndrome*, some compelling films have depicted corporate wrongdoing. These films will be the basis of the remainder of the book.

Reference List

Bollier, D. (2021). Ralph Nader entry in the Encyclopedia of the consumer movement. https://nader.org/biography/ralph-nader-entry-encyclopedia-consumer-movement/

Cook, D.A. (2002). *Lost illusions: American cinema in the shadow of Watergate and Vietnam, 1970–1979* (Vol. 9). Univ of California Press.

Croce, N. (Ed.). 2015). *The history of film*. Encyclopedia Britannica.

Doherty, T. (1999). *Pre-code Hollywood: Sex, immorality, and insurrection in American cinema, 1930–1934*. Columbia University Press.

Eller, C. (2000, June 9). Nader's Goal: Crash hollywood. *Los Angeles Times*. https://www.latimes.com/archives/la-xpm-2000-jun-09-fi-39101-story.html

Hamilton, M. (1980, September 20). Ralph Nader goes to hollywood – to film social issues. *The Washington Post*. https://www.washingtonpost.com/archive/business/1980/09/20/ralph-nader-goes-to-hollywood-to-film-social-issues/e1048a1d-cfee-4039-b442-ea7950212ad6/

Hurst, R.M. (2007). *Republic Studios: Beyond poverty row and the majors*. Scarecrow Press.

Kenny, K. (1998). *Making sense of the Molly Maguires*. Oxford University Press.

Koppes, C.R., & Black, G.D. (1990). *Hollywood goes to war: How politics, profits and propaganda shaped World War II movies*. Univ of California Press.

Lorence, J.J. (1999). *The suppression of salt of the earth: How Hollywood, big labor, and politicians blacklisted a movie in Cold War America*. UNM Press.

Mulvey, L. (2017). *Citizen Kane*. Bloomsbury Publishing.

Munby, J. (2009). *Public enemies, public heroes*. University of Chicago Press.

Navasky, V.S. (2003). *Naming names: With a new afterword by the author*. Macmillan.

Neve, B. (2016). Our daily bread: 'Cooperation,' 'independence' and politics in mid-1930s cinema. In I. Morgan & P.J. Davies (Eds.), *Hollywood and the great depression: American film, politics and society in the 1930s*. Edinburgh University Press.

Noakes, J.A. (1998). Bankers and common men in Bedford falls: How the FBI determined that "It's a Wonderful Life" was a subversive movie. *Film History, 10*(3), 311–319.

Owen, N. (2017, December 25). Dickens' A Christmas carol – The problem with benevolent capitalism. *The Panoptic*. https://thepanoptic.co.uk/2017/12/25/dickens-a-christmas-carol-the-problem-with-benevolent-capitalism/

Partnoy, F. (2010). *The match king: Ivar Kreuger, the financial genius behind a century of Wall Street scandals*. PublicAffairs.

Schatz, T. (1999). *Boom and bust: American cinema in the 1940s* (Vol. 6). Univ of California Press.

Schindler, C. (2005). *Hollywood in crisis: Cinema and American society, 1929–1939*. Routledge.

Shor, F. (2016, August 2). It's time to put Ralph Nader's role in the 2000 election into historical perspective. *History News Network*. https://historynewsnetwork.org/article/163522

Thomson, D. (2004). The decade when movies mattered. In T. Elsaesser, N. King & A. Howarth (Eds.) *The last great American picture show* (pp. 73–82). Amsterdam University Press.

3 Harm to the Environment

> *These people don't dream about being rich. They dream about being able to watch their kids swim in a pool without having to worry that they'll have to have a hysterectomy before the age of twenty.* Erin Brockovich (Julia Roberts), *Erin Brockovich (2000)*

After World War II, the United States began its ride of post-war global industrial supremacy with the unwavering belief in the vigor of enterprise. Underlying this spirit was the misguided assumption that nature was infinitely exploitable and renewable. In the 1960s, the politics of environmentalism had a difficult beginning as the denial of the problems was normalized, and the undesirable side-effects of progress were generally ignored. The recognition of impending environmental disasters and harms expanded as smog blanketed major cities such as Los Angeles, radioactive fallout from nuclear weapons testing spread across the Midwest, and pesticide-contaminated agricultural products proliferated. In 1962, Rachel Carson's impactful book *Silent Spring* was a watershed moment in the emergence of environmentalism. The book vividly highlighted the harmful impact caused by the undiscriminating use of pesticides. Carson alleged the chemical industry of propagating disinformation to curry public favor with public officials and consumers. However, interests hostile to environmental regulation dismissed Carson as a hysterical woman. However, her book helped swing public opinion, leading to the curtailing of DDT and inspiring an environmental movement that preceded the establishment of the US Environmental Protection Agency (EPA).

In the 1970s, the environment became a legitimate political issue that gained widespread support with the first Earth Day on April 22, 1970. The issue of environmentalism became an important, albeit divisive, issue in politics, business, and among the public. In 1971, the avowed socialist Barry Commoner wrote the bestseller *The Closing Circle*, in which he argued that the capitalist economy and ecology were incompatible. The struggle for higher profits was at the expense of Earth's clean air and water, which were contaminated to save costs for waste disposal. Despite the catastrophic consequences of disrupting the ecological system, free-market ideology received a considerable boost from the

Reagan presidency, with deregulation and denial of environmental harms. This trend continued through various Republican presidencies, with the most recent iteration in the Trump presidency, whose administration rolled back more than 100 environmental rules and regulations (Popovich et al., 2021). The continual shift of political discourse impedes the environmental movement, while corporations become enriched by polluting the planet and destroying the ecological system, killing humans and wildlife. Despite the overwhelmingly harmful consequences, relatively few Hollywood scripted films directly tackle the issue of environmental harm perpetrated by corporations.

The Early Films: Pre-1970

Prior to the 1970s, there were very few films that had environmental themes. There were even fewer that presented corporate or industry-directed environmental wrongdoing. One of the earliest scripted films to depict industry-driven environmental harm was Warner Brother's *Gold Is Where You Find It* (1938), directed by Michael Curtiz. Although fictional, the story was based on a dispute between wheat farmers and the mining industry. During the California Gold Rush, the use of hydraulic mining techniques destroyed fertile lands in the Sacramento Valley. The rivers were choked with sediment, sludge, and chemicals, flooding farmlands, destroying crops, and spoiling the land. However, the film focused on a melodramatic romance between a mining engineer and a prominent wheat farmer's daughter. True to the production code-era, the movie had a happy ending, showing the ravaged farmland-bearing fields of orange groves. In real life, California wildcat miners used an estimated 10 million pounds of mercury from the 1860s to the early 1900s. Today, regions near historically mined sites have high mercury and methylmercury concentrations, often exceeding thresholds set by the US Environmental Protection Agency (Gerson et al., 2020).

In a similar vein, *Thunder Bay* (1953) depicted a confrontation between shrimp fishermen and the oil industry. The film stars James Stewart as Steve Martin, a former navy engineer who arrives in a small Louisiana town to start offshore oil drilling. The local shrimpers are concerned that the tests will harm marine life and the local landscape. Financed by Big Oil, Martin is hard-headed and resolute in his belief in progress, while the residents view him with skepticism and disdain. Again, the film features a happy ending, as Martin's drilling uncovers a new bed of shrimp, proving that both industries can co-exist and happily work together. Life on the bayou was also depicted in Robert Flaherty's *Louisiana Story* (1948). A work of "docu-fiction," the film garnered an Academy Award nomination for best story. Standard Oil produced the film to show that oil drilling was humane and beneficial to the southern American wetlands. The film was a propaganda film that showed the oil industry's encroachment into the natural environment in a positive light. The film displayed the beauty of the Louisiana swamplands, as well as the lifestyle of the inhabitants. However, long before the film was produced, the Louisiana wetlands were gradually being destroyed. The Mississippi River Levee deprived the region of sedimentary deposits required for renewal. The incursion of Big Oil accelerated the erosive process by contaminating leaks and spills, both big and small. The refineries and chemical factories emitted carcinogens, while the ugly, grimy, and sometimes flaming oil rigs damaged the gulf, resulting in an irreplaceable loss of a unique ecosystem and culture (Allen, 2006). Finally, conservatism was featured in a couple of films in the 1950s. *The Roots of Heaven* (1958) told the story of a crusading environmentalist who sought to save the elephant from extinction. At the same time, the *Wind Against the Everglades* (1958) featured a game warden (Christopher Plummer) that confronts bird poachers in Florida. Both films did not feature industry or corporations as villains. However, they were ahead of their time in presenting ecological concerns in scripted films.

Types of Environmental Harms Depicted

In Hollywood, films that depict environmental issues or ecological concerns are not uncommon. However, films that squarely place the blame on real-life corporations are rare. There is a subgenre of science fiction films with corporations or their proxies serving as the villain. In these films, the corporation is responsible for unleashing viruses on the general population or dumping toxic waste that creates zombies, mutants, or other supernatural beings (*Return of the Living Dead*, 1985; *The Last Winter*, 2006; *The Bay*, 2012). For the most part, many of these films are "campy" and poorly contrived. They do very little to advance social commentary about the ill effects of pollution. There are also several family-based films in which corporate developers play the villain, contributing to the degradation of the environment. The protagonists serve as "eco-warriors" trying to save forests, parks, and the natural habitats of animals (*Yogi Bear*, 2010; *The Lorax*, 2012; *Pete the Dragon*, 2016). Moreover, several children's films explore the consequences of climate change, including *Ferngully: The Last Rainforest* (1992), *Ice Age 2: The Meltdown* (2006), and *Happy Feet 2* (2011). Again, the social commentary is limited as the films are geared toward younger audiences and tend to be lighthearted in their depiction. Albeit, some of the films can provide younger audiences with important social messages regarding environmentalism and pollution. For instance, Disney's *WALL-E* (2008) follows a solitary robot left to clean up the garbage on the uninhabitable planet Earth. The film was an intelligent social critique of consumerism and pollution. Unfortunately, this important social message is not regularly depicted in films geared toward adult viewers. That said, several scripted films depict environmental wrongdoing perpetrated by corporations. These films can be categorized into four major types: (1) The Poisoning of the Public, (2) The Oil Spill, (3) The Nuclear Accident, and (4) Climate Change/Global Warming.

Poisoning the Public: Water, Air, and Land Pollution

Pollution refers to the undesirable alteration in the air, water, or land's physical, chemical, or biological characteristics. Pollution threatens or harms the health, survival, or activities of humans or other living creatures. Most pollutants are emitted when industrial facilities release harmful by-products or waste into the environment. In the mid-1700s, the Industrial Revolution accelerated severe environmental problems, especially pollution. Initially, the primary culprit was coal, which became the primary energy replacing wood. Coal-powered engines allowed for the widespread use of machines, eventually powered by oil and natural gas. It was a watershed moment that transitioned human society from small-scale, manual production to large-scale, automated production. The Industrial Revolution significantly boosted the production and consumption of goods, which greatly impacted the quality of the environment and public health.

In the 18th and 19th centuries, coal burning was responsible for most air pollution, with America's largest cities darkened by foul-smelling and disease-causing smog. As the urban population proliferated in the 19th century, coal mines, metal-working factories, and textile mills developed rapidly, leading to even more industrial pollution, including drinking water contaminated by industrial wastes such as oils, benzene, tars, and acids. At the turn of the 20th century, the automobile emerged as the leading contributor of air pollution in modern industrialized society. The transportation industry accounts for approximately 29 percent of greenhouse gas emissions, the largest contributor in the United States (EPA, 2021). After World War II, many new products and materials, such as detergents, synthetic fibers, plastics, and pesticides, placed an even greater burden on the environment. These chemical plants generate excess heat, toxic gases, and hazardous waste. The workers and adjoining residents suffer from some of the highest cancer rates in the country. The actions of corporations such as DuPont, General Electric, and General Motors have depleted the ozone layer, contributed to acid rain, and caused massive amounts of groundwater contamination. These corporations reap enormous profits at the expense of the planet and human health. Several films hold corporations accountable for the poisoning of the environment, some of which are based on true stories.

Based on True Stories

Largely unknown, *Bitter Harvest* (1981) was a made-for-television movie that documented the worst mass poisoning in US history, the toxic contamination of Michigan's food supply. The film starred Ron Howard as Ned De Vries, a Michigan dairy farmer who lives with his wife, Kate (Tarrah Nutter), a teenage son, and a baby girl. After finishing an engineering degree, Ned returned to run the family farm but struggled as cows acted strangely. Some calves are dying, and his prize heifer, whom the family affectionately calls "super cow," is not producing milk. Their neighbor, farmer Walter Peary (Art Carney), suggests calling the Michigan Farm Bureau (MFB) to seek help identifying the problem. Seemingly helpful, the officials from MFB arrive at the farm, euthanize a calf, and take samples back to their headquarters. After receiving no information, Ned visits the Farm Bureau, where he is told that his cows were suffering from "malnutrition" and that it was a "question of management." Ned angrily defends his farming practices, telling the bureaucrats that he feeds his livestock the recommended protein-enriched AF10 feed marketed by the Michigan Farm Bureau.

Meanwhile, Walter's herd is getting sick, and the De Vries' baby girl has a terrible rash. Seeking answers, Ned makes a breakthrough when he discovers a nest of dead rats and performs an amateur autopsy that reveals that the rats were eating the cattle feed. Ned dramatically brings the dead rats to the agricultural board and angrily throws them on the table, asking the officials to conduct tests. The officials tell Ned that they are a regulatory laboratory and are unable to conduct research. A sympathetic lab technician with the Farm Bureau conducts clandestine tests but cannot interpret the results and tells Ned to seek help from Dr. Morton Freeman (Richard Dysart), a respected scientist and expert on chemical poisoning. Dr. Freeman identifies the unknown substance as polybrominated biphenyl (PBB), a flame retardant used in FireMaster extinguishers. In a chilling scene, Dr. Freeman tells De Vries that PBB is the toxin stored in body fat and is cumulative, meaning that it can be passed to humans from eating beef or drinking milk, even breastfeeding. Despite the harms, the bureaucrats refuse to alert the public or quarantine the livestock. Ned travels the state, gathering evidence by speaking to other farmers who have experienced the contaminant's impacts. Although the corporation is not named, it is revealed that the PBB was being stored in identically colored bags on pellets directly adjoining the feed nutrient. In particularly compelling testimony to the Farm Bureau, Dr. Freeman advocates for a quarantine:

> Mr. Chairman, this is a toxic chemical we're talking about, and I don't think anybody here understands the significance of that. You can't just inoculate the population, and it will all go away. It won't go away. If it gets inside your body, it's there forever. And you won't even know it. It is not like the measles. And there are no set symptoms. You could get anything on this list, in any combination, or none of them. It could lie dormant within you for twenty years, and then all of sudden, you've got crippling arthritis, kidney failure, cancer, and nobody knows why. Or it could skip you completely and hit your children or their children. And God knows what is going to happen a generation from now. Mr. De Vries cows are dying, and his baby's sick, and nobody gives a damn! [pauses for a moment and calmly states] There is at this moment an odorless, colorless, tasteless poison in your food chain. And it is spreading unchecked throughout this state.

In the concluding scene, the cows are herded into a pit, where Ned and his neighbors shoot and bury the cows with bulldozers. The postscript reveals that public pressure forced the state to test for PBB, which led to 500 farms closing and 30,000 livestock being driven into mass graves and slaughtered. In 1976, 90 percent of area residents had shown PBB in their system, and one year later, laws were enacted to eliminate contaminated meat and milk from the marketplace. Most disturbingly, the final postscript reads, "it is now estimated that eight million men, women and children carry the toxic chemical inside their bodies." Yet, the food supply contamination has largely been forgotten, except for researchers who continue to study the long-term effects, including thyroid problems, reproductive health, menstrual cycles, altering puberty timelines, higher rates of miscarriage, urinary conditions, and breast cancer. Overall, the film was a very subtle and honest depiction of the consequences of corporate negligence. That said, *Bitter Harvest* did not focus on the wrongdoing of Velsicol Chemical Corporation (formerly known as the Michigan Chemical Corporation) that made the grievous error through obvious negligence in safety regulations and protocol. Although the factory closed in 1978, in 1982, Velsicol was placed on the Superfund list because of the contamination of the Pine River, which adjoined the Michigan Chemical Corporation. The cleanup of the DDT-contaminated sediment cost over $100 million, and the no-fishing advisory is still in place (Walton, 2018).

Featured as the CBS movie of the week, *Lois Gibbs: The Love Canal Story* (1982) was the first non-science fiction film to depict the impact that toxic dumping had on a community. The telefilm starred Marsha Mason as Lois Gibbs, an ordinary housewife who led a campaign to save her family and neighbors from the health hazards of a nearby toxic chemical dumpsite. The television film was a subdued and thoughtful depiction of the challenges and skepticism that Lois Gibbs faced as she tried to get answers from various government bureaucrats and officials. Love Canal is an abandoned canal project in upstate New York off the Niagara River, just south of Niagara Falls. Approximately 800 single-family homes were built directly adjacent to the failed canal project. The Hooker Chemical Company used the partially dug canal to dump chemical waste with the government's approval. It is estimated that 21,000 tons of toxic chemicals, including known carcinogens, were dumped from 1942 to 1953. The 16-acre area was sealed in clay and sold to the Niagara Falls School Board. After recurrent wet winters in the late 1970s, the chemicals began to leech into nearby creeks, basements, yards of residents, and the elementary school playground directly over the canal. At the same time, public awareness of the danger commenced after investigative newspaper reports and grassroots door-to-door health surveys showed an unusually high number of illnesses, including epilepsy, asthma, migraines, and kidney diseases. There was also a very high rate of congenital disabilities and miscarriages in the working-class neighborhood. With Lois Gibbs as spokesperson, activists were primarily working-class women who lived in the neighborhood and had seen the adverse health effects on their children. Despite raising the alarm, officials in New York State were apathetic to the crisis, dismissing activists' concerns as hysterical and uneducated housewives. The persistence of the activists led to President Jimmy Carter declaring two states (1978 and 1981) of emergency in the region and the relocation of some 800 families. The crisis also pushed lawmakers to pass the Comprehensive Environmental Response, Compensation and Liability Act (CERCLA) in 1980, better known as the Superfund. The legislation held corporate polluters to be financially responsible for the cleanup of toxic waste contamination (Newman, 2016). Love Canal also contributed to the rise of the grassroots environmental justice movement that identified the failure to address the disproportionate impact of toxic pollution on working-class and minority communities, which became popularly known as environmental racism.

Almost 16 years later, *A Civil Action* (1998) debuted on Christmas Day. The film was based on Jonathon Harr's book, *A Civil Action,* published in 1995. The film documented the infamous court case involving toxic poisoning in Woburn, Massachusetts. The complaint alleged that factories owned by W.R. Grace & Co. and Beatrice Foods Co, two of the largest corporations in America, negligently disposed of industrial solvents, and the waste seeped into the underground water supply serving the town. The film is essentially a lawyer's story, telling only a tiny element of the Woburn tragedy. The film stars John Travolta as Jan Schlichtmann an ambulance-chasing attorney attracted to a big payout by two large corporations. However, Schlichtmann soon becomes obsessed with the lawsuit, sinking all the firm's financial resources into the unwinnable case. The film shows how Schlichtmann was outspent and outmaneuvered by high-powered defense attorneys hired by the corporate giants. Robert Duvall received an Oscar nomination for his depiction of Jerry Facher, a cunning lawyer who represented Beatrice. Schlichtmann admits that he failed his clients when the plaintiffs settled out of court for a nominal amount and never received an apology. In the end, Schlichtmann sends the unwinnable case to the EPA. Intertitles reveal that the companies were forced to pay $69.4 million to clean up the sites. Jan is last seen in bankruptcy court, where he is asked where it all went. The postscript reveals that Jan was able to pay his debts and now practices environmental law. Despite the lack of an apology, the film has a social conscience, painting corporations and their lawyers as unfeeling and heartless.

Two years later, *Erin Brockovich* (2000) debuted and instantly became the most notable depiction of corporate wrongdoing. Julia Roberts won an Oscar for best actress for portraying the relentless and determined Brockovich. In 1993, the divorced, unemployed mother became an activist for clean water after working for Ed Masry (Albert Finney), a lawyer who represented her in a failed accident claim. She begins to work on a real-estate case involving Pacific Gas & Electric (PG&E), where she discovers water contamination in Hinkley, California. Since the 1950s, the utility corporation Pacific Gas & Electric has operated a natural gas pumping station. Until 1966, PG&E used chromium 6 to prevent rust. The toxic chemical leaked into the water supply, which caused the residents numerous health problems, such as chronic cough, rashes, headaches, nosebleeds, and even cancer. Despite the gloomy message, the film was upbeat as it focused on Brockovich's quirky personality and tenacious demeanor. There are several dramatic and compelling moments, with the film ending with a historic settlement. The plaintiffs were awarded $333 million, at the time the largest in US history.

While Erin Brockovich was a success, *Bhopal: A Prayer for Rain* (2014) failed miserably at the box office and received mixed critical reviews. The film starred Martin Sheen as Warren Anderson, the CEO of Union Carbide, while Kal Penn played Motwani, a local journalist inspired by real-life Indian investigative journalist Rajkumar Keswani. The film detailed the events leading up to the worst case of industrial poisoning in history. On December 3, 1984, approximately 45 tons of methyl isocyanate was discharged from an insecticide plant owned by Union Carbide Corporation. The gas spewed over a densely populated Bhopal, killing at least 7,000 within the first three days and approximately 25,000 overall. The groundwater continues to have high toxic levels of chlorinated solvents, and the aftereffects continue to afflict approximately 500,000 survivors. The film depicted the woefully inadequate safety standards and measures, revealing how multinational corporations exploit underdeveloped regions with poor governmental oversight.

Similarly, *Minamata* (2020) explored the destructive effects of corporate greed and local government complicity. The film starred Johnny Depp as W. Eugene Smith, a noted American photographer made famous by his work published in Life Magazine. Through photography, Smith documents the ill effects of mercury poisoning in coastal communities of Japan. Minamata disease results from the daily consumption of large quantities of fish and shellfish heavily contaminated by toxic chemicals dumped into the sea. The disease was named after Minamata, a small coastal town on the Yatsushiro Sea in Southern Japan. Starting around 1908, Chisso, a large chemical company, released toxic waste into the Minamata Bay. For years, Japanese government officials refused to take action, minimizing and deflecting blame, even after Minamata disease was discovered in 1956. It was not until 1969 that the Japanese government finally officially recognized the disease. However, the legacy of Minamata continues to haunt Japan, as thousands of congenital victims continue to suffer, while Chisso remains a profitable company.

Dark Waters (2019) explores the legal battle against DuPont, a large corporation with deep pockets and high-priced lawyers. As the title infers, the film reveals that DuPont had deposited thousands of tons of toxic sludge into a landfill which seeped into nearby waterways. The film stars Mark Ruffalo as Robert Bilott, a corporate defense lawyer from Cincinnati. As a favor for his grandmother, Bilott agrees to talk to Wilbur Tennant, a farmer who lives next door to a DuPont factory in Parkersburg, West Virginia. The farmer is concerned about unexplained and bizarre livestock deaths, with 190 cows perishing with bloated organs, blackened teeth, and tumors. Initially skeptical, Bilott is transformed into a strong advocate after realizing that DuPont was using perfluorooctanoic acid (PFOA), an unregulated chemical used to manufacture Teflon. Worse yet, DuPont had conducted numerous tests that revealed that PFOA caused cancer and congenital disabilities but nefariously elected to keep the findings from the public. The film effectively depicts the legal wrangling, with Bilott stubbornly fighting for justice for his clients and the broader community whom the large corporation has poisoned. In the end, his persistence led to a large settlement, with DuPont paying out $671 million in damages to more than 3,500 plaintiffs.

Although appreciably less effective, *The Devil Has a Name* (2019) also revealed how corporate greed and corruption enable toxic dumping. Directed by James Edward Olmos, the quirky film was a fictionalized account of the so-called water wars in the San Joaquin Valley in California. The independent film was a dark comedy that starred David Strathairn as Fred Stern, an almond farmer who discovers that his groves were being poisoned by runoff from the fictional Royal Shore Oil company. The film also starred James Edward Olmos as his best friend, Santiago a Mexican immigrant, and Martin Sheen as Ralph Aegis, a crusading lawyer known as the man who killed the Pinto. The film is told through a flashback, with Gigi (Kate Bosworth), the regional director for Royal Shore Oil, telling the story to her superior, the "Big Boss" (Alfred Molina). Gigi recounts how the big oil company came to a $20 million settlement in a bizarre tale. Despite a stellar cast, the film was disjointed with a mixture of humor, stereotypical corporate bad guys, racism toward Mexican Americans, an eccentric lawyer, and even a murder. The film was very loosely based on a real farmer, Fred Starrh of Shafter, California. He won a large settlement against Aera Energy (owned by Shell and ExxonMobil) after it was found that the company knowingly allowed 600 million barrels of oil wastewater to leak into the subsurface of his farm, poisoning his orchard. The film had great potential for a dramatic, legal retelling of the corporate pollution, but the flimsy script resorts to standard cliches and caricatures of corporate villains, who employ absurd one-liners. That said, the ending postscript is a call for action:

DESPITE FRED'S LAWSUIT AND WIDESPREAD EVIDENCE OF GROUNDWATER CONTAMINATION, OIL COMPANIES ARE STILL USING UNLINED WASTEWATER PONDS THROUGHOUT CALIFORNIA'S CENTRAL VALLEY. WHERE MORE THAN HALF THE NUTS, FRUITS AND VEGETABLES IN THE US ARE GROWN.
IF YOU MAKE MORE MONEY DOING IT THAN IT COSTS TO GET CAUGHT FOR DOING IT CONTINUING DOING IT: NET PRESENT VALUE

Fictional Accounts

A handful of fictional films feature corporate polluters. *The Fire Down Below* (1997) starred action star Steven Seagal as EPA agent Jack Taggert. The film is set in the Appalachian hills of eastern Kentucky, where toxic waste was dumped into abandoned coal mines by the Hanner Coal Company, owned by Orin Hanner Sr. (Kris Kristofferson). The residents are helpless, as the company is the only source of employment and wields much power in the region. Taggert goes undercover as a volunteer carpenter at a local church, where he uncovers the evil plot that is sickening the children. The film features a lot of martial arts heroics, with Taggert battling rattlesnakes, a crooked local sheriff, "hillbilly" mercenaries, corrupt FBI agents, and local judges to stop the evil plot. Similarly, *Taffin* (1988) starred Pierce Brosnan as the titular character, a debt-collector and tough guy who locals hire to prevent Sprawley Enterprises from building a chemical factory on the outskirts of Ballymoran, a quaint little Irish village.

Appreciably better, *Michael Clayton* (2007) starred George Clooney as the titular character, an attorney and "fixer" for a prestigious law firm, Keener, Bach, and Ledeen. The film is essentially a legal thriller that involves pollution, coverups, hitmen, and murder. Clayton's firm represents U-North, an agribusiness corporation embroiled in a six-year multi-billion dollar lawsuit alleging that their weed product killed 458 people. The lead attorney, Arthur Edens (Tom

Wilkinson), has a manic episode, stripping off his clothes during a deposition, ranting and raving about his shame and love for Anna, one of the young plaintiffs. The firm sends Clayton to conduct damage control, by attempting to contain Edens. While being held in custody, Arthur tells Michael that he has "blood on my hands,"

> Six years I've absorbed this poison. Four hundred depositions, a hundred motions, five changes of venue … 89,000 documents in discovery. Six years of scheming and stalling and screaming, and what have a I got? I've spent 12 percent of my life defending the reputation of a deadly weed killer! They killed them, Michael. Those small farms, the family farms. Did you? Did you? Did you meet Anna? You gotta see her, you gotta talk to her. She's a miracle, Michael. She's God's perfect little creature. And for fifty million dollars in fees, I've spent 12 percent of my life … Destroying perfect Anna and her dead parents and her dying brother.

The lawsuit in jeopardy, U-North's newly appointed chief counsel, Karen Crowder (Tilda Swinton), discovers that Arthur possessed an internal memo that revealed that U-North knew the brand weedkiller was carcinogenic and could quickly enter the water supply. In a phone message to his law firm, Arthur colorfully reads the memo, interjecting his commentary, "You don't even have to leave your house to be killed by our product. We'll pipe it into your kitchen sink. Not only is this a great product … It is a superb cancer delivery system." The inexperienced Crowder callously okays the murder of Arthur, with the two hitmen (who are employees of U-North) making it appear to be a suicide. Clayton is suspicious and begins an informal investigation, uncovering the memo that implicated U-North. Clayton is targeted by the hitmen, who mistakenly believe they have blown him up in a car bomb. Fearing that the memo will surface, U-North decides to settle the case, but their plan is thwarted when Clayton reappears to confront Crowder, tricking her into a taped confession of the murder of Arthur.

Set in smog-infested Los Angeles, circa the 1970s, *The Nice Guys* (2016) was an action-buddy comedy that starred Russell Crowe as Jackson Healy and Ryan Gosling as Holland March. Healy is an enforcer paid to "beat up" people on behalf of clients, while March is a down-on-his-luck private investigator. The pair become entangled in a complicated case in which Auto Industry executives and the head of the Justice Department, Judith Kuttner (Kim Bassinger), conspire to suppress the catalytic convertor. In a humorous scene, Kuttner's daughter, Ameilia, who is also an environmental activist, tells the pair about the plot,

> [Referring to her mother] one of the capitalist corporate suppressors. You know, they want us dead, man! We're just in their crosshairs, you know! We're just pawns! The automakers, she's gonna let em walk … Yes, they have evidence. They have memos proving that Detroit conspired to suppress the converter, proving they would rather poison our air then spend a little bit of money.

Amelia explains that she performed in *How Do You Like My Car, Big Boy?* An "experimental film" combining pornography and investigative journalism to out Detroit's involvement in the conspiracy. Where, Holland March dead-panned, "so let me get this straight, you made a porno film where the point was the plot?" The conspirators hire contract killers to destroy the film and murder anyone involved in the production, including porn producer Sid Shattuck and actress Misty Mountains. While being pursued by "John Boy," a psychotic hitman, the protagonists (with the help of Holland's Daughter Holly) retrieve a copy of the film, and the criminal scheme is revealed to the authorities. In the end, Judith is arrested, but the auto industry is not held to account for their collusion in the repression of pollution controls. That said, themes of corporate wrongdoing and environmental pollution were minimized, as the primary narrative was action and comedy, not a call to action to end pollution.

Compared to *Michael Clayton* and *The Nice Guys*, *Main Street* (2010) was considerably more restrained. Set in Durham, North Carolina, Colin Firth starred as Texan Gus Leroy, a representative of Environmental Services Corporation. The corporation specializes in hazardous waste disposal, and Leroy rents a former tobacco warehouse to store canisters until they are transported. The warehouse is owned by the elderly Georgina Carr (Ellyn Burstyn), a tobacco heiress that has fallen on hard times. The small city has also experienced economic decline, with chronic unemployment, crumbling businesses, and urban decay. At a council meeting, Leroy proposes a plan to build a sister plant that safely converts toxic waste into a form that can be safely buried and disposed. He vigorously touts safety, claiming that "waste of any kind, hazardous, toxic or nuclear cannot harm you if it is properly managed." He boasts how his company has built community parks and swimming pools, where residents enjoy almost full employment. He ends his proposal, saying, "I refuse to live in the past. I look to the future!" Recognizing an opportunity to restructure their fledgling economy, the mayor and council enthusiastically accept the proposal. In a pivotal scene, the truck transporting the canisters of toxic waste are involved a major accident. Although the canisters are not damaged, LeRoy has a revelation, deciding to resign from the company, declaring, "I'm tired of being a cheerleader. I'm going to be a truthteller." Despite a slow-moving plot, the film extolled the dangers of toxic waste and how corporations peddle notions of growth and prosperity to the stakeholders.

Conversely, both *The East* (2013) and *Night Moves* (2013) featured eco-terrorists that intend to send overt messages about the environment by targeting corporations. *The East* starred Brit Marling as Jane, an undercover agent for a private intelligence firm. Taking the identity, Sarah, she infiltrates the East, an underground activist, anarchist, and environmental organization. The group is involved in a series of "jams," vandalistic attacks against corporations and their leaders accused of wrongdoing. The leader of the East, Benji (Alexander Skarsgaard), utilizes social media to highlight their actions and to educate the public on corporate wrongdoing. The film features several types of corporate wrongdoing, including oil spills, unsafe pharmaceuticals, and toxic dumping. The group kidnapped a petrochemical CEO and a senior-level manager responsible for dumping toxic waste into waterways. They attempt to force the pair into the contaminated water, with Izzy (Eliot Page) telling the pair,

> It is pretty simple, really. You make your living by poisoning this creek, and other rivers, and lakes. And you separate yourselves, in your gated communities, with golf courses from the world you're destroying. From the families who cannot afford to move away from this creek. Or from the cancer their children are dying of. You create, for a living! Toxic chemicals that will outlive us all and feel nothing! But tonight, you will feel something. Strip!

The group forces the CEO to admit on tape that they knowingly poisoned the water as it was cheaper and more profitable. The film features a melodramatic twist, with Jane/Sarah falling in love with Benji. In the end, Jane is enlightened to the damages of corporate wrongdoing. She quits her job and attempts to reveal the truth about corporations. Set in Oregon, *Night Moves* stars Jesse Eisenberg as Josh and Dakota Fanning as Dena, two environmentalists who join with Josh's brother, Harmon, to blow up a hydroelectric dam as a form of protest. Unfortunately, they accidentally killed a hiker who was camping near the dam. The brothers fear that the remorseful Dena will disclose her secret to the police. In a surprise ending, Josh confronts Dena, strangling her to death. On his brother's advice, Josh "disappears," ending up in California applying for a job at a camping supply store. The film was dark and morose, a character drama that feeds off stereotypes about environmentalists as "outsiders" and social misfits.

Also very dark, *First Reformed* (2017) starred Ethan Hawke as Ernst Toller, the pastor at the First Reformed, a historic church in Snowbridge, New York. The church is suffering from dwindling attendance. It is now mainly a tourist attraction celebrating its 250th anniversary. The celebration is being planned by Abundant Life, an evangelical megachurch in Albany that also owns First Reformed. One of the key benefactors of Abundant Life is mega-capitalist Edward Balq, who owns several industries and is underwriting the reconsecration of First Reformed. Toller is asked by a parishioner, Mary (Amanda Seyfried), to counsel her husband, Michael, a radical environmentalist activist for the Green Planet Movement. Michael wants Mary to get an abortion, feeling that it would be unethical to raise a child that will experience the climate crisis. After counseling, Michael commits suicide, leaving behind a suicide vest and tons of material about the environmental crimes of Balq industries. Michael requests that his ashes be buried at a toxic dumpsite. With a sparse crowd, the pastor gives a eulogy accompanied by the Abundant Life youth choir singing a Neil Young Protest song, *Who's Gonna Stand Up (And save the Earth)*.

At a meeting, Edward Balq confronts Toller, angry about the memorial's political message. After Balq questions climate change, Toller asks the industrialist, "will god forgive us for what he is doing to his creation." After reviewing Michael's laptop, the pastor becomes increasingly concerned about the environment, discovering that Balq Industries is one of the heaviest polluting corporations and has considerable influence over government policy. Toller is a heavy drinker who suffers from stomach issues, presumably cancer, and decides to send a message by bombing the church celebration with Michael's suicide vest. However, after Mary enters the service, Toller decides to abort his plan and painfully replaces the vest with barb wire. The movie ends after Mary walks in on Toller attempting to commit suicide by drinking toilet cleaner. The pair embrace and kiss as the film abruptly fades to black. *First Reformed* was written and directed by Paul Schrader, who was best known for writing *Taxi Driver* (1976) and *Raging Bull* (1980). Schrader also received an Oscar nomination for best screenplay for *First Reformed*. The bleak film gave important messages and visualizations about the business elite's complicity, the church's hypocrisy, environmental pollution, and the climate crisis.

Similarly, *Promised Land* (2012) was a thought-provoking film that explored the controversy of fracking. The film came on the heels of the Oscar-nominated documentary *Gasland* (2010), which highlighted the concerns of hydraulic fracking. Environmentalists contend that fracking can poison groundwater, pollute surface water, impair wild landscapes, and threaten wildlife. The film starred Matt Damon as Steve Butler, an employee for Global Crosspower Solutions, who is tasked with convincing landowners to grant drilling rights to acquire natural gas. Butler arrives in an economically depressed region in Pennsylvania, where the local farmers are experiencing downtimes. With his partner, Sue Thomason (Francis McDormand), Butler uses his small-town, folksy charm to convince the residents to agree to hydraulic fracking. However, at a town meeting, former engineer, and current high school science teacher, Frank Yates (Hal Holbrook) complicates the plan after raising environmental concerns about the safety of fracking. The council decides to delay the vote for weeks, pushing Butler into a race to convince the residents of the plan's economic benefits and allay their safety concerns. However, Dustin Noble (John Krasinski), an unknown environmental activist, further complicates Butler's proposal. Noble starts a grassroots campaign, claiming his family lost its Nebraska farm after Global's fracking methods poisoned their cows. He even provides a dramatic photo of the dead cattle. It appears that Butler is losing the fight until he discovers that Noble accusations are based on a falsehood. On closer inspection, Butler sees a lighthouse in Noble's photo of dead cattle and realizes that the picture could not have been taken in Nebraska. Buoyed by this startling new information, Butler is convinced that the town will now vote for Global's offer. In a twist, Butler learns that Noble was an employee of Global, sent to the town to purposely discredit the environmental movement and deflect the issue to obtain a winning vote. In the end, Butler makes a speech to the town, where he tells the residents of the corporation's deception and he is subsequently fired by the company. Interestingly, the energy industry engaged in a public relations campaign to discredit the film. They organized on social media platforms to protest the depiction of fracking and even resorted to buying pro-fracking advertisements to run in select Pennsylvania theatres that showed the film (Curry, 2013).

The Oil Spill

The federal government has prioritized the development of fossil fuels over environmentalism and ecological concerns. Big Oil receives unparalleled access to public land, tax breaks, and subsidies. Many politicians kowtow to the oil and gas industry, dismissing environmental concerns and opposing regulations. Research consistently finds that the oil industry accounts for a large percentage of environmental violations. Oil and gas drilling have harmful impacts on the environment, fueling climate change, disrupting wildlife, and destroying marine ecosystems. The oil spill is common in the industry, with upwards of 2000 spills reported in Colorado, New Mexico, and Wyoming in 2020 (CWP, 2021). Oil spills result from accidents at oil wells or through the transportation from oil from wells to refineries. These spills contaminate soil and water and can cause devastating fires. Oil spills can kill wildlife, pollute the air and water, and alter the ecosystem for years. There have been numerous oil spills that have occurred, both globally and in US waters. However, only a handful of oil spills are depicted in Hollywood features and made for television movies.

On March 24, 1989, the oil tanker Exxon Valdez struck the Bligh Reef in Prince William Sound, Alaska, spilling 11 million gallons of crude oil. The oil slick covered 1,300 miles of coastline and killed thousands of wildlife in the region, including seabirds, otters, seals, and whales. *Dead Ahead: The Exxon Valdez Disaster* (1992) was a docudrama that told the sinking of the infamous tanker. The film was produced for and aired on HBO, which has a solid reputation for making quality films that are thought-provoking and fact-based. The film was a straightforward depiction with no melodrama or hyperbole and used archival news footage to augment the story. The film featured an ensemble cast of characters, starring Christopher Lloyd as Frank Iarossi, the President of Exxon Shipping, and John Heard as a local conservation officer, Dan Lawn. The film depicted the accident, followed by the cleanup efforts botched by lack of equipment, indecision, red tape, and political posturing.

In sharp contrast, *On Deadly Ground* (1994) was a fictional movie that used harm to the environment as a central plotline. Set in Alaska, the movie starred action star Steven Seagal as Forest Taft, a firefighter specializing in extinguishing oil fires. Sir Michael Caine starred as Michael Jennings, the CEO of Aegis Oil and the unequivocal villain. He employs henchmen, mercenaries and delivers several cheesy and formulaic lines that reveal his wickedness. The fictional Aegis Oil operated various oil refineries and oil rigs in Alaska and faced opposition from environmental groups and indigenous communities. The corporation knowingly employs substandard safety equipment and plans on intentionally causing an oil spill so that they can reuse the empty oil field as a toxic dump. Naturally, the hero uses his martial arts abilities to save the region from an impending ecological disaster. The film was primarily an action film with overt environmental messages about the dangers of oil pollution. However, most audiences likely lost the message with the excessive violence, poor dialogue, bad acting, and lack of realism. Not surprisingly, the film received largely negative reviews from critics, with

Variety's Leonard Klady (1994) writing that the film was "a vanity production parading as a social statement." Even so, the film finished 37th at the box office for the year, grossing almost $39 million.

Also fictional, *Free Willy 2: The Adventure Home* (1995) featured an oil spill as an integral plot-line. The family-friendly movie continued the story of the unique friendship between Jesse, a young boy in foster care and Willy, an Orca whale. In the sequel, an oil spill traps three killer whales, including Willie, in a cove. The whales, one of which is injured, are in extreme danger, so Benbrook Oil CEO John Milner devises an altruistic plan to move the orcas into captivity to treat their injuries until they can be released back into the ocean. However, Milner greedily opts to sell the orcas to a marine park. Jesse, his friend Nadine, and his younger brother Elvis race to save the whales from the oil spill and being forced into captivity. As a family-based film, it did not provide a strong critique of corporations and their role in hurting the environment but at least illustrated the dangers of oil spills on whales.

On April 20, 2010, twenty-one years after the Exxon disaster, the oil drilling rig Deepwater Horizon exploded and sank, resulting in the death of 11 workers. The BP tragedy was the worst oil spill in US history, with 4 million barrels of oil flowing into the Gulf of Mexico, just off the coast of Louisiana. BP oil paid a $20 billion settlement for the environmental toll and another $4 billion in the criminal probe. *Deepwater Horizon* (2016) documented the horrific explosion that killed the unfortunate workers. The film was action-oriented, featuring chief electronics technician Mike Williams (Mark Wahlberg), who rescues several crew members, including rig-chief Jimmy Harrell (Kurt Russell). The film was a harrowing tale loaded with spectacular and believable special effects. Although the accident took an enormous toll on the region, the film itself was not focused on the environmental or economic consequences of the oil spill. The film's primary focus is the events that led up to the explosion, followed by a lively depiction of the harrowing escape by the survivors. The ending credits honor the 11 men who needlessly lost their lives.

Conversely, *The Runner* (2015) was a political-based drama that used the BP Oil spill as a backdrop to the main plotline. The melodramatic film starred Nicholas Cage as Colin Pryce, a congressman representing a district in Louisiana, negatively impacted by the oil spill. The devasting consequences are shown in the opening, followed by Pryce giving passionate and heartfelt testimony at Capitol Hill. He pleas for help for his district from the government and the oil corporation. As a result of his impassioned testimony, his popularity rises, and he considers a run for senate. However, his political ambitions are derailed after being caught having an affair with a fisherman's wife. Pryce resigned from congress and started working as a pro-bono attorney for claimants against BP, experiencing first-hand the challenges and bureaucracy in forcing a large corporation to settle financial claims. Unexpectedly, as a goodwill gesture, BP delivers money to his non-profit. Naturally, the gesture has a stipulation, and corporate lobbyists are willing to back his run for senate if he supports their economic interests. In an unhappy ending, the once idealistic Pryce capitulates to the interests of energy companies, caving

74 *Harm to the Environment*

to Big Oil. The film ends with the conflicted Pryce staring gloomily into the distance, with Capitol Hill in the background.

The Nuclear Accident

The use of nuclear weapons and energy has always been controversial. After the atomic bombings of Hiroshima and Nagasaki, the public became more aware and concerned about the testing of nuclear weapons. Starting in the 1950s, the public became more concerned about testing weapons in the Pacific Ocean. In 1961, the anti-nuclear group Women Strike For Peace organized marches in 60 cities, with approximately 50,000 women protesting nuclear weapons. At first, the protest focused on nuclear disarmament, a reflection of the Cold War era. At the same time, several films illustrated the threats of nuclear war, such as *Fail Safe* (1964) and the satirical *Dr. Strangelove* (1964). The aftermath of nuclear war was shown in *On the Beach* (1959), *Panic in Year Zero!* (1962) and the pseudo-documentary, *The War Game* (1965). The fear of nuclear war was revived in the early 1980s, with several films including *Special Bulletin* (1983), *War Games* (1983), *The Day After* (1983), *Testament* (1983), *Threads* (1984), *When the Wind Blows* (1986), and *Miracle Mile* (1988). *The Day After* aired on ABC and attracted over 100 million viewers. The film followed everyday citizens in Kansas before, during, and after the attack. Similarly, *Threads* depicted the death and destruction of a nuclear attack, rife with starvation, radiation sickness, and cancer. Even the protests over nuclear weapons became fodder for film. The made-for-television movie, *The Rainbow Warrior* (1992), depicted the real-life story of the sinking of a Greenpeace ship in Auckland Harbor in 1984. The ship was destined to protest French nuclear testing, and the French government was responsible for its sinking.

In the mid-1950s, the production of nuclear power was opened to private industry. At present, almost all commercial reactors in the USA are owned by private companies. Since the late 1960s, the resistance toward nuclear power has become more prominent. Throughout the 1970s, large demonstrations against nuclear power were organized. The real possibility of a nuclear accident was particularly concerning, with several "close calls" that occurred, including one at Fermi 1, in Monroe, Michigan, on the shores of Lake Erie. Published in 1975, the book *We Almost Lost Detroit* by John Fuller gives an account of the 1966 partial nuclear meltdown of the United States' first commercial breeder reactor. Fortunately, the crisis was averted, and no one was killed. However, it served as a cautionary tale for the nuclear industry.

In 1979, Hollywood expounded on those fears, with the debut of *The China Syndrome* on March 16, 1979. Albeit fictional, *The China Syndrome* (1979) illustrated the dangers of nuclear energy, with a chilling look at corporate greed eclipsing public safety. The film starred Jack Lemon as Jack Godell, Jane Fonda as Kimberly Wells, and Michael Douglas as Richard Adams. Kimberly Wells is a KXLA television station reporter specializing in "fluff" pieces rather than hard news stories. She is tasked with doing a special on the Ventana nuclear power plant, illustrating both the importance and safety of the plant. While visiting the plant, the news team witnessed a terrifying malfunction that led to a shutdown. Initially, the "turbine trip" is believed to be a routine event that poses no danger to the plant or the public. Unbeknownst to the public relations executive at the plant, Adams had secretly filmed the incident, with the excited Wells hoping to show it on the nightly newscast. The network executives thwarted the plan to show the tape, leading the pair to further investigate nuclear energy's safety. At the same time, shift-supervisor Jack Godell begins his investigation and determines the plant is unsafe. However, the corporate executives at the nuclear plant dismissed the incident as harmless and refused to conduct a thorough safety inspection. They even resort to attempting murder to silence the whistleblowers, with Godell taking the drastic measure of using a gun to hijack the control room. His one demand is to speak to Wells to give a live interview to tell the public about the unsafe reactor. Unfortunately, at the beginning of the interview, a SWAT team arrives, killing Godell and preventing him from informing the public. The reactor experiences another malfunction, which causes it to shut down once again. The film concludes with the public relations official characterizing Godell as an emotionally disturbed employee that had been drinking. However, his co-worker, Ted Spindler (Wilford Brimley), disagrees, telling reporters that an investigation will prove that Godell was a hero, not a "looney." Also, live on air, Wells gives an emotional recap, telling viewers that Godell was "not a drunk or crazy man" and that he just wanted the plant shut down. She concludes her live report by declaring, "let's hope it doesn't end here." Unsurprisingly, the film received a hostile response from the nuclear power industry, who asserted that it was "sheer fiction" and a "character assassination of the entire industry." Ironically, just 12 days after the theatrical release, the Three Mile Island nuclear accident transpired in Dauphin County, Pennsylvania.

While *The China Syndrome* is the most noteworthy film, *Red Alert* (1977) was the first movie that featured a malfunction at a nuclear power plant. The made-for-television film aired on CBS on May 18, 1977, with the story taking place at a nuclear plant in Birchfield, Minnesota. A leak in the reactor caused the mainframe computer, Proteus, to close the containment room, trapping and killing 14 workers. Proteus begins to detect several other malfunctions, which leads Harry Stone (Ralph Waite), the leader of central control, to send in investigators, Frank Brolen (William Devane) and Carl Wyche (Michael Brandon) to inspect. The pair report that the computer is incorrect, leading to a clash with Stone, who has an uncompromising faith in the computer system, and its decisions. The by-the-book Stone is unwilling to believe that the computer could be wrong, leading to a struggle between the inflexible bureaucrat and the investigators. As a meltdown is imminent, panic ensues with residents desperately fleeing the area. In the end, the crisis is averted with the heroic investigators determining that a mentally deranged employee planted several explosives, with the plan of tricking the computer into triggering a chain reaction. The telefilm was a tense, albeit sensational depiction of a potential disaster at a nuclear power plant. In a similar vein, *Atomic Twister* (2002) was another television film about an impending meltdown at a nuclear facility. As the title suggests, the storyline features a tornado that damages a plant in West Tennessee, which starts a nuclear meltdown. Once again, the individual heroics of the protagonists avert a disaster, and the film ends happily. Nevertheless, the mad bomber and tornado angles supplant any concerns over corporate control of safety measures in the nuclear industry.

On April 26, 1986, the worst nuclear accident occurred at the Chernobyl Nuclear Power Plant. The accident was the result of a flawed reactor design that was operated with insufficiently trained personnel. The explosion and fires discharged a minimum of 5% of the radioactive reactor core into the environment, the radioactive material reaching many regions in Europe. The initial explosion resulted in the death of two plant workers, and 31 others perished because of acute radiation syndrome. However, the impact was immeasurable, with thousands of residents exposed to cancer agents. The fallout impacted both agricultural and natural ecosystems in Belarus, Russia, Ukraine and other European countries. Radioactive materials were found in milk, meat, forest food products, freshwater fish, and wood. In popular culture, the story of Chernobyl has been shown in documentaries, scripted films and television series. The made-for-television production, *Chernobyl: The Final Warning* (1991), interlaces the story of a fireman at the plant and the heroics of Dr. Robert Gale (John Voight), who led an international medical team that treated survivors. However, the most notable depiction was the Emmy Award-winning *Chernobyl* miniseries, which aired on HBO in 2019. The five-part limited-run series was a chilling depiction of the events leading up to the disaster, the political bickering, and the cleanup efforts. The series painted Soviet officials and plant management as evil and conniving, in what critics called typical Hollywood inflation that used the biased Western perception of Soviet history (Tlis, 2019). However, the series was an entertaining, albeit unsettling, interpretation of the Chernobyl disaster.

Climate Change and Global Warming

The climate crisis has emerged as a significant social, political, and economic issue, with ramifications that reverberate globally. In August of 2021, the UN-sponsored Intergovernmental Panel on Climate Change released a damning report warning of increasingly extreme heatwaves, droughts, and flooding. The UN chief, Antonio Guterres, grimly stated that the report "is a code red for humanity." The prognosis is not new, as scientists have sounded the alarm about a climate catastrophe for decades, with global temperatures rising because of human pollution of the planet over the last two-and-a-half centuries, particularly in the last 50 years. Climate scientists contend that governmental leaders, businesses, and other stakeholders must act with a sense of urgency, cutting greenhouse emissions before the planet hits a tipping point. In terms of popular culture, Hollywood can play a vital role in educating the public about impending devastation, with thoughtful and provocative narratives that encourage ecological responsibility and action. That said, Hollywood has been criticized for either ignoring or depicting unrealistic representations of the climate crisis. Numerous films feature natural disasters, such as hurricanes, tsunamis, tornadoes, wildfires, and earthquakes. However, the connection between climate change and the apocalypse is tenuous, at best. While end-of-the-world films are typical fodder, the notion that our carbon footprint is responsible for the crisis is rarely mentioned in Hollywood films. In a *New York Times* article, Cara Buckley (2019) argues that Hollywood depictions are decidedly unrealistic with the hyperbolic end of world scenarios involving extreme weather events. Some scholars argue that fictional works about climate change have developed a new genre, termed "cli-fi." In an exhaustive review of 60 "cli-fi" films, Svoboda (2016) argued that these films are characterized primarily by extreme weather events or the planet's destruction. They include films about rising sea levels that result in flooding (*Waterworld*, 1995; *Noah*, 2013), extreme weather events (*Twister*, 1996; *Into the Storm*, 2014; *The Fire Next Time*, 1993), the advent of the ice age (*The Day After Tomorrow*, 2004; *Snowpiercer*, 2014), the melting Arctic (*The Last Winter*, 2016; *The Road*, 2009), and famine or drought (*Interstellar*, 2014; *Mad Max: Fury Road*, 2015).

The vast majority of films that represent themes of climate change are science fiction. The sci-fi classic *Soylent Green* (1973) envisions the planet in the midst of a chronic heatwave due to the greenhouse effect. Essentially a murder mystery, the film highlights pollution, poverty, overpopulation, and lack of food. Similarly, *The Fire Next Time* (1993) dramatically illustrated the consequences of global warming, featuring a family suffering from droughts, floods, and hurricanes. At the same time, the box-office flop *Waterworld* (1995) was a post-apocalyptic action film that imagined the disastrous impact of global warming. The melting of polar ice caps resulted in water covering nearly all the land. However, the most famous depiction of climate change was *The Day After Tomorrow* (2004). The film's premise was that US governmental inaction had precipitated an environmental apocalypse, in which extreme weather events precede the new ice age. The film served as a wake-up call for climate action but was criticized by right-wing pundits and politicians as hyperbolic, alarmist, and "leftist propaganda." Conservatives have minimized the danger, even rejecting the very existence of climate change. Critics argued that the film was based on "bad science" and may be used as publicity to pass legislation to cut back on the use of fossil fuels. The pundits argue that environmental regulation will lead to economic deprivation. No doubt, the film, like many Hollywood productions, took creative license with the science. The director, Roland Emmerich, admits that he took liberties, claiming, "I always knew I had to make it as exciting and spectacular as I can … We sped up the climate change dramatically, so it made a movie." (Kaltenbach, 2004). More importantly, critics of the film's environmental and political message did not disclose that many policymakers, both Republican and Democrat, are beholden to industry and multinational corporations. Interestingly, *Vice* (2018), a biographical black comedy about former Vice President, Dick Cheney included references to the Republican Party's minimization of climate change.

Although *The Day After Tomorrow* brought some much-needed attention to the climate crisis, the reality is that it had little impact politically, socially, and culturally. It was just another disaster movie that Hollywood likes to churn out frequently. Since the film's release, there have been some notable sci-fi films that depict climate change. *Take Shelter* (2010) is a psychological character study in which the protagonist envisions climate change ending the world. The Korean-produced *Snowpiercer* (2013) is a thriller set in a world encased in ice after failing to stop global warming. *Avatar* (2009) depicts a futuristic Earth destroyed by global warming, ozone depletion, and overpopulation. The film was visually stunning and featured the nefarious Resource Development Administration (RDA), a quasi-governmental corporation that owns all the resources outside Earth. Set on the planet Pandora, the RDA destroys natural resources and displaces the indigenous population. The sci-fi comedy, *Downsizing* (2017) explored both wealth inequality and climate change. Set in the not-too-distant future, Earth is overpopulated and experiences the devastating consequences of global warming. A scientist invents a procedure in which humans can be "downsized" to five inches, presumably reducing humans' carbon imprint. Finally, *Geostorm* (2017) features a series of superstorms that occur after the malfunctioning of climate-controlling satellites.

Aside from the overabundance of science-fiction films, a key element in climate change films is that corporations or their proxies are rarely villains. This, despite the reality that industry is the primary driver in the destruction of the environment, Hollywood has not taken industries such as Agribusiness or Big Oil to task for their profiteering at the behest of environmental sustainability. Documentarian and actor Fisher Stevens argued that "we need a pop culture 'Forest Gump' movie now to wake people up … because the fossil fuel industry is doing everything to stop us in America from believing that fossil fuels are causing climate change" (Buckley, 2019). Naturally, Hollywood itself is partially responsible as the standard film is brimming with messages of consumerism, and consumption, epitomized with unsubtle product placements. Moreover, film production exerts a considerable carbon footprint, with producers, directors, and actors that live opulent lifestyles. In response to the climate crisis, The British Academy of Film and Television Arts (BAFTA) created the Planet Placement Initiative as a resource for film and television content creators to "make positive environmental behaviors mainstream" and transform film narratives from doom and loss to one in which positive actions can make a tangible difference in the world (BAFTA, 2019). The project hopes to infuse narratives of climate crisis without resorting to typical Hollywood hyperbole.

Some non-sci-fi films have embedded global warming in their storylines and depicted big business as the villain. Although not exclusively "environmental" films, *The Emerald Forest* (1985) and *Medicine Man* (1992) highlighted the deforestation of the Amazon rain forest. *The Emerald Forest* features the story of Bill Markham (Powers Boothe), an engineer who relocates to the Amazon to work on a hydroelectric dam. While picnicking on the edge of the depleted forest, Markham's young son is abducted and subsequently raised by an indigenous tribe called the "Invisible People." The haunting story is a morality tale that explores how humanity is corrupted in the name of progress and capitalism. *Medicine Man* features a logging company building a road through the rainforest, threatening the native population and destroying the natural habitat. Similarly, *Fire in the*

Amazon (1993) was a B-Movie that highlighted the destruction of the rainforest. The film's postscript reads,

> For years, the rainforest has spawned bloody feuds. Ranchers and loggers have sought to clear the land, while rubber tappers and Indians have fought to save the forest. Many have died in the conflict. Rafael Santos, leader of the rubber tappers, was one such man.

The film starred Sandra Bullock as environmentalist Alyssa Rothman and Craig Sheffer as photojournalist R.J. O'Brien. Set in Bolivia, the fictionalized story follows Rothman and O'Brien as they investigate the murder of an indigenous environmental activist. The dialogue was cheesy, as illustrated when O'Brien and Rothman meet for the first time,

Alyssa: I'm with the Rainforest Preservation Society
RJ: Oh yeah. What do you—What do they do?
Alyssa: We're a privately-endowed foundation that supports Santos's work
RJ: Oh, so you're the good guys in this whole rainforest enchilada, huh?
Alyssa: It's just a little bit more than an enchilada to me, Mr. O'Brien.
RJ: Well, see, as far as I am concerned, that's the problem—everybody takes this thing too seriously. I mean, in America, you got the politicians, you got the singers and the Hollywood actors all jumping on the bandwagon doing speeches about the poor birds and the bees in the Amazon [laughs]. You know what I mean? It's just like—it's like the fucking fashion, you know?
Alyssa: Well, I'm not in Hollywood, as you can see here. Its been a long time since I've known that this cause is a lot more than just the birds and the bees, okay? There're people out there with rights, the right to live the way—the way that they want. And Santos and I have been working to protect that right. So yes, it is very serious, Mr. O'Brien, and it's not an enchilada, which by the way is a Mexican dish, not a Bolivian.

The pair unearth a nefarious scheme involving corporate bribery, corruption, and murder, amongst the backdrop of environmental destruction. Produced by Roger Corman, the schlocky film was loosely inspired by the murder of Chico Mendes, the Brazilian Rubber Tappers National Council (CTN) leader, by two wealthy landowners. The subsequent trial uncovered a long history of murder, intimidation, and corruption by landowners, loggers, and the authorities.

Also set in South America, *Salt and Fire* (2016) was written and directed by acclaimed German filmmaker Werner Herzog. The film begins as three UN scientists are taken hostage by Matt Riley (Michael Shannon), the CEO of a large international consortium. The consortium is responsible for the "Diablo Blanco disaster," a toxic salt flat spreading rapidly through the region. Riley enlists the help of a scientist, Dr. Laura Sommerfield (Veronica Ferres), to investigate the ecological disaster's possibility to spread to a nearby supervolcano. Riley tells Dr. Sommerfield that if the volcano erupts, "we will disappear as a species."

However, Dr. Sommerfield is more concerned about the rapid expansion of salt flats, where Riley retorts:

> But what may overtake it all is the fire lying underneath. We must face both. Salt and fire. Here lies a monster, on the verge of waking. My guess is one day soon, everyone will know how to pronounce Uturuncu … Uturuncu.

With that, Riley strands the doctor with two nearly blind indigenous children in the middle of the salt flat. The trio attempts to survive on meager supplies of rice and water. After a few days, Riley returns and tells Laura that he adopted the boys after their mother died from the toxicity of the region. The guilt-ridden Riley explains:

Riley: You see, I am the CEO of the consortium, which is responsible for all this. The toxins, the desiccation of the lake, the transformation of a whole landscape … into salt. The failure of a "glorious" irrigation system which diverted two large rivers. Both of which are now beyond repair. And the salt here is expanding. There were fish here … a few decades ago. Boats. Fisherman. Hard to imagine, isn't it?
Laura: But I was prepared to report on this. Why did you take me hostage?
Riley: I wanted a report back to the United Nations that contained something more than scientific data, graphs, and lifeless statistics. A report with something different in it. A report of a lake so poisonous … that two boys who grew up near its shores became blind! They will never see a world like this again.

The film is visually stunning and was an allegory for global warming and climate change, the salt flats representing "an alien planet, not of our world." However, the critical message was lost amongst the confusing plot and poor dialogue. Finally, the eco-friendly miniseries, *Burn Up* (2008), is one of the only depictions of Big Oil's role in global warming. BBC and Canada's Global television produced the miniseries. Set in Calgary, Alberta, the miniseries followed oil executives, political lobbyists, and climate scientists. The story is noteworthy as it dramatically examined the environmental impact of oil sand projects.

Concluding Thoughts

The corporation is a substantial contributor to the global climate crisis; they produce and profit from everything consumers buy, use, and discard. Corporate sources of pollution include an overreliance and abundance of plastic products, runoff from agriculture pesticides, herbicides, and fertilizers, and greenhouse gas emissions. Aside from the climate crisis, industry-driven pollution has destroyed entire regions – generating cancer clusters, poisoning lakes, rivers, and streams, and producing nasty smelling and hazardous air. The stretch of the Mississippi River between New Orleans and Baton Rouge is dubbed "Cancer Alley" because of the high concentration of petrochemical facilities. Predominately comprised of African Americans, the region has an incredibly high rate of cancer deaths and a long history of political indifference and inaction. Yet, the story of these unfortunate victims – many who suffer through long, agonizing deaths – is not told in Hollywood. At best, victims of corporate pollution are secondary characters that occupy minor roles in the film. The narratives revolve around heroic lawyers – or a famous paralegal — fighting for justice on their behalf.

Reference List

Allen, B.L. (2006). Cradle of a revolution? The industrial transformation of Louisiana's lower Mississippi River. *Technology and culture*, *47*(1), 112–119.

BAFTA (2019, April 3). BAFTA and Albert celebrates the launch of new resource 'Planet Placement' [Press Release]. https://www.bafta.org/media-centre/press-releases/bafta-and-albert-celebrates-the-launch-of-new-resource-planet-placement

Buckley, C. (2019, August 14). Why is Hollywood so scared of climate change? *The New York Times*. https://www.nytimes.com/2019/08/14/movies/hollywood-climate-change.html

Carson, R. (2002). *Silent spring*. Houghton Mifflin Harcourt.

Center for Western Priorities. (2021). 2020 western oil and gas spills tracker. https://westernpriorities.org/2020-new-mexico-oil-and-gas-spills-tracker/

Commoner, B. (2020). *The closing circle: Nature, man, and technology*. Courier Dover Publications.

Curry, C. (2013, January). Fracking group buys ads to run in front of Matt Damon's 'Promised Land.' *ABC News*. https://abcnews.go.com/US/gas-industry-buys-ads-counter-matt-damons-promised/story?id=18132574

Environmental Protection Agency. (2021). *Sources of greenhouse gas emissions*. https://www.epa.gov/ghgemissions/sources-greenhouse-gas-emissions

Fuller, J.G. (1975). We almost lost Detroit. https://www.osti.gov/biblio/5271154

Gerson, J., Wadle, A. & Parham, J. (2020, June 18). The long, toxic tail of the Gold Rush. *Greenbiz*. https://www.greenbiz.com/article/long-toxic-tail-gold-rush

Kaltenbach, C. (2004, May 30). 'Day After Tomorrow': Drowning in rhetoric. *The Baltimore Sun*. https://www.baltimoresun.com/news/bs-xpm-2004-05-30-0406010406-story.html

Newman, R.S. (2016). *Love canal: A toxic history from colonial times to the present*. Oxford University Press.

Popovich, N., Albeck-Ripka, L., & Pierre-Louis, K. (2021, January 20). The Trump administration rolled back more than 100 environmental rules. Here's the full list. *The New York Times*. https://www.nytimes.com/interactive/2020/climate/trump-environment-rollbacks-list.html

Svoboda, M. (2016). Cli-fi on the screen (s): patterns in the representations of climate change in fictional films. *Wiley Interdisciplinary Reviews: Climate Change*, *7*(1), 43–64.

Tlis, F. (2019, June). Russian politician calls HBO Chernobyl 'Anti-Soviet' Filth', falsely accuses producers of distortion. *Polygraph.info*. https://www.polygraph.info/a/fact-check-russia-hbo-chernobyl/30004231.html

United Nations. (2021). Secretary-general calls latest IPCC climate report 'Code Red for Humanity', stressing 'Irrefutable' evidence of human influence. [Press Release] https://www.un.org/press/en/2021/sgsm20847.doc.htm

Walton, B. (2018). Remembering Michigan's PBB crisis. *Circle of Blue*. https://www.circleofblue.org/2018/world/remembering-michigans-pbb-crisis/

4 Harm to Workers

They all looked like they died before they were dead. [Describing former employees at Kerr-McGee Plutonium Plant]

Angela (Diana Scarwid) in *Silkwood* (1983)

The corporation wields enormous, widespread, and grotesque levels of power, both domestically and globally. Ultimately, the primary goal of the corporation is profit – at any cost. This profit-maximization model has allowed the corporate mentality to seep into the public good, where corporations pay few taxes, infringe on human rights, and have excessive political influence. The increasing power of the corporation results in lower compensation, fewer benefits, less stable employment, and poorer working conditions for their employees. Corporations reap enormous profits, while CEO pay has skyrocketed. The average pay for CEOs at the top 250 firms falls between $14 million and $17.2 million per year. The compensation for CEOs has risen 940 percent since 1978, while workers' compensation had risen only 12 percent during that period. More importantly, the net productivity of workers has grown four times the pay of the average worker (Mishel & Wolfe, 2019). The income, wages, and wealth generated over the last four decades have failed to trickle down to the vast majority largely because public policy aligns with corporations and the uber-rich, in which corporate governance strategies prioritize Wall Street and shareholders. Moreover, the decline in the power of labor unions, outsourcing, and increase in contract labor has seriously diminished workers' ability to secure wage increases and maintain adequate health and pension benefits.

Globalization has also exacerbated the plight of workers, as corporations take advantage of lower operating costs, lack of labor regulations, and a large pool of exploitable labor to further their profits (Green et al., 2019). A particularly nasty feature of corporate globalization is the sweatshop. Workers are packed into unsanitary small spaces, breathing unsafe air, and working 14–18 hours a day for poverty-level wages. For example, brand-name sportswear manufacturers Nike and Adidas, clothing traders H&M, Levi Strauss, and Walt Disney have all profited from these harsh, subhuman conditions in sweatshops. That said, workers in American restaurants, farms, domestic labor, and workplaces attached

DOI: 10.4324/9781003163855-4

to corporations such as Walmart, McDonald's, and Wendy's are also exposed to sweatshop-type working conditions. This is especially true for Americans whose first language is not English who may be unfamiliar with US labor law. Unfortunately, recent immigrants, both documented and undocumented, are the most exploited workers in the United States, suffering wage theft, dangerous working conditions, and discrimination.

Nonetheless, all workers in the United States continue to face health and safety issues, with one worker perishing every 99 minutes from a work-related injury, accounting for approximately 15 deaths a day. This is a significant improvement from the 1970s, where about 38 employees died per day. Similarly, employee injuries and illnesses were also down from 10.9 incidents per 100 workers in 1972 to 2.8 per 100 in 2019 (BLS, 2020). That said, many workplace injuries are preventable, and worker rights must continue to be safeguarded, especially as corporate giants lobby to deregulate hard-fought industry protections. Unfortunately, the erosion of worker rights leads to increasingly large gaps between the rich and poor, creating even more division within an already divisive society. Yet, corporations continue to reap the benefits, enjoying cheaper labor, less regulation, and tax breaks – on the backs of labor.

How You Going to See Me Now

The race to the bottom – where workers' rights, compensation, and safety continue to erode – is not a popular topic in Hollywood. Generally, Hollywood movies provide a form of escapism for audiences, where the good vanquish evil and where comic book heroes become movie icons. Movies that feature strong messages that critique or question societal norms are generally absent from the box office. Although important, the exploitation of workers by corporations is a subject that is rarely depicted on film. On the one hand, it may be challenging for general audiences, many of whom face exploitation at work, to gaze upon that level of realism on the silver screen. More importantly, the film industry is a corporation with a dark history regarding workers' rights (Sainato, 2021). Film producers curry political favors, receive tax credits, attempt to halt labor activities, and transfer productions to regions where they receive economic benefits and political favors. That said, Hollywood has not entirely ignored the plight of workers. The silent film era was particularly progressive with several films that depicted the plight of workers, with examinations of low wages, unsafe conditions, child labor, and labor organizing. In the 1920s, the red scare precipitated increased film censorship, leading producers to increasingly avoid themes of socialism, worker rights, and any critique of capitalist enterprise. In the 1930s, pre-code Hollywood and New Deal sensibilities allowed for a handful of films that depicted the struggle between labor and capital. However, by the 1950s, World War II and McCarthyism resulted in few depictions of industry exploitation of labor. Through the 1960s and 1970s, unionism became increasingly associated with corruption and organized crime, with honest depictions of the realities of the working class a rarity. Until the 1980s, very few films place blame for the erosion of worker rights squarely on industry, and even fewer show workers as expendable pawns in the capitalist machinery.

However, the debut of *Norma Rae* in 1979 helped inspire several films that explored the plight of workers, including films that depict the harms that corporations have inflicted on their employees. In film, these harms can take many forms, such as injury to physical, psychological, and emotional well-being. Harms can also include unfair labor practices, including low pay, the busting of unions, lack of health and safety protocols, and unjust layoffs or terminations. As such, the remainder of this chapter will explore the films that depict corporate harms of workers categorized by (1) The Whistleblower; (2) The Toiler; (3) Race and Ethnicity; (4) The Farmer; and (5) Mistreatment of White-Collar workers.

The Whistleblower

The whistleblower serves a crucial role in shedding light on injustice, calling truth to wrongs perpetrated by the rich and powerful. The whistleblower can expose corruption, racial discrimination, sexual harassment, fraud, and dangerous working conditions. The whistleblower is beset with significant legal, ethical, financial, and personal challenges, especially within the insular corporate world. Once the wrongdoing is exposed, managers often utilize unfounded and defamatory tactics to denounce the whistleblower as a "disgruntled employee" that is unbalanced, untrustworthy or self-serving. In Hollywood, the whistleblower is an inspirational character that arouses justice and fairness within viewers. The whistleblower appears in many film genres, including films that depict corporate wrongdoings perpetrated toward workers. Without a doubt, *Norma Rae* and *Silkwood* are the most famous examples of whistleblowers that out industry misdeeds and attempt to right the wrongs by helping to organize labor unions.

Norma Rae was a groundbreaking depiction of work in a cotton mill. The film depicts poor working conditions, low pay, and hopelessness that engulf O.P. Henley, Textile Mill employees. The film stars Sally Field as Norma Rae Webster, a single mother who lives a meager and depressing existence. She has affairs with married men and lives with her mother and father, who work at the mill. Norma is feisty and is vocal about the poor conditions at the mill. Her life changes when she meets Rueben Warshowsky, a sarcastic yet determined union organizer who works for the Textile Workers Union of America. They have instant chemistry, with Norma liking the "Jew" from New York and Reuben spotting the untapped potential of the uneducated, seemingly broken single mother. Norma's fortunes soon change. After a quick courtship, she marries Sonny Webster (Beau Bridges), a divorced father and former mill employee. After listening to Warshowsky giving a speech to a small gathering at a church, Norma is inspired to help unionize the mill. She dedicates herself to promoting the union, becoming even more determined after her father dies of a heart attack on the job, which could have been prevented if he was allowed to take a break. In a pivotal moment, she is fired from her job and refuses to leave the mill. She writes the word UNION on a piece of cardboard and stands on a table. In a show of defiance, the workers stop their machines, and the deafening noise becomes silent. In a dramatic ending, the workers vote for the union, with Warshowsky and Norma parting ways, with the Oscar-winning song, *It Goes Like It Goes*, concluding the film.

Sans the happy ending, *Silkwood* was also an emotional and raw depiction of employees at a chemical factory. The film starred Meryl Streep as Karen Silkwood, an employee at Kerr-McGee Cimarron Fuel Fabrication Site in Oklahoma. The movie was loosely based on Karen Silkwood, who was a real-life whistleblower at the facility. The plant is woefully unsafe, with workers routinely exposed to radiation, which the plant doctor calls "acceptable body burden." Karen is not shy about voicing her concerns and becomes involved with the union, which is on the verge of decertification. As part of the union team, she travels to Washington, DC, to meet with union officials. The officials led by Paul Stone (Ron Silver) appearing disinterested in their concern until Karen privately tells them about doctoring radiographies of fuel rods to hide shoddy work. Concerned about a nuclear accident, Stone asks Karen to find evidence of the altering of safety records so that they can get the *New York Times* to print a story and use it as leverage for contract negotiations. Silkwood becomes obsessed with gathering evidence, putting herself at risk from management and Winston (Craig T. Nelson), an employee complicit in the scheme to alter the safety measures. The film concludes on a sad note after Karen is killed in a single-car crash on her way to meet with a *New York Times* reporter. The film insinuates that Karen was being followed and may have been forced off the road. The murder theory was propelled when no documents were found in the car wreckage. The postscript suggests that the circumstances surrounding her death were "unknown" and that she had high levels of tranquilizer and some alcohol. The plant was shut down one year after her death.

Similarly, *Radium Girls* (2018) was based on a true account of women poisoned while working at American Radium, renamed the United States Radium Corporation. The young women used the toxic substance to paint watch dials, urged to "dip, lick, paint" for one penny per watch face. The workers are told that the paint is harmless, despite management knowing that radium was toxic. The film featured Bessie and Josephine Cavallo, two sisters who work at American Radium. The elder sister, Josephine (Abby Quinn), becomes seriously ill, and Bessie (Joey King) becomes involved with communist supporters. Bessie becomes an activist and urges the other girls to seek compensation through litigation. The film features court proceedings, where the girls receive only $10,000 for their pain and suffering. The epilogue revealed that the judge, who negotiated the settlement, was a shareholder of American Radium. Despite the incredible importance of the story, the film lacked grit, substance, and suspense. Generally, it is a poor rendition of one of the most shameful acts of corporate wrongdoing in American history. Kate Moore's 2017 book, *The Radium Girls,* is a more detailed account of the tragedy. That said, the concluding intertitles did reveal that the Radium girls impacted labor law in the United States, leading to changes in worker's compensation and the creation of radiation safety standards. It is also noteworthy, as it is one of the only films that depict the dangerousness of working with noxious substances, such as radium paint, asbestos, or lead.

Also, based on true stories, systemic sexual harassment and widespread sex trafficking were uncovered in *North Country* (2005) and *The Whistleblower* (2010), respectively. Set in 1989, *North Country* followed Josey Aimes' (Charlize Theron) journey to expose widespread sexual harassment in the local Iron Mine. The film was inspired by the true story of Lois Jenson, a mine worker in Minnesota who faced a continual barrage of hostile behavior, including sexual harassment, abusive language, threats, stalking, and intimidation. Likewise, the mine women are relentless targets for sexual harassment and degradation by many male co-workers in the film. The management is complicit in inattention to the widespread abuse, ignoring the problem and refusing to rectify the untenable and incredibly cringeworthy harassment. The film was transformed into a courtroom drama, as Josey instigates a class-action lawsuit against the company, which results in the mining company paying damages to the women and establishing a landmark sexual harassment policy at the workplace. *The Whistleblower* was based on the true story of Kathryn Bolkovac (Rachel Weisz), a Nebraska police officer who served as a UN Peacekeeper in post-war Bosnia and Herzegovina. She unearths a sex trafficking ring serving and facilitated by DynCorp employees, an American private military contractor. DynCorp fired Kathryn, which precipitates her taking the story to BBC News and winning a wrongful dismissal lawsuit against DynCorp.

The whistleblower was also an integral element in *Concussion* (2015). The film revealed that the National Football League (NFL) suppressed data revealing that players were at increased risk for chronic traumatic encephalopathy (CTE), a brain injury that occurs as the result of repeated blows to the head. The film starred Will Smith as Dr. Bennet Omalu, a forensic pathologist who uncovers the risk that concussions have on the health of NFL football players. The film opens with actual footage of Pittsburgh Steelers center Mike Webster giving a speech at his Hall of Fame induction. He tells the audience that it was "painful playing football ... [and] banging heads [was] not a natural thing." A few years later, Webster (David Morse) is homeless and visited by another former Steeler, Justin Strzelczyk, who confides that he is losing his memory, hearing voices, and becoming violent toward his wife and children. The mentally unstable Webster repeats his Hall of Fame speech, telling Justin to "just finish the game." Soon after, Webster dies of a heart attack, which sets the motion for Dr. Omalu to investigate why a seemingly healthy 50-year-old would die of a heart attack. After watching football, Dr. Omalu believes that the sport's violent nature led to Webster's neurotrauma. He begins a relentless investigation, seeking out the brains of other deceased football players to prove his theory. He attempts to warn the NFL, but they do not take his research seriously, denying and minimizing the risk of concussions. Former Steeler team doctor Julian Bailes (Alec Baldwin) tells Omalu that the NFL knew about the risks of concussions but commissioned several studies that minimized the risks. The NFL and their public relations experts use their vast revenue to discredit Omalu and his supporters. Eventually, Omalu is forced to leave his position, relocating to California. In the end, Dr. Omalu is vindicated after Dave Duerson, a former NFLPA representative, who strongly disagreed with Omalu, commits suicide, leaves a note saying that Omalu was right, and donates his brain for future research. Dr. Omalu is invited to speak to the NFLPA, telling them they should know the real risk of playing football. In the end, the NFL began to take concussion safety more seriously due to increased public awareness, scrutiny from Congress and a major lawsuit from former players. The ending intertitles reveal that over 5,000 former players sued the league for concealing the dangers of concussions, with the league settling on the condition that they did not have to disclose what they knew and when. Further, the intertitles reveal that 28 percent of professional football players will suffer severe cognitive impairment, including CTE.

Concussion was a revealing look at how profit overrides safety concerns in sport. However, it was not the first sports film to depict its apathy toward players and their health. The fictional *North Dallas Forty* (1979) starred Nick Nolte as Phillip Elliot, an aging wide receiver that relied heavily on painkillers to perform on the field. In the opening scene, the viewer sees Elliot slowly crawl out of bed, painfully trudging to the bathtub to smoke a joint. The film was based on a novel written by Peter Gent, a retired wide receiver of the Dallas Cowboys. The film depicted the dark side of professional football, including violence against women, drug and alcohol use, and the business's inhumanity. Similarly, in *Any Given Sunday* (1999), James Woods plays Dr. Harvey Mandrake, an unscrupulous team doctor encouraged by the team owner to risk players' health for the sake of winning and profits. In the sports film, the ethos of winning at all costs and playing through pain is the more dominant narrative. Many viewers do not think that professional athletes are exploited, as they believe that the athletes are paid handsomely and are living out a fantasy. However, corporations, such as the NFL, make billions of dollars at the expense of player safety. Although professional athletes are living out a dream, many suffer chronic pain and disabilities. Worse yet, this ethos permeates youth and college sports, recklessly leading to severe and chronic injuries for many athletes who are not even compensated.

The "Toilers": The Mining Industry

From the silent era to the present, the mining industry has been vibrantly depicted in Hollywood. Some of the most notable films include *Black Fury* (1935), *How Green Was My Valley* (1941), and *The Molly Maguires* (1970). Outside Hollywood, there are several distinguished British films, including *The Proud Valley* (1940), *The Stars Look Down* (1940), *Blue Scar* (1949), *The Brave Don't Cry* (1952), *Kes* (1969), and *The Price of Coal* (1977). The 1984–1985 mining strike that shut down the British coal industry was portrayed in *Brassed Off* (1996), *Billy Elliot* (2000), and *Pride* (2014). Moreover, Emile Zola's 1885 novel *Germinal* has been adapted into five films, including the large-scale production of *Germinal* (1993), a bleak and uncompromising vision of a coal miners' strike in northern France in the 1860s.

In Hollywood, the malfeasances of the mining companies have been richly depicted in several films. Based on a true story, *Matewan* (1987) documents a coal miners' strike in West Virginia. The film starred Chris Cooper as Joe Kenehan, an organizer for the United Mine Workers and Mary McDonnell as Elma Radnor, an owner of a boarding house in the town. Directed by John Sayles, the film depicts the low pay, unfair, dangerous working conditions, and racial/ethnic divisions among the coal miners. The Stone Mountain Coal Company brings in Black and Italian scab miners, who are quickly educated on the unfair company practice of forcing the miners to deduct services and equipment from their pay while making the miners buy living goods at inflated prices in company stores. The company also utilizes a spy, C.E. Lively (Bob Gunton), to stoke racial divide among the strikers. One of the "scabs," "Few Clothes" Johnson (James Earl Jones), attends a union meeting but is faced with resistance. Kenehan urges them to work together and not let racial/ethnic divisions define the movement. He passionately argues that the only division is between workers and owners, "them that work and them that don't." With the help of "Few Clothes," Kenehan convinces both the Italian and Black miners to strike with the white miners. The coal operator hires the ruthless Baldwin-Felts Detective Agency to terrorize the strikers, with the agents Hickey and Griggs serving as the primary villains in the story. The pair attempt to evict miners, engage in shootouts, scheme (with Lively) to falsely accuse Kenehan of sexual assault, and torture a young boy to death for information. In a tragic ending, Hickey and Griggs hire reinforcements to carry out evictions, which lead to a climactic gun battle that kills Kenehan and the town's mayor. Griggs is killed during the battle, while Hickey flees to the boarding house, where Elma Radnor shoots and kills him. In the concluding scene, the narrator tells the audience that the Matewan Massacre was the beginning of the Great Coldfield War, reiterating Kenehan's belief that the world is "one great big union."

Coal mining was also a focal point of the *Harlan County War* (2000). The movie was based on the incredibly riveting Barbara Kopple documentary, *Harlan County USA* (1976). The showtime original was certainly not as powerful as the documentary, but it was an incredibly straightforward depiction of the underhanded tactics that coal companies used to break a strike. Set in Kentucky in the early 1970s, the film starred Holly Hunter as Ruby Kinkaid, the wife and daughter of a coal miner. The film begins with an accident that kills two miners, almost killing her husband Silas (Ted Levine). Despite the trauma of the accident, Silas is forced to return to work the next day with the promise of "outside" work. Ruby and Silas share a squalid little house with Ruby's father, dying from black lung disease. Warren Jakopovich (Stellan Skarsgard), a union representative from United Mine Workers of America, arrives in town and attempts to convince the skeptical Ruby to help with the union. The admitted rabble-rouser, Jakopovich, encourages the workers to fight the injustice of low wages, poor working conditions, and lack of safety standards. Despite the previously crooked union representation, Jakopovich quickly wins over the miners with only a few dissenters. The company targets the more vocal strikers, sending out eviction notices, refusing to sell them goods at the company store, and firing them. A court order prevents the miners from mass picketing outside the property entrance, with the "company" influenced judge limiting only three picketers outside the entrance. Ruby decides to organize the woman to "man" the picket line, which leads to the women (and

90 *Harm to Workers*

their children) being thrown into jail. The lengthy strike continues, with Ruby's dad's health deteriorating and eventually succumbing to the black lung. At that point, Ruby becomes an even more impassioned supporter of the cause, going to New York to disrupt a Duke Power stockholder's meeting. She tells the stuff-shirt executives of the suffering of the miners, the lack of safety, and black lung disease. She implores the stockholders to "treat people that work for you with respect." The film parallels the real-life story of the Brookside strike with the murder of a young miner, precipitating the management to negotiate a contract with the miners. In the ending intertitles, it is revealed that the strikers received a wage increase, full medical benefits, and improved safety and housing conditions. However, the postscript also warned audiences that only half of all coal miners were unionized, and that each year 1,500 succumb to black lung disease.

Curiously, the controversy that entangled the United Mine Workers of America (UMW) was not prominently featured in *Harlan County War*. In 1969, the leader of UMW, Tony Boyle, paid $20,000 to have his rival, Joseph Yablonski, murdered. Boyle was a corrupt leader who embezzled union funds and appeared more concerned about owners' interests than miners. Under his leadership, the union lost much of its power, and many members became disillusioned. The made-for-television movie *Act of Vengeance* (1986) was a fact-based account of the corruption that plagued the United Miners Workers (UMW) elections of 1969. It was based on a true-crime book of the same title by Trevor Armbrister and aired on HBO. In the made for television film, Tony Boyle (Wilford Brimley) is depicted as in "cahoots" with the owners, as he rolled back bargaining rights and disregarded the safety of the workers. After a terrible mine accident, Boyle callously praises the company, claiming that "mining coal is dangerous work ... we don't go down in the mine to be safe. We go down to get the coal out."

Jock Yablonski (Charles Bronson), a union official, is upset with the union's direction and decides to run against Boyle in the national election. The film follows the campaign, showing that Boyle is losing momentum in his quest to maintain leadership. Boyle takes drastic action, deciding to hire a hitman to kill Yablonski, but they cannot execute the murder, and the election is held. The election is rigged, with Boyle winning in a landslide. Incensed with blatant cheating, Yablonski appeals to the National Labor Relation Board. The appeal spurs the hitmen into action, carrying out the gruesome murders of Jock Yablonski, his wife Margaret, and his 25-year-old daughter, Charlotte. The postscript reveals that the election was overturned and that the guilty parties, including Boyle, were convicted of murder. The planning of the murder played a central role in the storyline, with the issues of worker safety and union reform relegated to a secondary role. The Hollywood retelling of the story provided no information about how the tragic death of Yablonski impacted sweeping changes within the UMW. Throughout the 1970s, a determined group of Yablonski followers struggled to successfully democratize the union and bring back the focus of worker's rights. The remaining members of the Yablonski family, son Ken (who found the bodies) and his brother Chip, were not satisfied with the scripts and refused to sign releases for the production. Ken Yablonksi claimed that "the movie had little substance, as it became a true-crime story rather than a story of reform in the UMW and unsafe coal mining conditions" (Steigerwald, 1986).

Unsafe working conditions were also depicted in *Little Accidents* (2014) and *The 33* (2015). *Little Accidents* was a fictionalized story about a tragic coal mining accident in a small West Virginia town. The film was a character-driven drama that involved interconnecting storylines with the mining accident as the backdrop. The only survivor, Amos Jenkins (Boyd Holbrook), was severely injured, unable to use his left arm. He is conflicted about revealing that cost-cutting decisions led to the death of ten miners, as he is concerned that the mine will be closed and the town's economy will be destroyed. His father belabored this point, a retired coal miner who suffers from years of breathing in coal dust. Conversely, union representatives and lawyers for the victims want to sue the company for negligence and win a large settlement. At the same time, teenager Owen (Jacob Lofland) is grieving, as his father died in the accident. He lives with his mother and younger brother James, who has Down's syndrome. Meanwhile, the mine supervisor, Bill Doyle (Josh Lucas), defends his cost cuts by claiming that he was forced to make them by the company. The depressing story evolves as Owen is bullied by the rich kids in town, including Bill and Diane Doyle's (Elizabeth Banks) son, J.T. After J.T. insults James, the smaller Owen confronts J.T., which leads to Owen accidentally killing J.T. and hiding the body deep in the woods. The police started a missing person investigation, theorizing that J.T. was targeted because he was the son of the disgraced supervisor of the mine. After a month of searching for the missing boy, distraught and emotionally neglected, Diane begins an affair with Amos after meeting him at a Bible study group. The slow-moving story continued, with the primary characters' lives starting to intersect with each other. In the end, the remorseful Owen confesses to Amos, and they ride to Doyle's house so that Owen can tell Mrs. Doyle the bad news. The film concludes with Amos revealing that Bill Doyle dismissed safety concerns and threatened workers with retaliation for whistleblowing. The powerful scene juxtaposed against Owen showing the police where the body was concealed.

While *Little Accidents* was a depressing character study, *The 33* was an inspiring account of the true-life mine collapse and rescue in Chile in August 2010. The beginning intertitle sets the tone, telling the audience that 12,000 miners perish in mining accidents worldwide. In the opening, the shift foreman Don Lucho (Lou Diamond Phillips) warns a manager that the mountain has shifted and the gold mine is unsafe. Not only does the manager disregard the evidence, but he also callously tells Lucho that the quota has increased to 250 tons a day. Shortly after the men enter the mine to start work, the mine collapses and 33 miners are trapped. Miraculously, they all survived but could not escape as they were confined in the deepest part of the mine. They take shelter in the "refuge," where they find that the radio is broken, and they only have enough food for three days. Mario Sepulveda (Antonio Banderas) attempts to climb safety ladders but finds the company cut costs by not completing them. The miners are buried alive, with Mario rationing the food and water. Their fate seems hopeless, as Lucho tells the men that the "owners won't spend money to drill ... they didn't even finish the ladders!" He tells the men that "they will wait three days ... and put up the gravestones." Lucho attempts to take the blame, as he knew that the mine was a "death trap." However, Mario tells him that everyone knew it was unsafe, and the blame lay with the mine owners. The miners' families appear at the gates, protesting that they have not received any information and wonder why there is no rescue attempt. It appears hopeless until the Minister of Mines arrives and takes over the operations from the company. The rescue operations begin with drills attempting to discern their location. In a poignant scene, the borehole appears above the miners, who frantically bang on the drill bit and attach a note, saying that all 33 are still alive. The film intersperses actual news footage into the film, which helps tell the technical details about the rescue. After 69 days, the miners are rescued from their underground tomb. The ending intertitles tell audiences that the company was found not guilty of criminal negligence, and the survivors were never compensated for their ordeal. In an overly happy ending, the 33 miners are shown at the end of the film. However, the film serves as a grim reminder of the dangerous conditions of mining, the expendability of workers, and the corporation's blatant disregard of safety protocols.

Race, Immigration, and Exploitation: A Nexus

Mainstream Hollywood tends to ignore the struggles of the farmworker, servant, factory worker, miner, cleaner, and other essential members of the working class. In the global capitalist system, the exploitation of workers is inextricably linked to racism. Globally, foreign workers experience lower wages, unsafe conditions, and precarious employment. Domestically, statistics reveal that racial minorities experience lower pay and less secure employment. Migrant workers are treated as a disposable workforce that is vastly underpaid, overworked, and encounters incredibly hazardous working conditions. Albeit rare, some notable films depict corporate or business exploitation of racial and ethnic minority workers. These films provide a clever critique of capitalism while encapsulating the issues of racism, immigration, and exploitation.

The plight of Mexican Americans and migrant workers has been the subject of a handful of films, including the groundbreaking *Salt of the Earth* (1954). The independent film *Alambrista!* (1977) was an uncompromising and groundbreaking depiction of an undocumented farmworker. Directed by Robert Young, it is a work of political art, convincingly showing how migrant labor is essential, yet the workers are exploited and ostracized. Less acclaimed, *A Day Without a Mexican* (2004) was a satirical examination of the importance of Mexicans in the state of California. The entire Mexican population disappears in the mockumentary, leading to social, political, and economic disaster.

Set in Los Angeles, *Bread and Roses* (2000) depicted the plight of poorly paid custodial workers. It was directed by British director Ken Loach, who made several notable British working-class films, including *Riff Raff* (1991) and *The Navigators* (2001). The film took its title from a 1912 labor dispute in Lawrence, Massachusetts, where immigrant women demanded better wages and working conditions, with the slogan "bread but with roses, too." The film was based on the "Justice for Janitors" campaign by the Service Employees International Union (SEIU). The film highlights the exploitation that legal and illegal immigrants face, with declining wages, lack of healthcare, and no rights. It features two Mexican sisters, Maya (Pilar Padilla) and Rosa (Elpidia Carillo), who work as custodial staff for Angel Services, which cleans a downtown office building in Los Angeles. They are supervised by the mean-spirited Mr. Perez (George Lopez), who takes kickbacks from new employees and callously suppresses any effort to improve work conditions. The film also stars Adrian Brody as Sam Shapiro, a labor organizer who stirs up the workers and attempts to help them form a union to improve pay and working conditions. He uses confrontational tactics to gain media attention, drawing attention to the plight of the workers. Maya enthusiastically takes up the cause, while Rosa is resistant to the idea, pithily saying that "we could all lose our jobs, and then who would pay the bills?" With the help of the janitors, Sam and a group of custodians crash a party celebrating the merging of two law firms that occupy some floors in the building. The law firm represents Hollywood agents and actors, with some actors (such as Ron Perlman) appearing as extras in the comedic scene. The custodians sing and vacuum, while Sam gives out awards to mock the stingy pay practices of the cleaning agency.

Unfortunately, the stunt led to Perez firing several employees, including Ruben, a young man saving money for college. It is revealed that Rosa "ratted" out the workers for promotion and increased wages, leading to a heart-wrenching confrontation between Maya and Rosa. In the most poignant moment in the film, Rosa unapologetically admits her culpability, telling Maya that she was a survivor that once worked as a prostitute to keep the family from starving. Maya also discloses that she had sex with Mr. Perez to secure a job for Maya. The emotionally jolting scene spurred Maya to rob a convenience store, using the proceeds to pay the remaining tuition fees for Ruben. In the culminating scene, the janitors protest, marching through the streets with their red t-shirts and placards. They demand the reinstatement of the fired custodians and march into the office building. Sam makes an impassioned speech, calling for health care, respect, and the end to "powerful companies that are controlling your lives." The police arrive to remove and arrest the protestors, who are booked, fingerprinted, and photographed. While in jail, they learn that Angel Services has settled the strike, reinstated the terminated employees, and provided health care. However, the celebration is bittersweet, as Maya is arrested for the robbery (her fingerprints were at the crime scene) and is deported rather than being sent to jail. In the final scene, the custodians go to the deportation facility to watch Maya get on the bus, yelling their goodbyes and providing her emotional support. Rosa is reluctant to join the group but runs after the bus, saying goodbye to her little sister in a very emotionally uplifting moment. The film was a brilliant depiction of the plight of low-paid and powerless workers, with appropriate comedic moments interspersed with the intense drama.

The exploitation of migrant workers was also a featured storyline in *Fast Food Nation* (2006). The film begins with Raul (Wilmer Valderrama), Sylvia (Catalina

Sandino Moreno), and her sister Coco (Ana Claudia Talanco) crossing the US border with the help of coyotes. The trio ends up in Cody, Colorado, where they gain employment at Uni-Globe, an industrial meat processing plant. After the training orientation, Sylvia decides to work for lower wages as a hotel cleaner, as she cannot "stomach" the smells and sights of the meat plant. The shift supervisor, Mike (Bobby Cannavale), is verbally abusive and sexually exploits the female employees. He starts a sexual relationship with Coco, getting her addicted to drugs. One of the most dramatic scenes involves a workplace accident where Raul's friend falls into a machine, mangling his leg. In an attempt to save his friend, Raul falls and seriously injures himself. Uni-Globe refuses to take any responsibility, claiming that Raul was on methamphetamines which they believed caused the accident. Raul is permanently injured, and with no recourse, Sylvia is forced to financially support the now-married couple. Desperate, Sylvia seeks work at Uni-Globe and is forced to have sex with Mike to secure a position in the plant. The exploitation storyline was captivating and deserved more attention in the underrated film.

The maltreatment of Latino farmworkers was the subject of the biopic *Cesar Chavez* (2004), which starred Michael Pena as the titular character. Chavez was an iconic union organizer and civil rights advocate who used non-violent methods to advocate for change. The film depicts Chavez's efforts to organize 50,000 farm workers in California by forming the United Farm Workers (UFW). He faces opposition from the owners of large industrial farms, highlighting the poor working conditions, low pay, and unrelenting racism toward both Mexican and Filipino workers. The film depicts several UFW campaigns, including the Delano Grape Strike, the Salad Bowl Strike, and the Modesto March. Set in New Mexico, *The Milagro Beanfield War* (1988) details the struggle of Hispanic farmers to compete against much larger business and political interests. The farmers are forbidden to divert water from an irrigation ditch that runs parallel to their properties. The political establishment wants to force the farmers to sell their properties to land developer Ladd Devine (Richard Bradford) to build a gated community and country club. However, their plans are thwarted after unlikely hero Joe Mondragon (Chick Vennera) accidentally strikes a water pipe, which leads to the fields being flooded, allowing Joe to grow beans. The decaying and dying town of Milagro is resurrected, led by Ruby Archuleta (Sonia Braga). She helps mobilize the residents to fight the land development and hoarding of water by the company. Devine uses his connections with the Governor to bring in Kyril Montana (Christopher Walken) to quell the mini rebellion. The concluding scene features a large crowd of residents protesting the arrest of Joe, forcing the state authorities to leave empty-handed. Despite the seriousness of the topic, the film was a dry comedy that featured whimsical and mystical dialogue. As such, the gravity of big business tapping large revenue streams and currying political favors to displace long-term residents is somewhat mitigated. That said, the film remarkably illustrated how grassroots activism could galvanize the weak against seemingly impregnable business interests.

Racism was a central theme in Showtime's original movie, *10,000 Black Men Named George* (2002). Set in 1925, the film follows labor activist A. Philip

Randolph's (Andre Braugher) struggle to organize the porters employed by the Pullman Company. The porters were all African American and eponymously named "George," after George Pullman, the owner of the railway cars. The "George Boys" were poorly treated by management and railway passengers, with several dramatic examples depicted in the film. Ashley Totten (Mario Van Peebles) is the head of the company-run union and asks Randolph to organize a "real union" that provides improved pay and better working conditions. At first, Randolph is trepidatious, telling Totten that "to form a negro (sic) union in one of the most powerful corporations in the country ... well, that is very difficult. I know, I've tried." However, after experiencing the degradation of the job, Randolph is determined to join the cause and publishes an article in his socialist magazine, *The Messenger*.

> The Pullman Porters seems to be made to order to carry the gospel of unionism in the colored world. His home is everywhere. His struggle is universal. For justice, decent wages and honorable working conditions. The days of ruthless exploitation and mistreatment at the hands of the Pullman Company are numbered. I personally witnessed these events in the course of my investigation. The company officials use their political influence, courts, company spies and violence to stop the unionization.

As the film progresses, Randolph and his associates experience several setbacks, including personal melodrama, beatings, firings, and divisions with his supporters. Championed by the New Deal policies of the Roosevelt administration, the Porters finally got to vote, and the Brotherhood of Sleeping Car Porters (BSCP) was officially certified in 1935. The postscript reveals that "On August 25th, 1937, the Pullman Company signed the first-ever agreement between a union of black workers and a major American corporation. It was 12 years – to the day – of the founding of the Brotherhood of Sleeping Car Porters." The film presented an interesting and often forgotten chapter in the American Civil Rights movement. Randolph was an integral figure in Civil Rights, advocating for the so-called "freedom budget," which recognized that "true" freedom must include addressing poverty, employment, fair wages, housing, and healthcare.

Set in 1917, *The Killing Floor* (1984) follows Mississippi sharecroppers Frank Custer's (Damien Leake) journey to work in a meatpacking slaughterhouse in Chicago. Frank experiences virulent racism while working in a dangerous work environment. Initially reluctant, Custer became an active member of unionization efforts. His black co-workers are not convinced, believing that the union will cater only to white members. After World War I, many veterans returned to seek their jobs back at the stockyards, increasing racial tensions. The bosses used the racial rift to "divide and conquer" the workers, culminating in the Chicago Race Riot of 1919 and the dismantling of the union. However, the film concludes with a hopeful metaphor, with Custer providing the narration.

> It's nice to see healthy stalks of corn growing tall in the field or some tomatoes growing red and juicy on the vine. But somebody's got to get out there

in that boiling sun and plant them seeds before they can grow. You can hold a little seed in your hand till doomsday, but nothin's gonna happen till you put it into the ground.

The film's postscript informs the viewers that "Twenty years later, on the great wave of labor organizing of the 1930s ... Chicago Stockyard workers successfully rebuilt their unions and gained recognition from the major meatpacking companies." The compelling film exhibited how the labor movement can transcend racism and prejudice to enhance workers' rights.

At the turn of the century, many immigrants experienced horribly unsafe working conditions. The lack of safety protocols was the primary storyline in *The Triangle Factory Fire Scandal* (1979). The television movie aired on NBC and retold the infamous fire that killed 146 garment workers who labored at the Triangle Shirtwaist Factory in 1911. The resultant investigation revealed that the company disregarded the safety of the primarily young immigrant women. The public inquiries resulted in the passage of new labor laws and helped spur the formation of the International Ladies Garment Workers Union. The film follows four young women who work in the factory, with the standard romantic and family melodrama. The movie dramatically recreated the fire, starting in an innocuous and non-threatening manner, morphing into a raging inferno that forces the desperate and terrified workers to flee to the fire escapes locked by management. While some of the characters escape or are rescued, many perish in the preventable fire. In particularly horrifying moments, the film shows the helpless young girls jumping to their deaths, holding hands for emotional support. In the closing, the narrator tells the audience that the fire inspired the events, which lasted a mere 20 minutes. He concludes by saying that sweatshop conditions, blocked exits, and inadequate fire escapes caused much tragedy. After various lawsuits, the owners paid $75 per life lost. However, the narrator did not reveal that the owners were paid $400 per worker from their insurance company. Moreover, the narrator also failed to reveal that the owners were criminally charged for manslaughter but were acquitted despite clear evidence of negligence (Stein, 2011).

"Hard Row to Hoe": The Exploitation of Farm Laborers and the Family Farm

The farmer is a mythic figure in American culture, conjuring patriotism, integrity, and images of the simple life. Surprisingly, excepting the Western genre, farming is rarely depicted in movies. In the 1940s and 1950s, the Ma and Pa Kettle film series reduced farmers to "country bumpkins." That said, one of the greatest films of all time, *The Grapes of Wrath* (1940), depicted the plight of farm laborers in California. The film was based on John Steinbeck's classic novel of the same title and was a stinging indictment of the Great Depression and the exploitation of migrant workers from Oklahoma. The struggle of farm laborers was a prominent feature in several works of Steinbeck, including the classic novel *Of Mice and Men*, which has been adapted to film four times. The most recent iteration of Steinbach's work was *In Dubious Battle* (2016), which explored the plight of migrant farmworkers during the Great Depression.

The film focused on the exploitation of fruit pickers in California. The intertitles at the beginning tell the audience that one-quarter of Americans were without jobs and suffered long hours, unsanitary living conditions, and starvation wages. The film starred James Franco (who also served as director) as Mac McLeod and Nat Wolff as Jim Nolan. The pair are labor organizers with the Industrial Workers of the World, a radical labor organization described as communists and anarchists. The narration by Nolan indicates the film's focus, telling audiences that "My pop always told me to watch the scales. Said the world will always find a way to cheat the workin' man." McLeod and Nolan are tasked with stirring up apple pickers in the fictional Torgas Valley, hoping that a strike will inspire other farmworkers to act. McLeod even resorts to sabotaging a ladder, injuring an elder worker, blaming the supervisors for the lack of safety equipment.

The pickers go on strike, demanding that the owner restore their wages to the promised $3 a day. To ensure the strikers' anger does not fade, Joy (Ed Harris), an elderly radical, willingly gives up his own life at the hands of an unknown gunman. It is presumed that Mac had set up the murder to spur on the strike. The slow-moving drama includes betrayal, violence, and some melodrama, with a love story between Nolan and Lisa (Selena Gomez), the daughter-in-law of London (Vincent D'Onofrio), the leader of the pickers. In the end, Mac gives up his life becoming a martyr for the cause, just like Joy. The postscript read:

> Across the nation countless workers engaged in battles like these in the ongoing fight for fair treatment.
>
> In 1934 alone, over 1.5 million workers took part in over 2,000 labor strikes.
>
> Most ended in failure, with many of the strikers arrested, wounded, or even killed.
>
> But out of these struggles arose change. In 1935, Congress passed the Wagner Act ... guaranteeing workers the right to unionize, collectively bargain, and strike.
>
> In 1938, President Roosevelt signed the Fair Labor Standards Act, establishing the federal minimum wage, overtime pay, and the forty-hour work week.
>
> These rights are a part of the very foundation of modern society.

Although technically true, the producers of the film omitted one key fact. The Wagner Act excluded agricultural laborers from unionizing. Moreover, the FLSA did not apply to farmworkers until 1966, when they were finally granted a minimum wage. However, to this day, farm laborers are not guaranteed overtime pay, while minimum wage provisions of the FLSA do not protect farms that employ less than seven workers. Essentially, in the 1930s, the focus of Congress was on industrial employment, with the belief that collective bargaining and a minimum wage were too burdensome for the typical, family-run farm. However, the family farm has been in steep decline, with large-scale "factory farms" increasing rapidly and at an alarming pace. These factory farms are like industrial firms, in both scale and organizational mode, with farmworkers earning poor wages and few benefits (Farm Aid, 2009).

The challenges of the family farm were highlighted in the 1980s, with Farm Aid benefits and in 1984, several "farm-based" films appeared, including *Places in the Heart, Country*, and *The River*. The films all shared similar plots of the challenges of farming, unsympathetic bureaucracy, and a determined woman who holds the family together. Set in Texas during the Great Depression, *Places in the Heart* (1984) starred Sally Field as the recently widowed Edna Spalding. After the tragic death of her husband, Edna is pressured by the bank to sell her small cotton farm. However, with the help of Moze (Danny Glover), a destitute "negro" cotton-picker and Mr. Will (John Malkovich), a blind veteran of World War I, Edna can save the family farm from foreclosure. The film had several uplifting moments interspersed with racism and the harshness of the depression era. Set in the modern era, the struggles of the small family farm were brilliantly portrayed in *Country* (1984). The decidedly human drama was realistic, with an intelligent and honest depiction of the family farm. The film starred Sam Shepard as Gilbert "Gil" Ivy and Jessica Lange as his wife, Jewell. The couple lives with Jewell's father, Otis (Wilford Brimley), and three children.

The family is struggling and facing the possibility of foreclosure after a spate of low crop prices and a high debt load. The Farmers Home Administration (FmHA) pressures the bank to get "tougher," insisting that the bank pressures the Ivy family toward voluntary liquidation. The film was an implicit critique of Reaganomics, with negative depictions of government bureaucrats and the banking industry. The FmHA and banks were encouraged to expand their farm operations, providing large loans based on inflated property values. Unfortunately, grain and livestock prices plummeted, and many farmers were forced to sell their family farms to pay off the loans. *Country* had several heart-wrenching scenes, including the bank repossessing the Ivy's flock of sheep, the suicide of a neighboring farmer who had lost his farm, and an unsettling domestic dispute, which led to the separation of Gil and Jewell. However, the most memorable scene was the farm auction at the end of the film. At the behest of the FmHA, the bank holds an auction to sell the Ivy's land and property. The auction represents the sad reality of vulture capitalism, as bidders scavenge through the possessions of the defeated farmers. In an emotional moment, Gil and Ivy's son, Carlisle bids $28.65 on a horse bridle that belongs to his grandpa Otis and promptly gives it back to him. This spurs the crowd to revolt by bidding low amounts for the expensive farm machinery. The crowd starts to passionately chant "No sale," forcing the incredulous auctioneer to terminate the auction, temporarily halting the foreclosure proceedings and providing some optimism for a happy ending. In the end, there is a touching reconciliation between Jewell and Gil. The ending postscript reveals that a federal North Dakota judge ordered all foreclosures be paused to give farmers loan extensions and deferrals.

Set in East Tennessee, *The River* (1984) featured the struggle of the Garvey family, who have farmed in the area for generations. The film starred Mel Gibson as Tom Garvey, a stubborn farmer who refuses to sell his land to Joe Wade (Scott Glenn), a greedy businessman who owns several businesses and properties in the region. Sissy Spacek depicts Tom's wife, Mae, a devoted mother of two children in an Oscar-nominated role. The region is experiencing an economic downturn, with dwindling grain prices and increasing debt load among the small farmers. Joe Wade is the owner of the Leutz Corporation, a mill that sets the grain prices for the farmers. Wade uses his influence with politicians and the local bank to "squeeze" farmers to sell their land so that he can build a dam to generate electricity and irrigate his properties. After a flood devastates the region, the cash-strapped family cannot secure a loan from the bank, and Tom unwittingly resorts to working as a scab in a strike at an iron foundry. The "scabs" are confined to the barracks, where they experience low pay and poor working conditions. Meanwhile, with the help of her young son, Mae works in the farm and almost dies after getting trapped in a piece of farm equipment. The film features some melodrama, as Joe Wade and Mae were formerly involved in a romantic relationship, which leads Mae to wonder if that is the reason that Tom is unwilling to sell his family farm. Like *Country*, there is a particularly heartbreaking scene in which an angry group of farmers at an auction chant "No Sale," believing that the unfortunate farmer is selling his land. However, the farmer tells the crowd that the property has already been foreclosed, and the auction is for his equipment and personal property. He tells the crowd that he needs the money so that he can move on with his life. There is a feeling of dread, as the farmers realize that they could also lose their way of life. Another poignant scene involves the scab workforce being forced to leave the steel factory. After the strike ends, the management refuses to truck them out safely, and the scabs are forced to walk through a crowd of unionized laborers. They are verbally berated and insulted, with an irate woman spitting on Tom's face and telling him that "he is scum." In the dramatic end, a rainstorm threatens to submerge the region. The neighboring farmers frantically work together to build a makeshift dam to save their crops from the flooding river. Wade hires some unemployed and homeless laborers to destroy the dam. The makeshift dam is partially destroyed in the ensuing standoff, with Tom desperately trying to patch the hole. In an uplifting moment, the destitute men turn on Wade, helping to repair the makeshift dam. Despite the decidedly negative critical reactions to the casting of Mel Gibson as the lead, *The River* provided some dramatic insight into the farm crisis, especially the struggle of the small family farm to compete with agribusiness.

Unfortunately, not much has changed, as the family farm continues to be the exception rather than the rule. Statistics reveal that the agricultural sector is concentrated in the hands of a few corporations, indicating that a handful of corporations control nearly all food production, processing, and distribution (Farm Aid, 2021). Farm laborers frequently contend with abusive labor practices at the hands of unscrupulous employers. Workers all too often toil for employers who evade the minimum wage laws or exercise other forms of wage theft, work under unhealthy or dangerous conditions or are made to live in utterly substandard housing. Employment abuses in agriculture are challenging to address because farm work is not covered by many important labor protections experienced by most other workers in the United States.

The Mistreatment of White-Collar Workers

The exploitation of workers is primarily associated with blue-collar workers in the manufacturing or energy sector. Although more work needs to be done, unionization has improved the welfare of many workers in these sectors (Pasquale, 2015). No doubt, working in the manufacturing and energy sectors can be difficult, but it would be remiss to ignore the mistreatment of white-collar workers. The largest layoff in US history took place in 1993 when IBM shockingly laid off 60,000 employees. It was noteworthy as IBM, or "Big Blue," had a reputation for valuing employees and fostering a positive workplace culture. After the dot-com bubble in 2000, over 200,000 jobs in Silicon Valley were lost, while corporations used the Great Recession as an excuse to restructure their workforces while still recording record-setting profits (EPI, 2009). They may lack sympathy compared to blue-collar workers, but the reality is that the comparison is problematic. Indeed, blue-collar workers in the United States have it better than foreign workers, who make meager earnings with considerably less safe conditions than their American counterparts. One could easily argue that cutthroat labor standards trickle down to the lowest workers, creating a culture of exploitation and abuse, where metrics are more critical than positive work values such as loyalty, job security, and compassion. Experts argue that white-collar employees in corporations experience a workplace culture that is both mentally and emotionally exhausting. The increased regimentation has allowed workplace bullying, harassment, and job stress to flourish. For example, Amazon CEO Jeff Bezos is obsessed with metrics, rigid numerical targets that require maximization. Similarly, Karen Ho's study of Wall Street Banking found that the environment was rife with abuse. Moreover, research has found that white-collar workers have the highest levels of depression, while there has been a substantial increase in substance abuse. There is a disturbing trend toward inhumane performance measures in which middle- and upper-level management are transformed into disposable employees. They are forced to sign non-disclosure and non-compete agreements, which limit their mobility and job prospects in their field (Kantor & Streitfeld, 2015). In Hollywood, several films depict harm toward white-collar workers. Generally, these harms tend to revolve around either downsizing or toxic corporate culture.

Corporate Downsizing

Corporate downsizing has been the subject of several notable films. *Mr. Mom* (1983) featured Jack Butler (Michael Keaton), a mid-level engineer in the auto industry who is laid off from his position and takes on a caregiving role in his home. At the same time, his wife, Caroline (Terri Garr), takes an executive position in an advertising agency, navigating the corporate environment and fending off sexual advances from her boss (Martin Mull). The film's premise is very dated, as gender norms have changed considerably since the film's release. Michael Keaton also starred in *Gung Ho* (1986), where he played Hunt Stevenson, an auto foreman who brokers a deal with a Japanese auto company to start production in a closed US plant. The film's central premise was the culture clash between American workers and Japanese management. Conversely, *Office Space* (1999) was a brilliant portrayal of the fictional software company, Initech. The film satirized "cubicle culture," where the persistently mundane work and office bureaucracy destroy the human spirit. The film became a cult classic, with the TPS report exemplifying the meaningless and mindless protocols imposed by incompetent and indifferent management. The protagonist, Peter Gibbons (Ron Livingston), explains his philosophy: "human beings were not meant to sit in little cubicles staring at computer screens all day, filling out useless forms and listening to eight different bosses drone on about mission statements!" A major storyline was the mass layoffs instigated by the two Bobs, corporate efficiency experts who interviewed employees and made cost-cutting decisions. Peter learns that his best friends, Samir and Michael, are to be fired and replaced by entry-level graduates. The two Bobs tell Peter that "we find it's always better to fire people on a friday. Studies have statistically shown that there is less chance of an incident at the end of the week." Peter decides to get even, partnering with Samir and Michael in a scheme to misappropriate funds from Initech, using a computer virus that takes fractions of a cent and places them into an external bank account. However, the trio mistakenly steals $300,000 in the first two days, making it easy for Initech to notice the scheme. Fortuitously, a disgruntled employee (Stephen Root) sets fire to the building destroying all the evidence of embezzlement.

Considerably more dramatic, the comedy *Up in the Air* (2009) starred George Clooney as Ryan Bingham, a traveling corporate downsizer who specializes in "employment termination assistance." The film opens with a memorable scene in which fired employees questioned their termination. One terminated employee said, "On a stress level, I've heard that losing your job is like a death in the family. But personally, I feel more like the people I worked with were my family, and I died." Ryan mentors Natalie Keener (Anna Kendrick), an ambitious new employee who advocates for terminations via videoconferencing. Although it cut costs, Ryan believes that it lacks empathy which leaves the fired employees emotionally vulnerable. In a poignant storyline, a terminated employee commits suicide, which causes Natalie to quit the agency. The film was an excellent depiction of the callous nature of corporate downsizing. In a similar vein, *The Company Men* (2010) illustrated how corporate strategy has become increasingly beholden to stockholders and the bottom line. The film was set after the stock market crash of 2008 and subsequent recession, which precipitated thousands of corporate layoffs. The film is centered around three main characters that work for Global Transportation Systems (GTX), a shipbuilding corporation. Ben Affleck depicts Bobby Walker, a sales executive who is unceremoniously fired from his six-figure position. His seemingly perfect life unravels, losing many luxuries – country club membership, Porsche – that he has grown accustomed to. After three months, the family is forced to sell their expensive house and move in with Bobby's parents. Bobby reluctantly works for his blue-collar brother-in-law, Jack Dolan (Kevin Costner), working construction. Meanwhile, the Chief Financial Officer of GTX, Gene McClary (Tommy Lee Jones), is clashing with CEO James Salinger (Craig T. Nelson) about restructuring the company, which involves factory closures and massive layoffs. Salinger coldly tells Gene that "we work for the stockholders now" and that GTX is in danger of a hostile takeover if the stock prices fall too low. McClary believes it is unethical to fire productive employees to appease shareholders, especially as the corporation spends millions on an opulent new corporate headquarters. McClary is protecting his good friend, Phil Woodward (Chris Cooper), a senior manager who rose from the factory floor to corporate offices after 30 years of employment. However, in another round of layoffs, Woodward is terminated, which leads to McClary angrily demanding that senior HR manager Sally Wilcox (Maria Bello) rehire him immediately, where McClary is told that he has also been terminated. The increasingly debt-ridden Woodward is unable to find employment due to his age and tragically commits suicide. After the funeral, McClary chats with Salinger in the lobby of GTX,

McClary: Hello, Jim.
Salinger: Gene. How ya been?
McClary: Not good. I was recently fired by my best friend. I missed you at the funeral.
Salinger: I am sorry to hear about Phil. How's Lorna holding up?
McClary: We build something here, Jim. Together. Together, it wasn't just you and wasn't just me. It was all of us.
Salinger: They got a paycheque every week. Medical if they got sick. Disability if they got hurt. Hell, it's a business, not a charity.
McClary: You took home 22 million dollars last year, and these people have lost their homes, their marriages, their respect, and their children.
Salinger: [interrupting] we did what the market required of us to survive. The board accepted Ally's bid last night, $39 billion, 97 a share.
McClary: I'm sorry.
Salinger: Don't be. My shares are worth 600 million.
McClary: [sullenly] Congratulations.
Salinger: What are your's worth, Gene? [awkward silence] I have to get to work.

The film concludes happily, as McClary uses the profits from his stock option to start his own shipbuilding business, hiring Bobby Walker as his first employee. While it is hard for blue-collar viewers to empathize with the plight of the well-off characters, the film was an excellent reflection of the economic climate after the Great Recession, including the dehumanizing impact of losing employment and starting all over again. The ending credits included audio of news reports of the economic crises, including extravagant CEO bonuses, bailouts, and difficulty finding employment.

Toxic Corporate Culture

The machinations of the corporate culture have been depicted in several films, including notable early films such as *Executive Suite* (1954) and *Patterns* (1956). In the 1980s, there were a series of comedies that parodied the cutthroat world of big business, such as *9 to 5* (1980), *Trading Places* (1983), *The Secret of My Success* (1987), *Baby Boom* (1987), *Working Girl* (1988), and *Big Business* (1988). The most notable business film was the drama *Wall Street* (1987), which introduced audiences to Gordon Gekko (Michael Douglas) and his infamous credo "greed is good." Gekko was a high-rolling corporate raider idolized by an up-and-coming stockbroker Bud Fox (Charlie Sheen). The 1990s also featured some notable business-based films such as *Bonfire of the Vanities* (1990), *Money* (1991), *Other People's Money* (1991), *The Hudsucker Proxy* (1999), *Pirates of Silicon Valley* (1999), and *The Big Kahuna* (1999). In the 2000s, the most notable films include *Boiler Room* (2000), *Wall Street: Money Never Sleeps* (2010), and *The Wolf of Wall Street* (2013). These films feature white-collar or occupational crimes, including insider trading, stock fraud, and Ponzi schemes. Some of the films include elements of toxic corporate culture, where middle management and lower-rung employees experience anxiety, dissatisfaction, lack of empathy, and dehumanization in extreme situations.

Nonetheless, a couple of noteworthy films highlight the problem with corporate culture that merit discussion. The television film *White Mile* (1994) was based on the true story of a corporate retreat – facilitated by DDB Needham, a large advertising firm – that ended with five corporate executives perishing on a rafting trip. The film starred Alan Alda as Dan Cutler, a ruthless and uncaring advertising agency CEO who believes that his subordinates have lost their competitive edge in business. Cutler arranged for his executives and their top clients to participate in a fishing and white-water rafting trip. Although hesitant about white-water rafting, the executives succumb to Cutler's manipulation, fearing that they will lose their standing within the corporation. At Cutler's demand, the group is placed into an overcrowded raft, as he does not want his group mixed into another tourist group. Unfortunately, the rafters were ill-prepared or trained to handle the difficult rapids. The overloaded raft crashed into a rock, propelling the group into the water, killing five members. Although the rafting accident and a rescue attempt were gripping entertainment, the film's depiction of corporate culture was more engrossing. The script addressed issues such as abuse of power, moral responsibility, and adhering to the cutthroat nature of corporate mentality. True to the actual case, the victims' families launched a successful lawsuit, establishing the corporation and their top executive partially to blame for the accident.

Corporate culture was also vividly depicted in *Glengarry Glen Ross* (1992), a star-laden drama featuring Jack Lemmon, Al Pacino, Alan Arkin, Ed Harris, Kevin Spacey, and Alec Baldwin. The film was based on a Pulitzer Prize-winning play written by David Mamet. It was a scathing indictment of American business practices, with ample cheating, stealing, and manipulation. The story features four salesmen engaged in "cold calling" to deliver new clients for Mitch and Murray, a fictional real-estate firm. Corporate sends Blake (Alec Baldwin), a sales trainer from Premier Properties, to chastise the salesmen, immediately telling Shelly Levene (Jack Lemon) to "put that coffee down. Coffee's for closers." While bragging about his success, Blake belittles the sales reps and sets the stakes for a new sales contest. The first prize gets a new Cadillac, the second gets a set of steak knives, and the third and fourth get fired. After he finishes demeaning the reps, he utters the famous line, "Always be Closing." The sales reps use deceitful and underhanded tactics to increase their sales, ending with one sales representative stealing prime leads to sell to a rival company. A cult classic, the film had a very clever script and memorable dialogue. The sales office is a microcosm of capitalist culture and sentiment highlighted by unscrupulous competition and an unhealthy obsession with masculinity.

In sharp contrast, *A Family Man* (2016) was a feel-good movie about a corporate "headhunter" who experiences a transformation. The film starred Gerard Butler as Dane Jensen, a corporate recruiter who works at Blackridge Recruitment Agency. Jensen is fast-talking and ruthless, competing with equally ambitious rival Lynn Wilson (Alison Brie) to take control of the company with the impending retirement of Ed Blackridge (Willem Dafoe). The film explored the survival-of-the-fittest world of big business, juxtaposed against Jensen's lack of involvement with his wife and children. His son Ryan is diagnosed with leukemia, which transforms Dane into a "family man". A parallel storyline features Lou (Alfred Molina) as an out-of-work engineer who cannot find employment because of his age. In the "out of character" moment, Dane waives his finder's fee to help Lou secure a position close to his grandchildren. As a result of his altruism and his plummeting sales, Ed callously fires Jenson. Disillusioned, Dane tells Ed, "You know I used to say our relationship with you was based only on the ability to make you money, just sounded tough. I never really believed it." In a feel-good ending, Ryan awakens from a cancer-induced coma, and Dane starts his own headhunting firm with the blessing of Ed, who ends a non-compete agreement. The melodrama critiqued the dog-eat-dog world of corporate culture, with themes of greed, ageism, and most importantly, the lack of work–life balance.

Concluding Thoughts

The exploitation of labor is a principal element of capitalism. Both globally and domestically, corporations profit on the backs of workers. In the United States, workers in restaurants, farms, domestic labor, retail, and fast food are poorly paid, work long hours, receive few benefits, and have little job stability. The so-called "gig economy" has rendered millions of American workers disposable, dependent on profit-minded big business to ensure that they can meet basic human needs, such as shelter and food. Globally, workers are crammed into tiny spaces with loud machinery, breathing dust-filled air and working long days for poverty wages. Their mistreatment allows multinational corporations to reap enormous profits from cheap and exploitable labor. The exploitation of workers has periodically appeared in Hollywood, primarily in historical films about the formation of labor unions. The anti-industry messages were muted, with depictions that blamed a few "bad apples" that exploited or harmed workers rather than the entire capitalistic system. Generally, the narratives revolved around "happy endings." The American way of life is restored, and workers are given a pay raise or better working conditions. Sans the happy ending, many films end with postscripts suggesting that workers' rights have improved or will improve, implying that workers' exploitation is an artifact of the past. Regrettably, the plight of workers has not magically disappeared – many perish from workplace injuries and diseases, work long hours for low pay, and are mistreated.

Reference List

Bureau of Labor Statistics. (2020). *Injuries, illnesses, and fatalities*. US Bureau of Labor Statistics. https://www.bls.gov/iif/home.htm

Economic Policy Institute. (2009, December 23). Many highly profitable companies cut jobs in 2009. [Commentary] https://www.epi.org/publication/many_highly_profitable_companies_cut_jobs_in_2009/

Farm Aid. (2009, September 9). Factory farms [Fact sheet] https://www.farmaid.org/issues/industrial-agriculture/factory-farms/

Farm Aid. (2021). *Corporate control in Agriculture*. Farm Aid. https://www.farmaid.org/issues/corporate-power/corporate-power-in-ag/

Green A., Weller, C.E., & Wall, M. (2019). *Corporate governance and workers*. Center for American Progress. https://www.americanprogress.org/issues/economy/reports/2019/08/14/473095/corporate-governance-workers/

Kantor, J., & Streitfeld, D. (2015). Inside Amazon: Wrestling big ideas in a bruising workplace. *The New York Times*. https://www.nytimes.com/2015/08/16/technology/inside-amazon-wrestling-big-ideas-in-a-bruising-workplace.html

Mishel, L. & Wolfe, J. (2019, August 14). CEO compensation has grown 940% since 1978. Economic Policy Institute [Press Release] https://www.epi.org/publication/ceo-compensation-2018/

Moore, K. (2017). *The radium girls: The dark story of America's shining women*. Sourcebooks, Inc.

Pasquale, F. (2015, September). How much sympathy do overwhelmed white-collar workers deserve? *The Atlantic*. https://www.theatlantic.com/business/archive/2015/09/how-much-sympathy-do-overwhelmed-white-collar-workers-deserve/403312/

Sainato, M. (2021, September 7). Union seeks Hollywood ending for film industry's tale of exploitation. *The Guardian*. https://www.theguardian.com/us-news/2021/sep/07/hollywood-film-industry-union-wages-conditions

Steigerwald, B. (1986, April 19). HBO's 'Act of Vengeance' movie shortchanges UWM reforms. *LA Times*. https://www.latimes.com/archives/la-xpm-1986-04-19-ca-634-story.html

Stein, L. (2011). *The triangle fire*. Cornell University Press.

5 Harm to Consumers

That's right, marketing 101. Don't kill the customer. Bad for repeat business.
Don Anderson (Greg Kinnear) *Fast Food Nation* (2006)

Unethical corporate strategies and policies can maim, injure, cause sickness, and even kill consumers. Corporations sell unfit goods, conspire to fix prices, use illegal sales/marketing practices, engage in deceptive advertising, and utilize false labeling to manipulate consumers. For instance, mega-corporations engage in wrongdoing in the food industry at all stages, including food production, distribution, preparation, and sale. Ultimately, consumers are over-charged, misinformed, made ill, or even succumb to unsafe or tainted food (Croall, 2012; Gray & Hinch, 2019). In the United States, the Centers for Disease Control (CDC) estimate that 48 million people get sick from foodborne illness, 128,000 will be hospitalized, and almost 3,000 will die (AMA, 2018). Globally, the World Health Organization estimates that 600 million, a whopping 1 out of 10 persons, will become ill from "bad" food, while 420,000 die each year (WHO, 2020). Moreover, the lack of regulation allows the food industry to market unhealthy foods to children, promote larger portions, and exploit schools for commercial gains.

Food production, particularly animal agriculture, is a guiding contributor to climate change, with a significant bearing on carbon footprints, air and water pollution, and land use. It is estimated that animal agriculture is responsible for up to 51 percent of greenhouse gas emissions. Essentially, methods that are standardized and normalized within food production are hazardous, unethical, and non-sustainable. However, agribusiness is unwilling to modify their industry practices, lobbying for less regulation and hiring teams of public relations experts to push shoddy science that deceives consumers about the safety of their food products (Gray & Hinch, 2019). For example, the sugar industry has worked tirelessly to misinform the public about the real danger of too much sugar by sponsoring research that minimizes the health hazards and lobbying to maintain misleading labels on food products (Taubes & Couzens, 2012).

The food industry is a primary example of harm inflicted on consumers by multinational corporations. However, they are not alone in disregarding consumers'

DOI: 10.4324/9781003163855-5

health, safety, and financial well-being. There is a long history in the auto industry of selling unsafe products while the pharmaceutical industry continues to profit off life-saving drugs that are criminally over-priced. Big Pharma has an extensive history of fraud, bribery, lawsuits, and scandals. According to Public Citizen, a consumer watchdog group, the pharmaceutical industry is the biggest defrauder of the Federal government under the False Claims Act. Big Pharma employs an army of lobbyists, almost 1,400, to gain influence on Capitol Hill. From 1998 to 2016, the industry expended nearly $3.5 billion on lobbying expenses, the most of any industry. Similarly, biochemical giant Monsanto engages in a public relations campaign that is incredibly deceptive. They paid scientists to "ghostwrite" academic papers and manipulate media, even going so far as posing as journalists to debunk any criticism of their product. Officials from Monsanto "cozy" up to regulators and target legitimate journalists that expose its weedkiller's possible link to cancer (Gillam, 2017). Finally, medical errors account for between 250,000 and 440,000 deaths each year, the third leading cause of death in the United States, behind cancer and heart attacks. These deaths are preventable, often caused by inadequately skilled staff, error in judgment or care, the hubris of some medical professionals, and, most importantly, an underfunded and under-resourced system that values efficiency over humanity. These tragic errors can result from computer malfunctions, mistakes with doses or types of medications administered to patients, and surgical complications that go underdiagnosed (Saks & Landsman, 2020). Unfortunately, when corporations harm consumers, they are not held criminally responsible. They are governed by regulatory agencies with little "teeth" and often yield to political will. Victims only recourse is civil law, which can drag on for years, with seemingly limitless corporate legal means to circumvent "true" justice from occurring.

In Hollywood, depictions of corporate harms to consumers are scarce. A handful of films backed the progressive agenda during the silent era, educating the public on the dangers of adulterated food and deceptive marketing practices in the pharmaceutical industry. From 1930 to the 1970s, only a few scripted films "touched" on harms to consumers, with most lighthearted depictions of the advertising industry. A plot featuring consumers getting sick, injured, or perishing from unsafe products or tainted food was non-existent. It is worth noting that consumer rights did not fully emerge until the 1960s, with JFK introducing the notion of consumer protections in a 1962 speech to Congress that outlined the basic tenants of consumer rights, including the right to safety, right to be informed, right to choose, and right to be heard. Moreover, the 1960s also introduced consumer advocate Ralph Nader to Americans, inspiring a generation of activists that attempt to hold corporations accountable to consumers. In Hollywood films, the harms that corporations wreak on consumers are negligible but not wholly absent. As such, this chapter will explore films that depict the harms inflicted on consumers by corporations.

The Health, Safety, and Financial Well-Being of Consumers

The health and safety of consumers are neglected in film depictions. In the movies, victims are most likely to die at the hands of serial murders or perish in gang violence. However, in real life, Americans have a greater chance of perishing going to the hospital to have a routine surgery or driving their "seemingly" safe automobile to work. Yet, those injuries are not "compelling" enough for mainstream Hollywood depictions. It is also feasible that the movie industry is so beholden to advertising and marketing that they ignore the problem for the sake of profits. That said, some notable films have depicted various forms of industry wrongdoing involving consumers, including the medical/pharmaceutical industry, automobile industry, food industry, and advertising industry.

Medical/Pharmaceutical Industry

In 2020, approximately 400,000 Americans perished from iatrogenic disorders, which simply means death from either an examination or treatment of a patient by a medical professional. While not all these deaths are based on negligence, there is a significant number of preventable deaths that are largely unnoticed by consumers. There is even less recourse for victims, as litigation for malpractice is not an effective deterrent to lessen medical errors. It is estimated that only 3 percent of negligently injured patients and their families collect any compensation (Saks & Landsman, 2020). Michael Saks claims that

> the focus was rarely on the big problem – hundreds of thousands of dead and injured patients ... the debate was almost always about taming litigation so it would not be annoying to healthcare providers. All the while, little was being done to improve patient safety.
>
> (CCR, 2021)

Moreover, this epidemic of preventable deaths is largely unnoticed by consumers, who generally have an abundance of trust in the medical establishment. Within this context, it is not surprising that Hollywood has generally ignored the issue of medical error, medical litigation, and lack of accountability of the corporate medical establishment. That said, there are some depictions which are memorable.

One of the most unforgettable, *The Hospital* (1971), was a satirical film that exposed the machinations within a large teaching hospital in Manhattan. The film starred George C. Scott as Dr. Bock, the Chief of Medicine at the Hospital. George C Scott is magnificent as Dr. Bock, a brilliant doctor who suffers from impotence and is a failed father and husband. He openly contemplates suicide and delivers impressive monologues that rail on the medical system and its incompetence.

> It is all rubbish isn't it? I mean ... transplants, antibodies. We manufacture genes. We can produce birth ectogenetically. We can practically clone people like carrots, and half the kids in this ghetto haven't even been inoculated for polio. We have established the most enormous medical ... entity ever conceived, and people are sicker than ever. We cure nothing! We heal nothing! The whole goddamn wretched world, strangulating in front of our eyes.

In the opening scene, the narrator colorfully tells the story of a patient who was misdiagnosed, given the wrong medicine, and died. The narrator tells the viewer that he "mentioned all this only to explain how the bed in Room 806 became available." It was revealed that a young intern, who made the misdiagnosis, used the bed to have sex with a technician in the Hematology Lab. Unfortunately, after the carnal deed is complete, the intern (Dr. Schaefer) is killed after a nurse mistakenly injects an insulin overdose. In a lively rant, Dr. Bock admonishes the head nurse, Mrs. Christie.

Mrs. Christie: I've got nearly a thousand nurses in this hospital.

Dr. Bock: (gathering rage) And every time one of them has her period, she disappears for three days. My doctors complain regularly they can't find the same nurse on the same floor two days in a row. What the hell am I supposed to tell that boy Schaefer's parents? That a substitute nurse assassinated him, because she couldn't tell the doctors from the patients on the floor? My God, the incompetence here is absolutely radiant! I mean, two separate nurses walk into a room, stick needles into a man — and one of those was a number eighteen jelco! — tourniquet the poor son of a bitch, anchor the poor son of a bitch's arm with adhesive tape, and it's the wrong poor son of a bitch! I mean, my God! Where do you train your nurses, Mrs. Christie? Dachau.

The brilliantly scripted film evolves into a murder mystery, as two doctors and a nurse mysteriously succumb to medical malfeasance on the part of the hospital. Meanwhile, the hospital administrators are faced with a protest of the hospital's annexation of a neighboring apartment building to be used as a drug rehabilitation facility. At the same time, the emotionally scarred Dr. Bock becomes romantically involved with the free-spirited Barbara Drummond (Dianna Rigg), whose father is Edward, who is in a coma, a victim of medical negligence. Dr. Bock colorfully summarizes Drummond's misfortune, "In short, a man comes into this hospital in perfect health ... and in the space of one week, we chop out one kidney ... damage another, reduce him to a coma, and damn near kill him." The elder Drummond was the victim of an unnecessary biopsy fabricated to facilitate research by Dr. Ivey. However, Dr. Welbeck (Richard Dysart) botched the operation that led to Drummond's ill-health. The villainous Welbeck is consumed by greed, more concerned about the well-being of his business and the price of his stocks than his duty to his patients. After Dr. Bock bans Welbeck from operating in the hospital, the head administrator, Dr. Sundstrom (Stephen Elliot), tells Welbeck:

> You're a whole medical conglomerate. You've got factoring service, a computerized billing company ... a few proprietary hospitals, a few nursing homes. Good heavens, Welbeck, you shouldn't be brought up before a committee of mere doctors. You oughta be investigated by the Securities and Exchange Commission

110   *Harm to Consumers*

In the end, it is discovered that Edward Drummond is the culprit, seeking biblically inspired revenge on those that triggered his coma. The mentally ill Drummond, a former doctor, refers to himself as the "Paraclete of Caborca" and reveals how he killed his victims. He wittily claims, "God clearly intended a measure of irony here. The hospital was to do all the killing for me. All I need do is to arrange for the doctors to become patients in their own hospital."

Drummond confesses that proper medical treatment could have saved all the victims. After he struck Dr. Ivey on the head, he administered a drug that caused a heart attack and brought him to the emergency room, where he was left to die. Drummond calmly explains:

> His vital signs were taken, an electrocardiogram ... which revealed occasional ventricular premature contractions. An intern took his history ... and then he was promptly ... simply ... forgotten to death.

Drummond then admits that he switched a patient identity with the dialysis nurse that caused his coma. Astonishingly, the nurse, who was noticeably younger than 53, was mistakenly operated on for a hysterectomy, leading to her demise. The remarkable scene included witty banter between the surgeons as the victim dies on the operating table, with the anesthesiologist incredulously saying, "I may be crazy, doctor. But I don't think this is your patient." The insane Drummond claims that God has ordered him to kill Dr. Welbeck. Rather than hold Drummond accountable, Dr. Bock decides to run off with Barbara, allowing her to take her father to Mexico rather than be institutionalized at a mental hospital. However, before Drummond's release from the hospital, Bock encounters Dr. Welbeck, angry about his banishment.

Dr. Welbeck: I like to know what it is you have against me, Doctor?
Dr. Bock: Eight days ago, you showed up half-stoned for a simple nephrectomy ... botched it, put the patient in failure, and damn near killed him. Then, pausing only to send in your bill, you flew off on the wings of Man ... to an island of sun in Montego Bay. This is the third time in two years we've had to patch up your patients. The other two died. You're greedy, unfeeling, inept, indifferent ... self-inflating, and unconscionably profitably. Besides from that, I have nothing against you. I'm sure you play a hell of a game of golf. What else do you want to know?
Dr. Welbeck: How much do you make a year, Bock? For a guy who makes a lousy $40 to $50,000 ... (Bock walks away)

In the conclusion, Dr. Welbeck attends to Drummond's neighboring patient in Room 806 and has a fatal heart attack after learning that he has lost his fortune to a crooked business partner. Ironically, Welbeck is mistaken for the comatose Drummond, who has once again left the room to continue his crusade against the medical profession. At the last moment, Dr. Bock decides to stay at the venerable institution while Barbara and her father escape to Mexico. The film was sharply written, with screenwriter Paddy Chayefsky winning an Oscar for his efforts. Despite being a satire, the plot was uncomfortable for audiences, as it was entirely plausible that medical errors of that sort could take place in a modern-day hospital. In fact, these types of medical errors occur daily across the United States, far more frequently than health consumers care to ponder.

A tragic medical error was the basis for *The Verdict* (1982). The film starred Paul Newman as alcoholic Frank Galvin, a disgraced lawyer who resorts to going to funerals to solicit potential clients. His former mentor delivered him a "slam-dunk" case involving medical malpractice. The lawsuit involves a young woman who received the wrong anesthetic and is now in a vegetative state, relying on a ventilator to breathe. The hospital is willing to settle out of court to avoid adverse publicity and protect its reputation. However, after visiting the woman, Frank has an epiphany and decides to reject the standard settlement. Without consulting his clients, he takes the case to court to face a prestigious and high-priced law firm run by Ed Concannon (James Mason). Frank has a very strong case, but it starts to unravel after his star medical expert disappears, and he hurriedly must replace him with an expert with questionable credentials. The trial judge is also biased and appears to be sabotaging Frank's rapidly deteriorating case. In the end, Frank unearths a key witness, Kaitlin Costello, a nurse who was in the operating room. In a dramatic moment, the surprise witness tells the jury that the doctor failed to read the notes and administered the wrong anesthetic. Costello admitted that she was pressured to change the notes to cover up the anesthesiologist's fatal mistake and produced a copy of the original notes. Despite the "smoking gun" moment, the judge is legally forced to strike the photocopied evidence from the record. Frank gives a short but passionate closing argument, where he pleads with the jury to provide justice to the victim, telling them, "And there is not justice: the rich win, the poor are powerless." True to the Hollywood happy ending, the jury comes back in favor of Frank, asking the trial judge if they can award more than what was requested. The film was nominated for an Oscar and is considered one of the best courtroom productions in film history. Conversely, *The Doctor* (1991) was a character study starring William Hurt as Dr. Jack McKee, a successful surgeon at a teaching hospital. His bedside manner lacks empathy, and he is emotionally distant. After receiving a cancer diagnosis, Jack experiences a life-altering transformation and becomes more compassionate and honest with patients. He even refused to participate in the suppression of a friend and colleague's medical negligence. The medical error and attempted cover-up were minor storylines but indicative of the medical industry, in which "whitewash" is standard practice. Unfortunately, the area of medical error and institutional cover-ups are under-recognized in film.

In a similar vein, wrongdoing in the pharmaceutical industry is also sporadically portrayed within scripted films. Arguably, *The Constant Gardener* (2005) is the most notable depiction of the sins of Big Pharma. The film unveiled cheap trials for unsafe drugs, uninformed consent, bribery and payoffs, and government cover-ups. The plot was inspired by Pfizer's antibacterial testing on children in Kano, Nigeria. The film was a murder mystery that utilized flashbacks to tell the story of Tessa Abbott-Quayle (Rachel Weisz), an Amnesty activist and Justin Quayle (Ralph Fiennes), a British diplomat. In the story, the fictional KDH corporation develops "Dypraxa," a drug that treats tuberculosis, while the company "Three Bees" was responsible for testing the drug's effectiveness and safety. The Three Bees begin drug trials in Kenya, using HIV patients as their "guinea pigs." Unfortunately, the drug is dangerous and kills several test subjects. To maintain cost efficiency and expand their profits, both KDH and Three Bees cover up the results and the drug is released to the public. However, with the help of Kenyan doctor Arnold Bluhm (Hubert Kounde), Tessa investigates and uncovers a massive cover-up that involves the corporations and Sir Bernard Pellegrin (Bill Nighy), a high placed British government official. As a result, Tessa and Arnold are brutally murdered, with the assassins making it appear that Tessa was raped and killed by Arnold. Although he is grieving his loss, Justin is not convinced, as Albert was a dear friend of Tessa and was also secretly gay. Justin begins a crusade to find the truth behind the murder. He uncovers a vast conspiracy that involves his boss, his friend and co-worker, Sandy Woodrow (Danny Huston), Bernard Pelligrin, and Big Pharma. In the end, Justin meets with Lorbeer (Pete Postlethwaite), a colorful and remorseful doctor who admits to the scheme and gives Justin a self-incriminating letter that Pelligrin had written to Sandy. Like his wife, Justin is also murdered, but before his death mails the letter to Tessa's cousin, Arthur "Ham" Hammond (Richard McCabe). At Justin's funeral, Pelligrin finishes his eulogy, telling the mourners, "That he chose to take his own life in the same remote spot ... where Tessa met her tragic death is a sad reflection of his tormented state of mind." In a clever ending, the smug Pelligrin sits, as Ham reads a noncanonical epistle. However, rather than the assumed religious parable, Ham reads the incriminating letter:

> My dear Sandy, your naivety is beyond belief. [the incredulous Pelligrin looks up] Knowing our arraignments with KDH and Three Bees, you send me this half-baked report ... by some bleeding-heart diplomatic wife and her black lover ... and ask me to take action. The only action required, apart from shredding the thing, its to keep a tighter rein on your resident harlot. I want to know what she does, where she goes, whom she meets. The issue here is deniability. If nobody told us Dypraxa was causing deaths, we can't be held responsible. [Pelligrin quickly exits the church] But, my dear Sandy, should it ever become known ... that we've closed our eyes to the deaths, none of us would survive the scandal. I still have great hopes of you—my love to Gloria. Yours Sincerely, Bernard.

Ham sardonically continues by telling the grievers that Justin's death was not a suicide,

> So who, of course, has got away with murder? Not, of course, the British government. They merely covered up, as one does, the offensive corpses. Though not literally. That was done by person or persons unknown. So who

has committed murder? Not, of course, the highly respectable firm of KDH Pharmaceutical, which has enjoyed record profits this quarter ... and now licenced ZimbaMed of Harare ... to continue testing Dypraxa in Africa. No, there are no murders in Africa. Only regrettable deaths. And from those deaths, we derive the benefits of civilization, benefits we can afford so easily ... because those lives were bought so cheaply.

The Constant Gardener was a subtle and intelligent thriller that exhorted both the pharmaceutical industry and corruption in higher levels of government. Conversely, *The Fugitive* (1993) was the prototypical Hollywood blockbuster with action and suspense. The film starred Harrison Ford as Richard Kimble, an eminent surgeon framed by pharmaceutical giant Devlin MacGregor. The film revealed that Devlin MacGregor was concealing evidence that showed that the fictitious drug Provasic was causing liver damage among trial patients. The Netflix original, *Sweet Girl* (2021), was also an action-thriller that starred Jason Mamoa as Ray Cooper, a widow and father to Rachel (Isabela Merced). Cooper's wife, Amanda, has a rare form of cancer that requires the life-saving drug, Infirmam. The Coopers cannot afford the drug but are scheduled to start treatment with Spero, a generic version of the life-saving drug. Unfortunately, BioPrime, the makers of Infirmam, paid the generic drug manufacturer to delay Spero's release indefinitely. On CNN, BioPrime CEO Simon Keeley (Justin Bartha) callously justifies his decision by claiming that it costs billions of dollars to produce the drug. Diana Morgan (Amy Brenneman), a congresswoman, tells the viewers, "Paying competitors to shelve generic drug brands of drugs? That is immoral, Mr. Keeley." As a result, Amanda succumbs to cancer, with Ray and Rachel deeply in debt and grief-stricken. Months later, Ray is contacted by a reporter, Martin Bennett, who tells him that BioPrime is involved in several illegal schemes, including bribery, cover-ups, and offshore accounts. While they talk on the subway train, Bennett is murdered by a hitman and Ray is seriously injured, propelling the film into a "revenge" flic, with plenty of action, chase scenes, and violence. Two years after the subway murder, Ray poses as a waiter, abducts Keeley and in self-defense strangles the CEO to death with a plastic bag. Ray takes Rachel on the run, where Ray fights would-be assassins while hiding from the FBI. At that point, the film takes an inexplicable twist, revealing that Ray died in the subway attack two years earlier. In a fugue state, Rachel (seen as Ray) is responsible for the revenge murders. In yet, another plot twist, Rachel discovers that the seemingly honorable Congresswoman, Diana Morgan, was taking bribes from BioPrime and that she ordered the contract murders of her father and the investigative reporter. In the end, Rachel secretly tapes Morgan admitting her crimes, where she tells Rachel that "I took the bribe. I ordered the hit. You don't understand anything. You're so young. The candidate with the most money wins. That is how it works." Rachel sends the audio to the FBI and escapes with a fake passport and cryptocurrency, and is last seen boarding a plane, whereabouts unknown. Although the film touches on the greed of Big Pharma, the message gets lost with the action and strange plot twists.

Big Pharma and the FDA were also disparaged in *The Dallas Buyers Club* (2013), set in 1985. The film was loosely based on the true story of Ron Woodruff (Matthew McConaughey), a homophobic rodeo rider who was diagnosed as HIV positive. He is desperate to live and volunteers for a trial program for AZT. The problem is that patients appear to be getting sicker, and the FDA has not approved other more promising medications. With the help of Rayon (Jared Leto), his transgender business partner, Woodroof, builds an HIV drug empire by smuggling and selling non-FDA-approved drugs to the gay community. The pharmaceutical industry is depicted as unethical and greedily promotes only drugs in which they can profit. The FDA (US Food and Drugs Administration) is depicted as beholden to the pharmaceutical industry and overridden in bureaucracy and incompetence. Set in the 1990s, *Side Effects* (2005) depicted the unethical world of pharmaceutical representatives. The film was based on producer/screenwriter/director Kathleen Slattery-Moschkau's career as a "legal pill pusher." Slattery-Moschkau begins the film with intertitles that tell the viewer that over 90,000 pharma reps attempt to persuade doctors to prescribe their products. It is an eight billion-dollar-a-year industry or 1 million per hour. The romantic comedy starred Katherine Heigl as Karly Hert, a 24-year-old representative of the fictional Braden-Andrews pharmaceutical corporation. Karly is unhappy with her position, telling her romantic interest that:

> You know, I read this article once by a physician that reps know just enough to get by. At first, I was really defensive about it. And then I realized we are all just one sentence away from complete negligence. I mean, there is just something fundamentally unethical about tying profit into educating doctors and helping patients.

She decides to quit the job in six months and starts telling doctors the truth about the pills. Her honesty propels her sales, and she becomes incredibly successful, even considered for a management position. Benefitting from the monetary perks, Karly is transformed into a corporate shill which causes problems with her boyfriend, who believes she is selling out to corporate greed. Braden-Andrews is heavily promoting a new antidepressant, Vivexx, which Karly learns is dangerous to consumers. The storyline was likely based on claims that antidepressants such as Prozac and Serzone were harming consumers. In several lawsuits, Eli Lilly, the maker of Prozac, was "grossly negligent" in its failure to warn doctors and consumers about potential dangers, including violent, aggressive, and suicidal behavior. At the same time, consumer watchdog Public Citizen sent warnings that Nefazodone under the brand name Serzone was causing deadly liver failure, with links to at least 55 deaths since the drug was introduced in 1994. In 2003, Bristol-Myers Squibb discontinued the sale of Serzone. However, generic formulations of Nefazodone are currently still available (Associated Press, 2004; Llamas, 2021). In the culminating scene, Karly receives an award for her high sales record and in a "whistleblower" moment, turns the microphone over to the widow of a man that died from taking the antidepressant.

The primary narrative in *Side Effects* involved the ethics of an uneducated sales force providing information to doctors about the efficacy of the pills. However, it also critiques the profiteering in Big Pharma, emphasizing sales rather than human health. One scene juxtaposes the production, marketing, distribution, and eventually sale of Glucadox, a fictional diabetes pill. Ironically, Braden-Andrews credo is "to protect and prolong life." However, the corporate executives happily reveal that it only costs 10 cents to produce, but they can sell it for $12 a tablet. The marketing team tells representatives that "it can save lives," but then the scene shifts to a pharmacy, where a pharmacist tells a consumer that his prescription costs $580 for 30 tablets. Unfortunately, the man does not have insurance and cannot afford the "life-saving drug." The movie itself was low budget and quickly shot over 18 days in the summer of 2004. As such, the film's low quality deflects from the important message – the greed, negligence, and fraud – of Big Pharma. It is estimated that the pharmaceutical industry spends an average of $25 billion on marketing its drugs. Concurrently, many antidepressant studies have been tainted by Big Pharma influence, rife with hidden conflicts of interest and financial ties to corporate drugmakers (Jacobson, 2015).

While the drugs in *The Fugitive, The Constant Gardener,* and *Side Effects* were fictitious, Thalidomide was all too real. The harmful side-effects of the notorious drug were powerfully depicted in the HBO produced *A Private Matter* (1992). In the 1950s and 1960s, Thalidomide was prescribed to thousands of pregnant women to relieve morning sickness. Unfortunately, the so-called "miracle drug" caused irreversible damage to the fetus, and thousands of children were born with congenital malformations. The drug was distributed to thousands of doctors, who claimed it held no risk for pregnant women. Based on a true story, *A Private Matter* starred Sissy Spacek as Sherri Finkbine and Aiden Quinn as her husband, Bob. Set in 1962, Sherri is pregnant and learns that the tranquilizer she used was causing deformities in babies. Without Sherri's consent, the doctor and husband schedule an abortion. Sherri is reluctant at first but decides that it is the best course of action for her unborn child. However, abortion is a criminal offense in Arizona, subject to two to five years in jail unless the mother's life is in jeopardy. The abortion is postponed and is subject to a court hearing to determine its validity. Sherri is a children's entertainer on a local television show and becomes a lightning rod of controversy. She is fired from her job, harassed by the media and the public. Even Bob is suspended from his teaching position, as the controversial abortion develops into a media firestorm. The court rules that the doctors must make the final decision on the abortion. In a symbolic scene, a group of elderly male doctors decide not to abort the fetus. The postscript revealed that Sherri went to Sweden to have an abortion in her twelfth week of pregnancy. Although Thalidomide was integral to the plotline, the teleplay focused on patriarchy and pro-choice rather than the condemnation of the pharmaceutical industry.

Also produced by HBO, *Breast Men* (1997) was a fictionalized telling of the invention, development, and marketing of silicone breast implants. The film stars David Schwimmer as Dr. Kevin Saunders, a medical resident who convinces his superior, Dr. William Larson (Chris Cooper), to partner with him on the ground-breaking usage of silicone breast implants in the 1970s and 1980s. The characters were adapted from real-life plastic surgeons, Dr's Frank Gerow and Thomas Cronin, who created silicone implants for Dow Corning Corporation. Despite some start-up problems, Saunders and Larson became incredibly successful with their breast augmentation clinic, with Larson touting the product as "*absolutely safe*." However, the partners have a falling out, end their friendship, and separate their business interests. The booze and cocaine-addled, Saunders begins a rapid downfall into the seedy world of strip clubs and porn, where he creates unnaturally larger breasts for "non-cosmetic" reasons. Conversely, Dr. Larson believes that breast augmentation contributes to the betterment of women's self-esteem and mental health. However, Larson's smug point of view collapses after a former patient confronts him at a trade convention by revealing her lumpy and deformed breasts. Through media footage, it is disclosed that several women were experiencing problems with the implants, and several lawsuits followed. Dow Corning is held responsible for willful misconduct, and the quick-rising industry experiences a rapid nosedive, as the FDA puts a moratorium on the use of silicone-based implants. However, the practice is quickly resurrected as the industry shifts to saline-based implants. In the end, Dr. Saunders reaps even more profit after replacing the silicone implants with saline, as several women question why it costs more to take the implant out than the original surgery. The ending postscript reveals that medical studies have found no link between silicone implants and chronic diseases like lupus or rheumatoid arthritis, but more studies are pending. The postscript also discloses that Dow Corning filed for bankruptcy in 1995 and offered a $2.4 billion settlement for women allegedly injured by the implants.

In the 1980s, Ralph Nader's Public Citizen sounded the alarm that silicone breast implants might be carcinogenic, triggering a wave of lawsuits and studies on the risks of silicone implants. There is a contentious debate about the risk of silicone, with no long-term scientific study that shows that silicone implants have caused serious disease. Conversely, tens of thousands of women have claimed many health problems, including the hardening of breast tissue, implant rupture, and autoimmune disorders. That said, at issue was that Dow Corning (a subsidiary of Dow Chemical) did not properly inform the recipients of the potential for health risks, even covering up research of the possibility of risks. Simply put, Dow Corning deceived thousands of women by marketing a potentially dangerous product without providing appropriate warnings.

Finally, the health insurance industry has also been pilloried in films. *The Rainmaker* (1997) was a legal drama based on a John Grisham novel of the same title. The film starred Matt Damon as Rudy Baylor, a recent law school graduate working for an "ambulance chaser." As a condition of employment, the idealistic Baylor must "find" clients at a local hospital. Baylor's first case involves an insurance company not paying out a claim for a young cancer patient. The inexperienced Baylor teams up with Deck Shifflet (Danny DeVito), a paralegal unable to pass the bar exam. The pair are pitted against much more experienced litigators from a large law firm led by Leo F. Drummond (Jon Voigt). In the film's climax,

Rudy cleverly cross-examines Wilfred Keeley, the president of Great Benefit. The jury finds in favor of the plaintiff, awarding the family $150,000 in actual damages and 50 million in punitive damages. The FBI arrests the company president for a scheme involving fraudulent insurance policies sold in poor neighborhoods. However, the Hollywood happy ending had a wrinkle; Great Benefit went bankrupt and avoided paying punitive damages to the grieving parents. Similarly, *John Q* (2002) also showed the callousness and greed of large insurance companies. The film starred Denzel Washington as John Quincy Archibald, a factory worker who takes E.R. patients and staff hostage at a major hospital. Archibald's son requires a heart transplant, and his insurance has denied his coverage. The dramatic film reveals the dark side of American health care, in which the poor do not enjoy the same access to treatment as the rich. It also villainizes health administrators, medical bureaucracy, and profit-driven insurance corporations.

The Auto Industry

Although automobiles have become appreciably safer, just over 37,000 Americans perish in automobile accidents each year, an average of 90 victims per day. The primary reasons for car accidents include driver behavior, highway engineering, traffic hazards, weather, and automobile design. Regarding design, the auto industry has a long history of valuing profit and marketability over the safety of consumers. There is ample research showing that the industry has ignored safety research findings, retained hazardous designs that cause injury or death and engaged in massive cover-ups to hide their negligence in protecting motorists. In 1965, Ralph Nader authored *Unsafe at Any Speed*, a muckraking book that exposed the auto industry's questionable manufacturing and design practices. Nader roused public interest by meticulously and passionately arguing that motorists were victims of corporate neglect. General Motors even went so far as to hire private investigators to shadow Nader to dig up dirt on the young activist. The powerful auto manufacturer was also accused of hiring young women to act as sex lures, making threatening and obnoxious telephone calls and interrogating his acquaintances. The insidious attempt to discredit Nader did not work, with GM settling a lawsuit for $425,000, funds used by Nader to fund various public interest groups. As a result of Nader's crusade and increasing pressure from the federal government, the auto industry was forced to create safer automobiles. That said, there have been very few film depictions of wrongdoings of the auto industry.

In the 1970s, the work of Nader was alluded to in the television miniseries, *Wheels* (1978) which appeared on the NBC network. The miniseries was based on a novel written by Arthur Hailey, who researched the auto industry, to create the fictional National Motors depicted in the novel and miniseries.[1] Set in Detroit, the novel included many topical issues within the auto industry, including race relations, corporate culture, politics, and business ethics. The novel and miniseries featured the fictional Emerson Vale, a high-profile critic of the auto industry and a thinly disguised version of Ralph Nader. To ensure that the reader does not miss the obvious connection, Hailey absurdly titles Vale's book *The American Car: Unsure in Any Need*. Hailey even goes as far as to make Vale a silly and screechy character that is a thorn in the side of auto industry executives, questioning safety records and business ethics. Hailey attempted to assuage the similarities between Nader and Vale by specifically mentioning Ralph Nader in the book, alluding to Vale being the "lesser" successor to Nader. Hailey's fictional retellings of industry engage the reader with social questions, including discrimination, pollution, inequitable distribution of wealth, and ethics of big business. That said, these elements of his books are superficial, as his work is centered on personal melodrama, not industry criticism (Sutherland, 2010). His work is more human interest than social justice, a blend of mild muckraking embedded within a soap opera format.

The soap opera format was also used to depict the auto industry in *The Betsy* (1978). The pretentious film starred Sir Laurence Olivier as Lorne Hardeman Sr., the founder of Bethlehem Motors, a fading manufacturer. Also referred to as number one, Hardeman Sr. hires race-car driver Angelo Perrino (Tommy Lee Jones) to design "The Betsy," a safe and fuel-efficient automobile. The film employs a flashback narrative with Olivier playing an 85-year-old confined to a wheelchair in 1975 and a younger version of himself at the age of 45, set in 1935. Faithful to the trashy Harold Robbins novel it was based on, the film features greed, betrayal, deception, and sexual depravity. There is even an affair between Hardeman Sr. and the wife (Katherine Ross) of his son, Brian, who was also secretly carrying on a homosexual affair. The angst-ridden Brian eventually commits suicide, with his young son, Lorne believing that it was caused by the affair between his grandfather and his mother. Consequently, the patriarch's grandson and president, Lorne Hardeman III (Robert Duvall), resents his grandfather and plans to eliminate the corporation's auto division. Lorne III is the typical type-A personality, ruthlessly pushing the elderly founder to the side, revealing the new truth in corporate economics to the ageing board of directors. Although obscured by the copious number of sexual shenanigans and horrible dialogue, the film did produce one scene that showed wrongdoing in the auto industry. In a fancy dinner party, Hardeman III and his financial guru, Dan Weyman (Edward Herrmann), discuss legislative emission controls with a member of the President's cabinet. They claim the costs will be passed onto the consumers and threaten to stop production, causing mass unemployment and more problems for the administration. Hardeman III indignantly says, "the Congress or the public because we're not giving one God damn thing to that son of a bitch, Nader. I tell you that." The image of Nader was also evoked, with Mark Sampson, a shady "consumer advocate," who was referred to as the "poor man's Ralph Nader." Sampson was paid by Hardeman III to falsely claim that the Betsy's engine could blow up at high speed. Perrino angrily confronts Sampson, telling him to "turn off the bullshit before we both drown in it," arguably the best line of the entire film. There is also a scene of pure fiction, in which Hardeman Sr. pushes for wage increases for workers at the height of the Great Depression. The notion that an industrialist would voluntarily offer large wage increases and overtime pay is laughable and non-sensical. Working conditions in the auto industry worsened during the Depression, as companies increased hours and cut wages. It was not until the late 1930s and early 1940s that the rise of unionization led to improved working conditions and pay for auto workers. Nonetheless, the film was primarily a clumsy melodrama with a tangled web of deceit and lust, only notable for its allusion to Nader's impact on the auto industry.

Automobile safety was also alluded to in the biographical comedy *Tucker: The Man and His Dream* (1988), which starred Jeff Bridges as the titular character Preston Tucker. The film documents the short-lived rise of the 1948 Tucker Sedan, followed by its rapid demise. Preston Tucker was depicted as a flamboyant showman who wanted to build a futuristic automobile. He boldly takes out an advertisement that generates tremendous public interest despite not having a prototype or capital. During a dinner with potential investors, Tucker grimly reports that every 25 seconds, someone dies in an automobile accident. He touts the safety of his model, advocating swivel headlights, pop-out and shatterproof windshields, and seatbelts. In a memorable speech, Preston condemns the auto industry:

> The Big Three in Detroit have been allowed to make billions of dollars without spending one dime on safety. But I know, what you know, what the public knows, is that they don't give a damn about people. All they care about is profits. Let me tell you something. I mean this from the bottom of my heart. The entire automobile industry of America is guilty of criminal negligence. And if it were up to me, they would be tried and convicted of manslaughter.

The film also depicts the Big Three as resistant to the competition, engaged in surveillance and political and media influence to sabotage the upstart company. Near the film's conclusion, Tucker is confronted with allegations of stock fraud, which essentially destroys his reputation. The prosecutors allege that Tucker swindled investors into paying money for cars never intended to be built and sold. On the last day of the trial, Tucker proudly delivers his entire production run of 50 Tucker Torpedoes to the courthouse. This proves that he has met his legal obligations to investors, but the jury is not allowed to see the cars. In a feel-good Hollywood scene, Tucker delivers the closing arguments to the jury and ardently decries the efforts of large corporations to stomp on small entrepreneurs like himself. He passionately argues:

> It's true! ... We're all puffed up with ourselves now because we invented the bomb ... Dropped the ... Beat the daylights out of the Japanese; the Nazis ... But if "big business" closes the door on THE LITTLE GUY WITH A NEW IDEA, WE'RE NOT ONLY CLOSING THE DOOR ON PROGRESS, BUT WE'RE SABOTAGING EVERYTHING THAT WE FOUGHT FOR! ... EVERYTHING THAT THE COUNTRY STANDS FOR! And one day, we're gonna find ourselves at the bottom of the heap, instead of king of the hill, having no idea how we got there; buying our radios and our cars from our former enemies! ... I don't believe that's gonna happen; I can't believe it, cuz ... if I ever, stop believing in plain old common

120 *Harm to Consumers*

horse-sense of the American people ... there's no way I could get out of bed in the morning ... Thank you

The film ends with a surprising acquittal, with the postscript revealing that 46 of the 50 cars are still roadworthy.

Nonetheless, the courtroom drama *Class Action* (1991) was the most noteworthy depiction of the auto industry's malfeasance toward consumers. The film parallelly addresses the lack of ethics in the auto industry and among corporate lawyers. The film starred Gene Hackman as Jedediah Tucker Ward, a showboating attorney specializing in fighting the underdog in civil cases. Gene Hackman is magnificent in this role, stealing scenes by depicting an idealistic civil liberties lawyer who can provoke standing ovations in courtrooms with his closing arguments. In his most recent case, he takes on Argo Motors, a fictional automobile manufacturer whose station wagon has a propensity to explode on impact. The film takes a melodramatic twist, as Jedediah's daughter, Maggie, is assigned as Argo's chief counsel in the lawsuit. Maggie Ward (Mary Elizabeth Mastrantonio) is a corporate attorney on the fast track for partnership in a prestigious law firm. Maggie and her father have a volatile relationship as Jed had placed his career ahead of his family, cheating on her mother, Estelle, years earlier. Jedediah believes that Maggie's firm is using her as a "parlor" trick to try to rattle him, but she stubbornly continues to work the case. Estelle (Joanna Merlin) attempts to be a peacemaker for the pair. However, she dies of a stroke after the trial begins, once again bringing the pair to clash in a particularly tense and heart-wrenching argument as the pair try to come to terms with their mutual loss.

In this way, the film is more than a courtroom drama with the ideals of the two central characters clashing throughout the plot. Jed relishes being a champion for the "little guy," using legal skills and persuasion to passionately fight David versus Goliath cases. Maggie strongly resents her father, believing him to be self-serving and hypocritical. She channels her rage into her work, where she is cold and calculating. Maggie is meticulous in her duty to her clients and investigates potential problems with the case. She stumbles across an elderly scientist who wrote a report condemning the safety of the fuel tank. She also learns that Argo motors utilize a "bean-counting approach" to risk management. Potential lawsuit payouts are weighed against costs of re-designing and re-manufacturing the product without the defect. Maggie discovers that her boss and lover, Michael Grazer (Colin Friel), has destroyed the safety report to ensure that Argo Motors will win the lawsuit. Despite her dismay with her firm's unethical tactics, Maggie fervently continues with the case, callously cross-examining an elderly scientist, whose damning report "disappeared." She disdainfully used his inability to "remember numbers" to make him appear senile. In a legal surprise, Jed calls Michael Grazer to the stand, demanding that he answer questions about the missing report. The sleazy Grazer mockingly doubts the very existence of the safety report, agitating Jed by not directly answering his queries. In her cross-examination, Maggie confidently asks Grazer directly about the safety report. Grazer lies, and then Jed calls a surprise witness, an employee from Argo, who discredits Grazer and reveals the contents of the safety report. In the end, it is divulged that Maggie, using the same legal trickery of her firm, had supplied her father with information about the witness that corroborated the report's existence. The plaintiffs settled out of court for $100 million, and in a sentimental closing, father and daughter are reunified. Maggie tells her father that she loves him, and they sentimentally dance in memory of Estelle.

Class Action was inspired by the infamous Ford Pinto case, which featured a faulty fuel tank design that killed several consumers. It was later uncovered that Ford knew that a design flaw in the gas tank led to unnecessary deaths, injuries, and vehicle burnouts. In 1977, *Mother Jones* printed an article revealing a memo in which Ford outlined that it would be cheaper to payout lawsuits than fix the problem with the cars. The Pinto case has never been the subject of a Hollywood film or television movie. However, in the comedy *The Devil Has a Name* (2019), there is a particularly compelling scene in which the Pinto scandal is parallelly told by attorney Ralph Aegis (Martin Sheen) and the "Big Boss" (Alfred Molina), a Big Oil CEO who once worked as an executive for Ford.

The dishonesty of the auto industry was also on full display in *Flash of Genius* (2008). The film starred Greg Kinnear as Robert Kearns, a college engineering professor and inventor. With the help of his friend and financial supporter Gil Previck (Dermot Mulroney), he invents, patents, and enters a deal with Ford to manufacture the intermittent wiper, which he calls the Kearns Blinking Eye Motor. However, Ford reneges on the agreement, steals his prototype, and sells it on its new cars. Robert is despondent but is determined to fight the large corporation. He has a nervous breakdown and resorts to stealing circuit boards from Ford models to prove that it is his invention. Afterwards, Robert is institutionalized after being found in his pajamas traveling to Washington on a Greyhound. As a condition of release, he agrees to stop obsessing over the case, but with the support of this wife, Phyllis (Lauren Graham), he decides to pursue legal action against Ford. He enlists a seemingly passionate lawyer, Gregory Lawson (Alan Alda), who tells Robert and Phyllis, "I am not in this for the quick score. This firm is in this for the long haul." Lawson nobly tells the couple, "I believe in what I do. I believe in a little thing called justice. These bastards think they can walk all over anybody they want. But we're here to tell them that they can't that it stops right here." Shortly afterwards, Lawson invites the Kearns to a celebratory dinner, where he enthusiastically tells them that he secured a $250,000 settlement from Ford. However, Kearns refuses, insisting that Ford must give him credit for the wiper and confess that they lied. Lawson hypocritically drops Kearns as a client, telling him that he cannot win a trial against a large corporation and that Ford will use their unending legal resources to prolong the case for years. Robert's stubbornness and obsession with justice compel Phyllis to leave her husband. As Lawson predicted, it took years before the case went to trial, where Kearns represents himself in court. Despite his legal inexperience, Robert brilliantly represents himself. He even puts himself on the stand, where he tells the jury the story of his "flash of genius," which led to the creation of the intermittent wiper. The representatives of Ford become worried about losing the case and offer him a generous settlement. With his family's blessing, Kearns turns down a $30 million settlement and decides to trust in the jury. The Ford defense team callously employs a dirty tactic, using the nervous breakdown against Kearns, making him appear mentally unstable. In the culminating scene, Kearns gives an impassioned closing argument about Ford's corporate power, deceit, arrogance, and lack of ethics. The jury agrees that Ford infringed on the patent, and he is awarded $10 million. The postscript tells the audience that he also received $18.7 million from Chrysler Corporation.

The Food Industry

Globally, the production, processing, sale, and consumption of food are responsible for a large amount of death and illness. Despite the vast economic and environmental costs that the food industry inflicts on consumers, "food crime" is not deemed a pressing issue within criminal justice. The corporations that control the food industry are subject to regulatory law, a quasi-criminal form of law that metes out minimal punishments with little deterrent impact, and whose agencies increasingly have fewer resources and authority. There are many forms of wrongdoing in the food industry, such as price-fixing, misleading advertising, and adulterated food sales. There is a long history of corporate food giants that monopolize and fix prices, from dairy to packaged seafood. Labeling practices are often deceptive, with frauds involving the sale of purportedly "free range" or "organic food" and the use of misleading terms such as "extra light," "fresh," or "natural," phrases which have no legal definition, fooling consumers into buying seemingly "healthy" products. Finally, adulteration can be lethal, the global nature of food processing contributing to the increasing amount of food poisoning outbreaks (Croall, 2012; Gray & Hinch, 2019).

To say the least, there is moral ambiguity in producing, marketing, and selling unhealthy food to consumers. In Western society, there is an epidemic of obesity, which is linked to processed food that is readily available, cheaply priced, and marketed to a progressively overburdened and uninformed consumer. The globalization of the food industry and domination of large corporations – aptly referred to as Mcdonaldization and Coca colonization – has resulted in massive profits for corporations that produce and sell processed food. Research reveals that profit margins from processed, sugary foods, and soft drinks are as high as 15 percent, while fruits and vegetables are in the range of 3–6 percent. Essentially, the food industry maximizes profits at the expense of consumers, who tragically die of preventable diseases such as type 2 diabetes, heart disease, and some forms of cancer. Despite the enormous health costs, governments favor the so-called "soft" regulatory policies that put the onus on consumers to make "informed" choices about healthier foods – for instance, providing calorie counts on menus and having manufacturers provide more transparent labeling. In contrast, "hard" regulations, such as increased taxes on sugary foods and restrictions on advertising unhealthy food to children, have met with intense opposition from the food industry, which has unlimited finances to lobby the government for political favors (Croall, 2012; Gray & Hinch, 2019).

Within this context, Hollywood portrayals of the food industry exist, albeit those depictions are uncommon. There is, however, a veritable cottage industry of documentary films that explore the harms perpetrated on consumers by the food industry. Some of the most compelling include *Super Size Me* (2004), *Food Inc.* (2008), *The World According to Monsanto* (2008), *The Sugar Film* (2014), and *Fed Up* (2014). Unfortunately, the structure of the typical scripted film makes it difficult to tell a compelling story about malfeasance in the food industry. It is very challenging for screenwriters to entertain audiences with stories of price-fixing, contaminated food, deceptive labels or advertising, and unhealthy eating dangers.

The potential danger of GMOs was the primary plotline in *Consumed* (2015), which follows Sophie Kessler (Zoe Lister-Jones), a waitress and single mother whose son is experiencing mysterious illnesses. He is vomiting at night, having skin rashes and painful body aches. Doctors are unable to make a diagnosis, believing that he might be experiencing a psychological disorder. Unconvinced, Sophie begins an investigation, discovering that food and skin allergies in children have increased dramatically. She suspects that it may be the result of GMOs and goes to the University science lab, where her mother works, to inquire about GMOs. The Dean quickly dismisses her concerns and touts the benefits of GMOs. The science lab is funded by Clonestra, a corporation that is developing genetically modified food. Clonestra has a new CEO, Dan Conway (Victor Garber), who firmly believes in the benefits of genetically modified food and spins the corporation as helping the world. Sophie is approached by Peter (Griffin Dunne), who offers to meet with Sophie clandestinely and tells her (and the viewer) about GMOs:

Peter: So, in the nineties, when GMOs were like flooding the market, food-related illnesses doubled. Now, is that a coincidence. I don't think so. Now, almost 90% of corn and more than 90% of soybeans that are planted in the United States are genetically engineered.
Sophie: So it's just in everything ...
Peter: Exactly, You know when you change the DNA of our food, You open up the possibility of all kinds of new allergies.
Sophie: Is that what you think my son has, ah, like an allergic reaction or something?
Peter: Children's immune systems, much more vulnerable than ours. See, none of these genetically modified crops have been tested on humans.
Sophie: Why Not?
Peter: Because the corporations are self-regulated.
Peter: [as Clonestra CEO and executives meet with two research scientists] They hold no independent studies. Hell, with all this lobby cash at hand. Washington deregulated all the crops. So they don't have to test longer than 90 days or release the raw data of their studies. They are the authority on the science. You get it?

Sophie is becoming increasingly paranoid and uses her mother's keys to access the science lab to gain more information. Along with Peter, she is caught and is told by security that Peter was a former scientist who now works as a janitor. She feels increasingly helpless and turns to Hal Westbrook (Danny Glover), an organic food farmer whom Clonestra is suing for patent violations. Sophie also visits an attorney, who tells her that there is no proof that GMOs caused the illness, and even so, GMOs are not on labels, so it would be impossible to prove. Meanwhile, Serge (Kunal Nayyar) is a university scientist researching the impact of GMOs on lab rats. His character serves as the whistleblower after discovering that research showing the harms of the product they are developing (biotech chickens) is being buried. After he is fired, he steals the research files and arranges to meet with Sophie. In a Silkwood-type moment, he is killed after being accidentally run off the road by two cops who work for the corporation. Sophie goes to the junkyard to retrieve the incriminating research files from Serge's car. She confronts the CEO, giving him the files that show him deformed rats. The confrontation is caught on a cell phone. It goes viral on social media, leading to the ending of the development of biotech chickens and the CEO's resignation, who had a pang of social consciousness. The film was well meaning but was a little too ambitious in scope, as it tossed in too much information in a short period of time. For example, the film explored many elements around GMOs, including the corruption of science in funding, peer review, and ghostwriting; suicides of farmers in India who were bankrupted by GMO foods; agribusiness litigation against small farmers; the lack of labels on GMO produced food; the latent harms of Glysophate; and most prominent narrative was the potentially harmful effects of GMOs on consumers, primarily allergies with children.

Like *Consumed*, *Fast Food Nation* (2006) ran the gamut in terms of wrongdoing in the food industry, with several implicit messages about the food industry, including the predominance of unhealthy processed and fast food; gimmicky marketing directed at children; the use of chemicals to enhance or flavor food items; exploitation of food workers; the reliance on a service-based economy; animal cruelty; factory farming; price-fixing and monopolies; lobbying; the tracking of consumers; and unsanitary conditions in processing plants. The film featured three interweaving stories that highlighted problems within the fast-food industry. The film was based on investigative journalist Eric Schlosser's ground-breaking and best-selling non-fiction book, *Fast Food Nation*, 2001. In the first storyline, the marketing director of Mickey's Burgers, Don Anderson (Greg Kinnear), is tasked with investigating claims of fecal matter in their highly popular burger, The Big One.

Jack: I have a friend that teaches food science over at A&M. Microbiology. And this semester, a couple of his grad students decided to culture some patties from a bunch of fast-food chains.
Don: Uh-huh.
Jack: Well (sighs), they got a hold of a couple of Big Ones. The frozen patties. Don't ask me how. And the fecal coliform counts were just off the charts. I'm concerned that this could be a problem for us. Do you understand what I'm saying?

Don: (shakes head). Not exactly.
Jack: I'm saying there's shit in the meat.

Don travels to Cody, Colorado, to investigate Uni-Globe, the meat processing plant that supplies the Big One. After he visits the seemingly pristine operation, he becomes suspicious and meets with locals and learns of the poor working conditions and unsanitary techniques. He tells executive VP Harry Rydell (Bruce Willis) about the problems. Ryder admits that he is aware and colorfully rationalizes the company decided to partner with Uni-Globe, claiming to buy "grade A-chuck at 40 cents a pound." Fearing that he may lose his position, Don "cops out" and does not become a whistleblower. He launches a new marketing campaign for the BBQ Big One, "a hickory-taste" chow-down.

The second storyline features Raul (Wilmer Valderrama), Sylvia (Catalina Sandino Moreno), and her sister Coco, Mexican migrants who journey to the United States to seek a better life. The trio also ends up in Cody, with Raul and Coco working at Uni-Globe under the supervision of Mike (Bobby Cannavale). This sleazy and cruel supervisor harasses and exploits his workers. In a particularly compelling scene, Mike admonishes an employee after they allowed Grade A meat into the burger, an unequivocal message about the low quality of the product that many fast-food chains utilize. Sylvia ends up working at a hotel because she cannot "stomach" the idea of working at a meat processing plant. In the end, Raul is hurt in an accident at work, and Sylvia has sex with Mike to seek work at the processing plant. In a disconcerting scene, Mike has Sylvia work on the "kill floor," which vividly shows the cattle being slaughtered. The third storyline features Amber (Ashley Johnson), an aspiring college student, a model employee at Mickey's Burgers in Cody. The storyline morphs from the reliance on the service economy to animal cruelty within the factory farm. After her radical "hippie" Uncle Pete (Ethan Hawke) comes to visit, Amber is inspired to quit working in the fast-food industry, as it "feels wrong." She starts to hang out with college students who are members of the Environmental Policy Discussion Group. They discuss the exploitation of animals and workers at the Uni-Globe Meat processing plant. The group decide that they will start a letter-writing campaign, which angers Paco, a more radical group member:

> You guys are going to write a letter. That company's the meanest fucking company I've ever seen. They treat their workers like shit, they treat their animals like shit. They're dumping tons of shit and piss into our river, and you guys are going to write a letter?

Amber convinces the group to sneak into Uni-Globe and set the cows free. However, when they cut the fence, the cattle do not escape, which perplexes the group who think that the "cows" are "stupid." Unbeknownst to the group, these "cows" have never left the stockyard and have never experienced grazing in a natural setting. Decidedly, *Fast Food Nation* was not nearly as impactful or insightful as the book. However, it had some very clever scenes and dialogue that highlighted several problems in the food industry. In a particularly clever scene, Don oversees the development of a new product and provides feedback to the food scientist developing the artificial flavoring. Without a sense of irony, the characters tout the use of a chemical to replicate lime flavoring, rather than using lime itself:

Lab Scientist: Yeah, I mean, these Caribbean seasonings are kind of tricky.
Don: Well, were calling them Calypso Chicken tenders. I think people are going to have an expectation for a ... maybe a touch of lime.
Lab Scientist: Oh, well, lime. Lime's easy. I just held back on the Terpinolene on this to keep the flavoring more subtle, but I can always go back and add more.
Don: Yeah, why don't we try that?
Lab Scientist: I will keep working on it.

Similarly, the comedy *Good Burger* (1997) also featured a storyline in which a corporate fast-food chain, Mondo Burger, artificially enlarged their burgers with the fictional Triampathol, an illegal chemical. Although the depictions are comical, the reality is much more sinister. Every day, consumers purchase foods brimming with additives and chemicals associated with several negative and behavioral conditions (Conscious Club, 2019).

Moreover, several films depict agribusiness corporations engaged in price-fixing, environmental pollution, and monopolization. *The Informant* (2009) was very loosely based on the Lysine price-fixing scandal in the 1990s. The film starred Matt Damon as Mark Whitacre, an executive with Archer Daniels Midland, an agribusiness giant. He becomes a whistleblower that records hundreds of tapes that implicates the industry in a global price-fixing scheme. The film was a very rare depiction of price-fixing, which impacts the "pocket-books of consumers." In a hidden tape, Whitacre explains the scheme to the international conspirators: "What he's saying is, the customers are our enemy. The competitors are our friends. This is why it is important that we have all the lysine producers involved, including the Cheil Corporation." However, Whitacre was also involved in a kickback scheme, in which he netted over $9 million and spent nine years in prison. The thriller Michael Clayton (2007) featured U-North, a fictional agribusiness conglomerate responsible for leaking pollutants that killed over 400 residents. The film was primarily focused on the cover-up, which included murder and the malfeasance of corporate lawyers. That said, there was a brief scene that questioned the safety of the seed product. Similarly, in 1973 the Velsicol Chemical Company (under the name Michigan Chemical) erroneously sent polybrominated biphenyl or PBB to the Michigan Farm Bureau, which is mistaken for a feed additive and mixed with grain. The toxic substance rapidly spread through Michigan's food chain through dairy, beef, and contaminated sheep, chickens, and eggs. The PBB crisis was one of the worst chemical poisonings in US history and was intensely depicted in *Bitter Harvest* (1981), a made-for-television production. Finally, *Percy vs. Goliath* (2020) featured the story of Percy Schmeiser, a farmer in Saskatchewan who was sued for seed piracy. The film's primary focus was on the unethical business practices of Monsanto. However, the film questioned the safety of GMOs, with fictional environmentalist Rebecca Salcau (Christina Ricci) arguing,

> What's going to happen when we spray these toxic substances onto our wheat? Wheat that is ground down into the flour that is baked into bread ... by the time it gets to our dinner plates, it contains glyphosate, the main ingredient in Monsanto's herbicide, Roundup.

The Tobacco Industry

In January 1964, the much-anticipated Surgeon General's Report on Smoking and Health was released to the public and revealed that cigarettes caused death from lung cancer, emphysema, and coronary heart disease. By contemporary standards, the news is not shocking. However, the findings reverberated through a country thoroughly immersed in a smoking culture, with upwards of 60 percent of the population engaged in the activity. The tobacco industry engaged in a widespread public relations campaign to hide the hazards of smoking, using doctors, nurses, actors, athletes, and even Santa Claus to promote the health benefits of smoking (Rabin-Havt, 2016; Sokol, 2010). Aside from the obvious public health issue, the campaign against tobacco became a battle over corporate influence, lobbyists in Washington, individual responsibilities, collective choice, deceptive advertising, and the extent of government power (Milov, 2019). The tobacco industry has a long history with the film industry, using movies to depict smoking as glamorous and cool. The depiction of cigarette smoking in film is controversial, as many opponents argue that it unduly influences children and young adults to engage in the dangerous habit. Conversely, some filmmakers contend that artistic license must be maintained. That said, the tobacco industry has paid handsomely to promote their products in movies and among Hollywood stars. For example, tobacco giant Lark paid $350,000 for their product in *Licence to Kill* (1989), while Sylvester Stallone was paid $500,000 to use Brown and Williamson products in five feature films. The marketing potential within movies was not lost on industry executives, as the president of Phillip Morris once claimed [in 1983],

> I do feel heartened at the increasing number of occasions when I go to a movie and see a pack of cigarettes in the hands of the leading lady ... We must continue to exploit new opportunities to get cigarettes on screen and into the hands of smokers.
>
> (Malaspina, 2014)

After the US prohibited advertising of tobacco products in the 1970s, the tobacco industry turned to popular entertainment until the 1998 Master Settlement Agreement banned the practice in television, film, and video games. However, the CDC found that film depictions of smokers have risen sharply, even though smoking is declining. That said, Hollywood depictions of the tobacco industry, either positive or negative, are very scarce, with only a couple of movies that depict corporate wrongdoing.

One of the earliest depictions of the tobacco industry, *Bright Leaf* (1950), is now considered a historical curiosity as it was a celebration of the invention of mass-produced cigarettes. Set in 1890s North Carolina, the film depicts the rapid ascension of Brant Royle (Gary Cooper) to become a tobacco tycoon after he supports the invention of a cigarette rolling machine. The film was primarily a melodrama, with romance, greed, and revenge but did feature automation of the industry and accusations of monopolization. Years later, the made-for-television *The Good Fight* (1992) appeared on the Lifetime network. The film starred Christine Lahti as Grace, a small-firm lawyer who advocates for Tony, a young athlete dying of mouth cancer. Grace instigates a lawsuit alleging that Federated Tobacco was negligent in marketing harmful chewing tobacco to young athletes. Grace reluctantly takes the unwinnable case, telling Tony that

> you have to understand if one person wins one of these things and sets a precedent. The entire tobacco industry would be flooded with suits. I mean they're willing to spend billions of dollars to make sure that nobody wins one.

The powerful tobacco corporation employs a mass of ferocious lawyers and dirty tricks to win the case. As a Lifetime film, it featured a romantic angle in which Grace enlists her ex-husband and prominent lawyer Henry (Terry O'Quinn). Henry urges her to fight the case, telling her that "big money is always going to win ... but if you quit, the light goes out."

Even though internal memos showed that smokeless tobacco was harmful, Federated Tobacco company promoted the product with prizes and gifts, marketing the product toward youth. In an atypical Lifetime ending, the case ends in a hung jury and the high costs of the trial bankrupt Grace. However, she renews a relationship with her former husband and resiliently vows to retry the case. The film held true to the reality of lawsuits against Big Tobacco. At that time, there was only one case in which a tobacco company had to pay damages to the family of a smoker who had perished. In 1988, Judge Lee Sarokin ordered Liggett to pay $400,000 to the family of Rose Cipollone, a 57-year-old smoker who died of lung cancer. Sarokin held the Liggett Group negligent for failing to warn smokers before 1966 (when warning labels started) and for advertising that could be construed as a guarantee of safety. Just two years later, the Cipollone case was overturned on appeal, and in 1992 the case was dropped, with big tobacco remaining seemingly untouchable. In another case, Sarokin referred to the tobacco industry as the "king of concealment" and argued that tobacco industry documents, which essentially revealed consumer fraud, should be made public. Sarokin's opinion inspired a federal probe into the wrongdoings of Big Tobacco and served as a watershed moment in the litigation against the tobacco industry (Milov, 2019).

The legal fight against Big Tobacco was prominently depicted in *The Insider* (1999), a fictionalized version of the struggle to produce and air the infamous *60 Minutes* interview with tobacco industry whistleblower Jeffery Wigand

(Russell Crowe). The film stars Al Pacino as Lowell Bergman, a senior producer of *60 Minutes*. Bergman is researching a story on Big Tobacco and seeks specialized knowledge about some documents. He meets with Wigand, a scientist who was the vice president of Scientific Research with Brown and Williamson Tobacco. Wigand agrees to help, but only within the limits of his confidentiality agreement. However, shortly afterwards, Wigand is threatened with litigation and asked to sign a revised, more strict confidentiality agreement. Becoming more paranoid, Wigand angrily calls Bergman accusing him of selling him out by not protecting his sources. Also angry, Bergman confronts Wigand telling him, "Big Tobacco is a big story, and you got something important to say. I can tell ... I came all the way down here to tell you, story, no story, fuck your story, I don't burn people." Wigand contritely offers to take Lowell for a ride. He tells Bergman that he cannot violate the confidentiality agreement because he needs the health insurance for his asthmatic daughter. The increasingly curious Bergman believes that Wigand has an important story to tell and asks his colleagues, including Mike Wallace (Christopher Plummer), how they can get Wigand to violate his corporate secrecy agreement.

> Mike Wallace: He's got a corporate secrecy agreement. Give me a break. This is a public health issue, like an unsafe air frame on a passenger jet or some company dumping cyanide into the East River. Issues like that. He can talk about it. They've got no right to hide behind a corporate agreement. Pass the milk.

Bergman believes that they can circumvent the confidentiality agreement if Wigand is deposed in a court of law, paving the way for Wigand to appear in *60 Minutes*. Wigand arranges for attorney Richard Scruggs (Colm Feore) to use Wigand as an expert witness in a lawsuit against the tobacco industry, which allows Wigand to appear on the program. Meanwhile, Wigand relocates to a modest house and takes a lower-paying teaching position. However, he learns that he is still being watched and is threatened with a menacing phone call. Wigand's wife discovers an emailed death threat, and Wigand finds a bullet in his mailbox. The FBI agents do not take the threats seriously, harass and even confiscate Wigand's computer. Wigand is furious and demands to be interviewed on 60 Minutes to tell his story. After the taping of the interview, Wigand faces a difficult decision as a Kentucky Court has placed a gag order on his testimony in Mississippi, threatening him with a hefty fine or jail time if he testifies in a Mississippi court. He courageously testifies, which allows for the *60 Minutes* segment to proceed. At this point, the story takes a dramatic turn, as CBS, urged by "corporate," airs an alternate story segment without the interview of Wigand. Bergman is enraged, arguing:

> I hear potential Brown & Williamson lawsuit jeopardizing the sale of CBS to Westinghouse. I hear, shut the segment down. Cut Wigand loose. Obey orders and fuck off." That's what I hear.

Bergman also learns that the *Wall Street Journal* will publish a "hit piece" that was based on Brown & Williamson's "investigation" of Wigand. Bergman uses his connections with the WSJ to delay the story, and his fact-checkers determine that the 500-page report on Wigand is not credible, with many exaggerated and false claims. Rather than smear Wigand, The WSJ prints Wigand's court disposition, with Bergman colorfully telling his colleagues:

> Don't invert stuff! Big Tobacco tried to smear Wigand, you bought it. The Wall Street Journal, here: not exactly a bastion of anti-capitalist sentiment, refutes Big Tobacco's smear campaign as the lowest form of character assassination!

At the same time, the *New York Times* prints a front-page story and a scathing editorial on CBS's role in burying the interview, also leaked by Bergman. At that point, CBS decides to air the full interview. However, Bergman decides to quit the show, realizing that he cannot trust CBS to support his journalistic integrity and support his sources. In the postscript, it was revealed that in 1998 the tobacco industry settled lawsuits across the country totaling $246 billion.

The Insider was deservedly nominated for several Academy Awards, including Best Picture and easily was the most damning indictment of the tobacco industry depicted in scripted film. Conversely, *Thank You for Smoking* (2005) was a satirical attempt to poke fun at Big Tobacco and Lobbyists. The comedy starred Aaron Eckhart as Nick Naylor, a spokesperson for the Academy of Tobacco Studies, a lobby group for Big Tobacco. Calling himself the "Colonel Sanders" of Nicotine, Naylor describes his job as a tobacco lobbyist,

> Few people on this planet know what it is to be truly despised. Can you blame them? I earn a living fronting an organization that kills 1,200 human beings a day.

Naylor vividly explains how the tobacco industry hires scientists to dispute harms associated with cigarettes, lawyers to fight potential lawsuits, and lobbyists to influence political policy. He shamelessly argues that there is no link between lung disease and tobacco on a television talk show. As a result of bad press, tobacco sales are plummeting, and Naylor boss, BM (J.K. Simmons) angrily tells his staff, "Teen smoking—our bread and butter, is falling like a shit from heaven. We don't sell tic tacs, for Christ's sake. We sell cigarettes. And they're cool and available and addictive. The job is almost done for us." BM is also concerned about Senator Finistirre (William H. Macy), who is crusading to have a poison warning, with skull and crossbones on cigarette packaging. The film takes several silly little turns, including the kidnapping of Naylor by an anti-tobacco terrorist group; the bribery of the Marlboro Man, who has cancer; and Naylor negotiating cigarette placement in a Hollywood film. Nick is also duped by Heather Holloway, a reporter with the *Washington Probe*. Holloway seduces Naylor, who writes a story detailing the secret information about his amoral life and career, which ruins his reputation and gets him fired. In the end, he appears before a Senate committee, admits that smoking is dangerous, but claims the public is already cognizant of the harms, and consumers can make their own choices without resorting to poison warnings. He also argues that Finistirre's state of Vermont is a major cheese producer and is similarly guilty of cholesterol-related deaths. Despite the apparent false equivalency, Naylor persuades the committee not to include a more graphic warning label, and he is offered his position back with the Academy. However, he decides to start his own agency, which is fortuitous, as the Academy of Tobacco Studies was eliminated after Big Tobacco was forced to pay out $246 billion in lawsuits. The film was obviously anti-smoking. However, it was considerably less critical than the novel, in which it was based. The film underplayed the insidious role that lobbyists and advertising can inflict on public health measures. That said, the film provides light entertainment value on an often-neglected element of corporate wrongdoing – lobbying and corporate harm to human health.

The Advertising Industry

The advertising industry serves a vital role in the corporate harm of consumers. False advertising and the misrepresentation of products continue to be a problem within the industry. Advertising is teeming with exaggerations, puffing ads, misleading claims, and deception. Yet criminal prosecutions for deceptive marketing are rare and generally non-punitive (Rabin-Havt, 2016). Food and pharmaceutical conglomerates spend billions of dollars on advertising their products at a higher rate than expenditures for research and development. No doubt, marketing impacts millions of consumers and has become normalized within our culture. In popular culture, advertising has been the subject of several television series and films. The television series *Mad Men* (2007–2015, *AMC*) is likely the most recognizable portrayal of the advertising industry in popular culture. That said, there have been several films that depict Madison Avenue, with satires such as *The Hucksters* (1947) *Will Success Spoil the Rock Hunter* (1957), *Lover Come Back* (1961), *Putney Swope* (1969), *Nothing in Common* (1985), *Beer* (1985), *How to Get Ahead in Advertising* (1989), *Crazy People* (1990), and *In Good Company* (2004). However, the depiction of corporate wrongdoing in the advertising industry is very rare, with only a handful of depictions.

The manipulation of television viewers by corporate executives at NBC and the makers of Geritol was the premise of *Quiz Show* (1994). Based on a true story, the film depicts the unbridled cheating on the set of Twenty-One, a popular quiz show in the 1950s. The "unstumpable" Herbert Stempel (John Turturro) is the reigning eight-week champion of the show. However, sponsors are concerned that his annoying personality is wearing thin and request that a more appealing contestant replace him. As luck would have it, the son of a prominent literary family, Charles Van Doren (Ralph Fiennes), auditions for the show and the producers immediately believe they have a suitable replacement. In contrast to Stempel, Van Doren is both charming and handsome, and the producers tell Stempel that he must lose on purpose with the false promise of more work on television.

Despite his objections, Stemple is humiliated after not answering an easy question on a popular movie. As he leaves the studio, he feels slighted by Van Doren and then overhears a show valet exclaim, "now we have a clean-cut intellectual, instead of a freak with a sponge memory." Stemple is quickly forgotten in the following weeks, and Van Doren becomes an even more popular champion and national celebrity. Van Doren is conflicted but allows the producers to give him the answers, which eventually leads a jealous and "broke" Stempel to become a "whistleblower," divulging all the secrets to a congressional lawyer, Richard Goodwin (Rob Morrow). Meanwhile, the conscience-stricken Van Doren intentionally loses after 14 weeks and becomes a correspondent with the Today Show. The House Committee for Legislative Oversight convenes a hearing into the scandal, and both the network head and Geritol executive deny any knowledge that Twenty-One was rigged. However, after Van Doren testifies about his role in the cheating, the producers of the show "take the fall," claiming that they acted alone, without the consent of the top brass. With Geritol executive Martin Rittenhome (Martin Scorcese) privately telling Goodwin, "Look, Dan Enright [the producer] wants a future in television, okay? You have to understand that the public has a very short memory. But corporations they never forget." The quiz show scandals of the 1950s highlighted the malfeasance of both the entertainment and advertising industry, further eroding viewers' and consumer trust. One of the more interesting but understated elements of the film was the misleading advertisements for Geritol. Geritol was a supplementary tonic that promised more vitality for consumers, a cure for iron deficiency. The Federal Trade Commission (FTC) investigated and penalized the false and misleading claims about the efficiency of the product (Whitney, 1970).

While *Quiz Show* was a thoughtful depiction, many films utilize satire to illustrate advertising impropriety. In the tradition of Putney Swope, *Pootie Tang* (2001) chronicled the titular character (Lance Crouther) battle against the Lecter Corporation, obviously a play on the villain in Silence of the Lambs. A popular culture icon, Pootie is a hero of the "ghetto" and engages in PSA campaigns to help his community. However, the PSAs are reducing the evil Lecter Corporation's bottom line. The corporation manipulates Pootie into selling out by endorsing addictive and harmful products to African American children. The silly film was not for all tastes, pilloried by some viewers and critics. Still, fans consider the film a "cult classic," spoofing various stereotypical aspects of African American pop culture. The film is considered a satirical indictment of harmful products marketed and sold to a vulnerable population. Likewise, *Fast Food Nation* satirizes unethical marketing practices in the fast-food industry. The film depicted marketing directed toward children that pushed unhealthy food such as the "The Little Big One," "Itty Bitties," and the "Teeny Weenies." They dispense toys to children and use kid's programming to schlep their products. In the opening scene, the executive team at Mickey's Burgers discuss marketing strategy directed toward kids:

CEO: How about Disney?
Don Anderson: No Word Yet.

Dave: Also, the PBS deal doesn't seem to be happening. Uh, apparently Burger King and McDonald's have the Teletubbies all locked up.
CEO: [Dejectedly] Fuck Em

Similarly, *The Founder* (2016) briefly alluded to the ethical issues of advertising in the fast-food industry. The film is a biographical retelling of the founding of McDonald's. The film starred Michael Keaton as Ray Kroc, a failing salesman who exploits the McDonald brothers by mass franchising their restaurant's revolutionary Speedee system. In a particularly sarcastic moment, Ray urges the brothers to allow sponsorship on their menus.

Ray Kroc: Let me explain. It'll be real small along the bottom. Very discreet.
Dick McDonald: We're just not comfortable with the notion of turning our menu into an advertisement.
Ray Kroc: See it's not an ad, it is sponsorship.
Dick McDonald: It's distasteful.
Ray Kroc: It's free money!
Dick McDonald: There are plenty of things we could do to make a quick buck that doesn't mean we should.
Ray Kroc: Loads of restaurants do it!
Dick McDonald: Well, we don't.
Ray Kroc: Why not?
Dick McDonald: Cause I have no interest in indulging in that source of crass commercialism. It is not McDonald's.
Ray Kroc: I didn't realize I was partnering with a beatnik.
Dick McDonald: I'll have you know I'm a card-carrying Republican.

As most viewers would recognize, McDonald's is a prime example of crass commercialism that dominates the fast-food industry. The film touched on some unethical issues regarding Kroc's takeover of the McDonald's restaurant and chain. However, the movie was primarily a celebration of American entrepreneurship, with no discussion of the negative health consequences of fast food, poor working conditions, union-busting, automation of food preparation, and the seemingly endless supply of cheap labor in the service industry (Mattera, 2015).

Misleading advertising in the fast-food industry was given slight treatment in *Falling Down* (1993), which featured William "D-Fens" Foster (Michael Douglas) as a downtrodden, former defense engineer who has a mental breakdown. In the opening, Foster is stuck in a traffic jam in Los Angeles, abandons his car, and slowly makes his way through the city in a quest to reach his estranged ex-wife's house and give his daughter a birthday present. As Foster angrily journeys through the city, he becomes increasingly violent and delivers sarcastic and cynical observations about the state of the world. In a memorable scene, Foster enters a fast-food establishment and becomes infuriated that he cannot order from the breakfast menu. He pulls out an Uzi and then orders a "whammy burger with cheese" and "whammy fries." After receiving his burger, he compares it to the picture on the menu and dejectedly tells the staff, "Look at this sorry, miserable squashed thing. Can anybody tell me what's wrong with this picture? Anybody? Anybody at all?" The scene resonated with many viewers who have purchased a food product that does not resemble the advertisement.

Comparably, unscrupulous marketing has also been depicted in films on the tobacco industry. The satire, *Thank you for Smoking*, mocked product placement in the movie industry. The protagonist, Nick Naylor, pitches an idea to push for more cigarette smoking in Hollywood.

Nick Naylor: In 1910, the US was producing ten billion cigarettes a year. By 1930, we were up to 123 billion. What happened in between? Three things. A World War, dieting ... and movies.

B.M: Movies?

Nick: In 1927, talking films – were born. Suddenly, directors need to give their actors something to do while they're talking. Cary Grant, Carole Lombard are lighting up. Bette Davis a chimney. And Bogart – remember the first picture with him and Lauren Bacall?

B.M.: Well, yea ... not specifically.

Nick: Oh, she sort of shimmies in through the doorway, 19 years old. Pure sex. She says, "anyone got a match?" And Bogie throws the matches at her ... and she catches them. Greatest romance of the century. How'd it start? Lighting a cigarette. These days when someone smokes in the movies, they're either a psychopath or a European. The message Hollywood needs to send out is smoking is cool. We need the cast of Will and Grace smoking in their living room. Forrest Gump puffing away between his box of chocolates. Hugh Grant earning back the love of Julia Roberts by buying her favorite brand – her Virginia Slims. Most of the actors smoke already. If they start doing it on screen, we can put the sex back into cigarettes.

B.M: Well, it's a thought.

Naylor sets up a deal with a sleazy entertainment agent, Jeff Megall (Rob Lowe), to have the Tobacco industry help finance a futuristic science-fiction film, *Message from Sector Six*, "a world where smokers and non-smokers live together in perfect harmony." Megall proposes that for $25 million, he can have Brad Pitt and Catherine Zeta-Jones smoke in the film after a steamy sex scene. Naylor responds, "well for that kind of money, my people expect some very serious smoking. Can Brad blow smoke rings? ... For $25 million, we'd want smoke rings."

Considerably more dramatic, *The Good Fight* also touches on Big Tobacco marketing their product to youth consumers. The film shows how smokeless tobacco products were marketed toward youth baseball players, appearing as candy flavors such as bubble gum and promoted with free baseball equipment. Moreover, the protagonist, Grace Cragin, also uncovers a report in which the head of advertising advocated for the marketing of smokeless tobacco to the youth market to "start a trend." Big Tobacco continues to market its product to vulnerable populations, advertising at small corner stores, lowering costs of tobacco in poorer regions in the country, and providing discounts on tobacco products at cash registers. In 2019, the five major tobacco manufacturers spent approximately $7.13 billion to advertise their products, of which $5.7 billion was spent on reducing the cost of cigarettes (CDC, 2021). The tobacco industry continues to mislead the public by marketing its products as "slims" or "light" while utilizing brightly colored packaging and logos that are attractive to youth. Big Tobacco also has developed strategies to market products to youth through social media platforms, such as rewarding social media influencers to pitch their products (Rowell, 2020).

Concluding Thoughts

Corporations kill – this is indisputable – thousands of Americans die each year due to adulterated food and unsafe products, including automobiles, pharmaceuticals, and cigarettes. Although the tobacco industry continues to deny, smoking cigarettes is responsible for the deaths of eight million consumers worldwide (WHO, 2020). Consumers are at the mercy of Big Business interests, as corporations expend millions on lobbyists to pressure politicians to lessen consumer protection regulations. Moreover, corporations manipulate consumers through advertising, spending millions on sending messages and images that have little by way of objective truth. The film industry is complicit, serving big business interests by trumpeting products on the big screen, bolstering commercial and materialistic culture. The so-called Big Five – Universal Pictures, Paramount Pictures, Warner Bros. Pictures, Walt Disney, and Columbia Pictures – reflect corporate interests, rarely producing scripted films that depict harm to consumers or any critique of corporations. That said, some notable films have attempted to illustrate the incredible harm that corporations inflict on consumers. These films highlight dirty tactics used by corporations to deny culpability for their actions. However, these important stories are sporadic, at best, hardly making a dent in the realm of public consciousness.

Note

1 Arthur Hailey was a best-selling author who produced several books based on industries. Many were adapted for films or television miniseries, including the hotel industry (*Hotel*, 1967); airline industry (*Airport*, 1970); banking sector (*The Moneychangers*, 1976); and pharmaceutical industry (*Strong Medicine*, 1987).

Reference List

AMA. (2018). AMA, FDA help America's physicians combat spread of foodborne illness [Press Release]. https://www.ama-assn.org/press-center/press-releases/ama-fda-help-america-s-physicians-combat-spread-foodborne-illness

Associated Press. (2004, March 15). Consumer group seeks ban on antidepressant. *NBC News*. https://www.nbcnews.com/health/health-news/consumer-group-seeks-ban-antidepressant-flna1c9445195

CCR. (2021, June 28). Michael Saks on the epidemic of death and injury from healthcare. *Corporate Crime Reporter*. https://www.corporatecrimereporter.com/news/200/michael-saks-on-the-epidemic-of-death-and-injury-from-healthcare/

CDC. (2021). Tobacco industry marketing [Fact Sheet]. https://www.cdc.gov/tobacco/data_statistics/fact_sheets/tobacco_industry/marketing/index.htm

Conscious Club. (2019, May 23). Food & chemicals. Ecological Footprint Bible. https://www.theconsciouschallenge.org/ecologicalfootprintbibleoverview/food-chemicals

Croall, H. (2012). Food crime. In P. Beirner & N. South (Eds.), *Issues in green criminology* (pp. 228–251). Willan.

Gray, A., & Hinch, R. (Eds.). (2019). *A handbook of food crime: Immoral and illegal practices in the food industry and what to do about them*. Policy Press.

Gillam, C. (2017). *Whitewash: The story of a weed killer, cancer, and the corruption of science*. Island Press.

Jacobson, R. (2015, October 21). Many Antidepressant studies found tainted by pharma company influence. *Scientific American*. https://www.scientificamerican.com/article/many-antidepressant-studies-found-tainted-by-pharma-company-influence/

Llamas, M. (2021, March 5). Prozac Lawsuits. *Drugwatch*. https://www.drugwatch.com/ssri/prozac/lawsuits/

Malaspina, A. (2014). *False images, deadly promises: Smoking and the media*. Simon and Schuster.

Mattera, P. (2015). McDonald's corporate rap sheet. Corporate Research Project. https://www.corp-research.org/mcdonalds

Milov, S. (2019). *The cigarette: A political history*. Harvard University Press.

Rabin-Havt, A. (2016). *Lies, incorporated: The world of post-truth politics*. Anchor.

Rowell, A. (2020, January 23). Big Tobacco wants social media influencers to promote its products – can the platforms stop it? *The Conversation*. https://theconversation.com/big-tobacco-wants-social-media-influencers-to-promote-its-products-can-the-platforms-stop-it-129957

Saks, M.J., & Landsman, S. (2020). *Closing death's door: Legal innovations to end the epidemic of healthcare harm*. Oxford University Press.

Sokol, K.C. (2010). Smoking abroad and smokeless at home: Holding the tobacco industry accountable in a new era. *New York University Journal Legislation and Public Policy*, *13*, 81.

Sutherland, J. (2010). *Popular fiction of the 1970s*. Routledge.

Taubes, G., & Couzens, C.K. (2012). Big sugar's sweet little lies. *Mother Jones*, San Francisco, CA: Foundation for National Progress. https://www.motherjones.com/environment/2012/10/sugar-industry-lies-campaign/

WHO. (2020, April 30). Food safety [Fact Sheet]. https://www.who.int/news-room/fact-sheets/detail/food-safety

WHO. (2020, July 26). Tobacco [Fact Sheet]. https://www.who.int/news-room/fact-sheets/detail/tobacco

6 Harm to the Economy

There are three ways to make a living in this business. Be first, be smarter, or cheat.

John Tuld (Jeremy Irons), CEO, Unknown Wall Street Investment Bank, *Margin Call* (2011)

The corporation is richer and more profitable than any other period in American history. Yet, corporations have also become preoccupied with maximizing short-term profits and appeasing shareholders. Corporations are no longer investing in the future, their workers, and the economy. The corporate-based economy is based on the tenant "every man for himself," where upper-level executives are accountable for shareholders and not consumers or their employees. These uber-capitalists are focused on short-term gains, where quarterly-earning reports and annual (and increasingly larger!) bonuses take precedence over long-term sustainability and stability. In this way, corporations hurt the economy by refusing to invest their massive profits back into the economy, as CEOs are more interested in increasing efficiency, which is just a catchphrase for cutting costs, which means firing employees and scrimping on research and development. These corporations reap generous government contracts or subsidies, do not pay their fair share in taxes, and even secure government bailouts during "tough" times. Unfortunately, corporate welfare does not "trickle" down to the average American. Instead, corporations can maximize their profits, allowing them to stockpile massive amounts of cash on their already bloated balance sheets. In this way, corporations starve the economy of revenue that could promote economic growth, and more importantly, spur economic inequality within an increasingly widening gulf between the rich and poor (Blodget, 2013; Reich, 2008). For instance, the wealth gap between America's wealthiest and poorest families more than doubled from 1989 to 2016. In 1989, the wealthiest 5 percent of families had 114 times the wealth compared to families in the second quintile. In 2016 that ratio increased to 248. Globally, 1 percent of the population has more than twice as much wealth as 6.9 billion people (Oxfam, 2021).

Despite these significant gaps, corporations and their proxies continue to lobby for less regulation, lower taxes, and enhancements to corporate welfare.

DOI: 10.4324/9781003163855-6

Corporations – both large and small – have excessive influence over public policy, lobbying for laws that benefit themselves, with little to no opposition (Speri, 2019). Furthermore, corporations kill the "spirit" of capitalism through mega-mergers and monopolization. Although the free market is the basis of the American entrepreneurial spirit, which "supposedly" operates to benefit consumers, the reality is much different. Corporations employ several "dirty" tactics to monopolize their industry or sector, including utilizing intellectual property rights, buying up the competition, and hoarding scarce resources. Monopolies allow corporations to control markets, set prices, and gouge consumers (Hubbard, 2021).

Finally, corporate theft and fraud erode the public's confidence in the stock market, ultimately hurting the economy. The financial crash, precipitated by shady financial practices within banking and real estate, underscored the economy's fragility. Characterized as "financial crime," corporate fraud and theft include bank interest rate fixing, insider trading, illegally leveraged mergers and takeovers, bribery, and various forms of tax evasion and illegal accounting. Although difficult to quantify, available evidence reveals that corporate financial crime is widespread. Studies reveal that 37 percent of the US population have been victims of some type of corporate fraud or theft (Rebovich and Kane, 2002). The collapse of Enron is the archetype of corporate financial crime, specifically illegal accounting practices. At its peak, Enron was one of the largest companies in the world, with shares trading over $90.00 before plummeting to $0.26 at bankruptcy. Enron's executives tricked regulators with fake holdings and off-the-books accounting practices to hide mountains of debt and toxic assets from investors and creditors. By the fall of 2000, the scheme was exposed, and the company collapsed, impacting thousands of investors and employees while upending trust in Wall Street. Although Enron was the most well known, its malfeasance was not an isolated event, with several "reputable" firms engaged in unethical and deceptive practices.

Likewise, the Great Recession was avoidable, precipitated by the government's failure to regulate the financial industry, especially predatory mortgage lending. Investment firms expanded to rival the depository banking system but were not under the same scrutiny or regulation. This shadowy banking system took on too much risk. Eventually, it failed, which impacted the flow of credit to consumers and businesses, who were already engaged in excessive borrowing at artificially low-interest rates. Several key players in the US finance industry could have been held liable and indicted for a range of serious frauds that triggered the 2008 financial crash. However, the crisis that financially ruined thousands of Americans prompted little or no criminal justice response. In the end, it was "business as usual" on Wall Street, with the government bailing out several firms and placing relatively modest regulations on the industry.[1] Unfortunately, the primary obstacle in the punishment of corporate wrongdoing is political will. Regulators require increased resources and logistical and partisan-governmental support to challenge some of the world's largest and most powerful corporations. At present, the system of corporate crime regulation guarantees minimal interference in the financial system. Only a tiny proportion of corporate thefts and frauds are penalized with nominal fines that have little impact on mega-corporations. These penalties are perceived as the cost of "doing business in America." In this way, most corporations are relatively free to engage in nefarious and criminal behavior with little to no penalty (Tombs & Whyte, 2020).

It is within this context that Hollywood depictions of corporate financial wrongdoing exist. However, it can be challenging to depict complex financial schemes to general audiences, especially in scripted films. Historically, films simplified corporate fraud or theft by utilizing an individual transgressor, which viewers could quickly identify as greedy, corrupt, and evil. Capitalism's systemic problems are reduced to depicting a "rotten apple" rather than a "rotten barrel." In this way, the line between white-collar crime and corporate crime is often blurred, with corporate culture or wrongdoing depictions misrepresented or distorted to fit Hollywood narratives and tropes. This chapter will examine films that depict financial wrongdoing perpetrated by corporations and their proxies. Essentially the actions of corporations weaken the economy, undermine the political process, and cheat taxpayers.

Bursting the "Bubble": The Great Recession in Film

On September 29, 2008, the Dow Jones Industrial Average fell 777.68 points, the largest single-day loss in Dow Jones history. The impact was catastrophic for many Americans, many of whom lost employment, retirement savings, and homes. The financial upheaval impacted many sectors, as investment houses collapsed and automakers were on the verge of bankruptcy. The federal government "bailed" out several companies, and the economy remained stagnant for years. The primary reason for the crash was the lack of regulation, which allowed lenders to relax standards and extend easy credit to consumers who were not qualified. The dream of homeownership became a reality for many unqualified buyers who were offered unconventional mortgages at subprime rates. At the same time, banks repackaged these mortgages and sold them to investors on the secondary market. Housing prices rapidly expanded, allowing the subprime mortgage market to thrive as an increase in home equity counterbalanced the accrual of bad debt. Rather than take losses on foreclosures, lenders could reap profit off the defaulting of mortgage loans by unqualified buyers. After the housing bubble burst, the economy crashed, and many regular Americans found themselves unable to pay their mortgages, and their houses were foreclosed. The financial misdealing that led to the so-called Great Recession of 2007–2008 was featured in several films, including *The Last Days of the Lehman Brothers* (2009), *Too Big to Fail* (2011), *Margin Call* (2011), and *The Big Short* (2015).

The first depiction of the financial crash was *The Last Days of the Lehman Brothers* which aired on the BBC in 2009. The quickly made-for-television movie was an account of the events that led to the declaration of bankruptcy by the prestigious and long-standing Lehman Brothers investment bank. The story is narrated by Zach (Michael Landes), a fictional employee who would occasionally break the fourth wall and speak directly to the viewer, explaining the intricacies of the complex fiduciary matters. This technique would also be used, much more effectively, in the Hollywood blockbuster, *The Big Short*. The BBC telefilm took place on the weekend preceding their bankruptcy on Monday, September 15, 2008. The stock has plummeted by 75 percent in one week, and CEO Dick Fuld (Corey Johnson) is running out of options, with large banks such as Bank of America and Barclays reluctance to take on much of Lehman's "toxic" assets. The film features the political wrangling that took place, with James Cromwell playing Treasury Secretary Henry Paulson. Paulson calls a meeting with the top investment banks, warning the group that Lehman is "not too big to fail" and that no bailout money is forthcoming. He bleakly persuades the top executives to aid their competitor by relieving Lehman of the toxic assets. Throughout the weekend, the banks engage in valuation to determine the extent of damage, with the trading of subprime mortgages being the primary culprit in the firm's downfall. Using narration by Zach's sister, Ezzy tells how she easily got a mortgage without a proper credit check and that risky mortgages, like hers, end up being bought and sold on Wall Street. This speculative and unregulated market led to the collapse, merger, and bailouts of the largest investment banks in the United States. The film reveals that Barclays had agreed to purchase Lehman Brothers, but British Law required shareholders to vote on the matter, which would delay the acquisition by a couple of days. Paulson refused to temporarily back Lehman, even for only two days, leading Fuld to declare the bankruptcy of Lehman Brothers. In the final narration, Zach reveals that the Fed bailed out other beleaguered firms after the collapse of Lehman.

Based on Andrew Ross Sorkin's book, *Too Big to Fail* chronicled the weeks preceding the 2008 financial meltdown that led to the Great Recession. The storyline is centered on the government response, featuring Treasury Secretary Henry Paulson (William Hurt) and Federal Reserve Chair Ben Bernanke (Paul Giamatti) attempts to avert the crisis. The film documents the inside negotiations and backroom deals between major banks, cabinet officials, and Congress. The HBO film was a rather tense depiction of the crisis, emphasizing the panic that encapsulated the most powerful stakeholders in the financial industry and government. Perversely, the companies that prompted the meltdown were allowed to dictate the bailout terms, even paying their CEOs large bonuses and stock options. The ending intertitle reveals that bank mergers continued and that only ten financial institutions control 77 percent of all US banking assets and have been declared "too big to fail." Unfortunately, the banks were not held accountable but were rewarded for a culture of greed that led to the economic devastation for millions of hardworking Americans. *Wall Street: Money Never Sleeps* (2010) featured Gordon Gekko being released from prison to warn the public of an impending economic collapse. The film was set with the backdrop of the recession, with archived clips from CNBC and CNN to demonstrate some realism. The story itself was a fictional telling of Gekko getting revenge on a former adversary while also reconciling with his estranged daughter. Although an entertaining melodrama, the film lacked insight into the economic collapse (Schurenberg, 2011).

Margin Call was set within an unnamed Manhattan bank in the hours leading to the financial crash. Although fictional, the film's plot closely resembled Goldman Sachs early move to hedge and reduce its position in mortgage-backed securities, which was based on the suggestion of two employees. It begins as a senior risk analyst, Eric Dale's (Stanley Tucci) employment is terminated. As Dale leaves the building, he leaves a flash drive with Peter Sullivan (Zachary Quinto) that reveals the firm's dubious mortgage practices. Working late, Sullivan learns that the firm's mortgage-backed securities are overleveraged, leading to the firm's potential bankruptcy. The upper management, Senior Manager, Sam Rogers (Kevin Spacey), division chief Jared Cohen (Simon Baker) and CEO John Tuld (Jeremy Irons) argue strategy, with Cohen and Tuld favoring a "fire sale" to rid themselves of the problematic assets and avoid insolvency. However, Rogers is concerned about the impact on the larger market, their reputation, and clients. In the end, Rogers reluctantly agrees to the fire sale and informs his traders to start selling off the assets, promising cash bonuses for employees that sell most of their assets by the end of the day. The "fire sale" results in massive losses for the firm, results in trader layoffs and triggers a stock market crash. The film shows the cutthroat and callous nature of the banking industry, where upper-level management is more concerned with covering their backs rather than looking out for their clients or the public's well-being. Roger Ebert (2011) penned, "I think the movie is about how its characters are concerned only by the welfare of their corporations. There is no sense of the public good. Corporations are amoral and exist to survive and succeed, at whatever human cost." Despite the intricate and complex topic, the film was rather suspenseful and tense, with compelling characterizations and dialogue.

Similarly, *The Big Short* was a compelling and entertaining film about the housing bubble and subsequent financial meltdown. The film was based on the book by renowned journalist Michael Lewis and featured an ensemble cast of characters that superbly narrated the story in a simplified manner. The film involved three primary storylines that preceded the housing market crash. The first storyline featured Scion Capital's Michael Burry (Christian Bale), a brilliant, eccentric hedge fund manager. Burry uncovers the incredible instability of the housing market, which was overburdened with high-risk subprime loans. He predicts that as interest rates rise, the market will collapse in the second quarter of 2007. Burry decides to create credit-default swaps, "insurance on the bond," permitting him to short or bet against the market-based mortgage-backed securities. Burry is considered "a crazy man" and invests 1.3 billion of Scion money and pays sizable monthly premiums to the banks, who happily take his "free" money. Simply put, Burry is gambling that the housing market will burst, and they will make an enormous profit. As predicted, the market collapses, and fund value increases by 489 percent, with a value over $2.69 billion.

The second storyline featured Mark Baum (Steve Carell), the hedge fund manager of FrontPoint Partners. Baum is approached by Jared Vennett (Ryan Gosling), an executive at Deutsche Bank, with a scheme to sell short on the housing market. Vennett learned of Burry's analysis and used his math expert to verify the housing bubble. Vennett tells Baum that the bank miscategorized the subprime loans at AAA ratings, guaranteeing their eventual collapse. The FrontPoint team travels to South Florida to perform a field investigation, learning that the mortgage industry is taking on increasingly riskier loans and profiting by selling these dodgy mortgages to Wall Street banks. Despite his hate of the banking industry, Baum agrees to buy the swaps from Vennett. In early 2007, mortgage defaults rose, but collateralized debt obligation (CDO) prices increased, and rating agencies refused to downgrade the bond ratings. Baum and his team conclude that banks and credit rating agencies are engaged in fraudulent activity to cover up the fact that the impending mortgage crisis will collapse the world economy. In the end, the market folds and FrontPoint earn over $1 billion in their swaps, with Baum bemoaning that the big banks will not be held accountable for their role in the economy's collapse.

The third storyline features Brownfield Capital, operated by young investors Charlie Geller (John Magaro) and Jamie Shipley (Finn Wittrock). The pair accidentally finds Vennett's marketing presentation on a large investment bank coffee table and decides to "short" the housing market. They are a low-level brokerage and are aided by retired securities trader Ben Rickert (Brad Pitt), another eccentric character disillusioned with the banking industry and Wall Street. They attend the American Securitization Forum in Las Vegas, where they discover that the SEC has no regulations to scrutinize mortgage-backed security activity. The pair take even more risk by shorting the higher-rated AA mortgage securities. As mortgage defaults rise, the pair angrily discover that the banks and rating agencies are fraudulently maintaining the value of their CDOs to sell before the unavoidable crash. The pair go to the press, with Jamie telling a Wall Street reporter:

> Casey, right now, every bank in town is unloading these shit bonds, onto unsuspecting customers. And they won't devalue them until they get them off their books. This level of criminality is unprecedented, even on fucking Wall Street.

The reporter rebuffed the pair, telling them that he does not want to jeopardize his position and contacts on Wall Street. In the end, the pair converted their $30 million investment into $80 million.

Excepting some creative license, the film was a startlingly accurate depiction of the financial misdealing in the bank and real estate sectors. For a scripted film, it provided a robust explanation of the global financial crisis. It was a scathing indictment of the banking industry, lack of government oversight, and Wall Street's greed. The predominant narrative was how the protagonists became even more prosperous by selling short on the American Dream of homeownership. In this way, the film is a celebration of greed and capitalism, as the protagonists appear as vultures, profiting off the remains of the American economy. That said, some of the characters were torn by their success, recognizing that their profit meant the downfall of the American economy. Apart from Vennett, the protagonists, particularly Baum and Rickert, were sympathetic toward regular folks, many of whom would lose their jobs, savings, and houses due to the fraud perpetrated by the banks. The postscript soberly tells the audience that $5 trillion in pension money, real estate value, 401k savings, and bonds had disappeared while over eight million Americans lost their jobs.

The consequences of the Great Recession were depicted in *99 Homes* (2011), an independent film that dramatized the foreclosure process. The film starred Michael Shannon as a predatory real estate agent, Rick Carver, who specializes in properties that are in foreclosure. Carver is cold-hearted and corrupt, taking advantage of loopholes in Fanny Mae regulations to make a small fortune. He even resorts to documentation fraud to ensure that his predatory business remains profitable. In the beginning, Carver dispassionately serves notice to Dennis Nash (Andrew Garfield), a young single father who works in construction but has fallen on hard times because of the recession. Unfortunately, Nash used his house as collateral for a loan, and he is now forced to relocate, with his mother and young son, to a motel filled with people in similar situations. Initially reluctant, Dennis begins to work for Carver, who mentors him on making money in the dirty business of foreclosures. Dennis is torn, as he clearly sympathizes with the plight of the former homeowners. However, his goal is to make enough money to buy back his former home and financially provide for his young son and mother. Carver is the epitome of a greedy and heartless capitalist, pithily claiming that the only way to get ahead is to "cheat" the system while scolding Dennis for feeling sorry for the evictees, telling Dennis that "America does not bail out losers." The scenes in which homeowners are dispossessed are both infuriating and heart-wrenching, as the evictees are entirely helpless to save their homes. Their possessions were strewn to the sidewalk like trash, and their lives were reduced to liabilities on a bank balance sheet. The film is essentially a morality play, as the viewer watches Dennis transform himself from a poor, unfortunate evictee to an efficient mentee of the very successful Rick Carver. The film highlights the real victims of the greed-driven 2007 recession, the regular folks that had misguided trust in the economy and the banking industry.

The "Money-Chase": Uber-Capitalism on Parade

In contemporary society, there is an ethos in which winning at any cost outweighs ethical and moral pronouncements, where success is measured by wealth. This "money chase" permeates every corner within society, in which the fetishization of the uber-wealthy is a popular narrative and cheating to get ahead is commonplace. The culture of cheating allows greed, dishonesty, and corruption to thrive. At the same time, regulatory agencies, such as the SEC, do not have the resources or political backing to stop the rampant abuse in the financial sector. Within this context, popular films will occasionally deliver depictions of the extravagances and greed of corporations and their executives. One of the best examples was the critically acclaimed, *Barbarians at the Gate* (1993). Set in 1988, the film starred James Garner as F. Ross Johnson, the President and CEO of RJR Nabisco. Self-made, Johnson is a natural salesman who enjoys the perks of being in charge. He is extravagant in spending the company's money, telling an executive that "the company is making so much money, we're shitting green. Hell, this [extravagant party'] comes out of petty cash ... every penny you think I am pissing away here comes back to us dressed up like a nickel." Johnson is worried that the market failure of the corporation's new smokeless cigarette will lower the stock price and jeopardize his position in the company. He decides to buy the company and move it from a publicly traded to a private company. This leads to a leveraged buyout – the acquisition of another company using borrowed money – with the acquired company's assets being used as collateral. Initially, Johnson meets with Henry Kravis, a billionaire who made his fortune as a corporate raider. Kravis explains his scheme to Johnson:

Henry Kravis: Everyone benefits when management takes over. It's simply a question of arriving at an attractive price to pay the stockholders to buy out their shares. I work the same way that you work with Don. Some of the money we borrow, some we raise from the public sale of securities, we pay off the debt incurred from buying the company with cash from its ongoing operation. And by selling out pieces of the business.
F. Ross Johnson: that's French for firing people, isn't it, Henry?
Henry Kravis: As few as possible, of course.
F. Ross Johnson: A few dozen, ten thousand?
Henry Kravis: As I said, as few as possible.
F. Ross Johnson: I couldn't do that. I couldn't live with the fallout.
Henry Kravis: I'll take care of that.
F. Ross Johnson: I don't shave your face in my mirror every morning. Wouldn't be your face in my mirror every morning. All that aside, I have never been a fan of debt.
Henry Kravis: Debt can be an asset. Debt tightens a company.
Johnson: Does wonders of the sphincter too [laughing]

Johnson does not trust Kravis, concerned that his control of the company, and the perks (corporate jet, golf club memberships), will be threatened. He is also sympathetic to the thousands of employees who may lose their jobs as collateral damage from the leveraged buyout. He decides to partner with Jim Robinson, the CEO of Shearson Lehman Hutton, a division of American Express. They offer $75 a share, which appears to be a substantial profit for the company. The deal is leaked to the press, which leads to a bidding war between Kravis and Johnson. Kravis is slighted because he believes that he gave Ross the idea of the leveraged buyout. However, other potential buyers emerge, including Ted Forstmann (David Rasche), who cannot hide his disdain for Kravis,

Ted: If Henry Kravis was CEO of any other company in the country except his own, they'd put him in a straight jacket. They'd take him away in a rubber limo. Henry Kravis pays out these incredible sums because his money is all junk bond crap! It's phony, he's phony! He's a fuckin fraud!

Ross: If you don't like him, don't beat around the bush, Teddy.
Ted: No, it's no, it's not personal. My focus is not on that goddamn megalomaniac. No, what kills me is these quick buck artists, like Kravis, they don't give a rat's ass about the companies they buy. Okay, hey, I have said this in the Wall Street Journal. All they want is their steady flow of these outrageous fees, they couldn't care less if they are going to throw the whole country into a depression. Let me tell you about Forstmann Little. At Forstmann Little, what you get is reality. My brother and I are real people with real money!
Ross: Alright, we'll talk, alright.

Later in the film, Ted tells Ross, "Ross, don't you see this is our last chance. The bastards are at the city gates. Let's stand at the bridge together. Let's stand at the bridge and push the barbarians back!" In the end, Johnson and his investors offer $112 a share. However, the RJR Nabisco board of directors took a lower bid, $109 from Kravis, because they were offended by an unflattering *New York Times* article that smeared Johnson and his apparent greed. The postscript of the film read,

> By the end of the 1980s, American business piled up nearly one trillion dollars in debt ... For his settlement with RJR Nabisco, Ross Johnson received fifty-three million dollars ... But that was only around twenty-three million after taxes.

The film was an excellent depiction of vulture capitalism, simplifying complex financial narratives for viewers.

Also produced by HBO, *Weapons of Mass Distraction* (1997) stars Gabriel Byrne as Lionel Powers and Ben Kingsley as Julian Messenger, a pair of media moguls intent on destroying each other. The rivals are competing to buy the Tucson Titans, a fictional pro football team. Certainly not as powerful as *Barbarians at the Gate*, the film was a satirical morality tale that highlighted blackmail, greed, and corruption in the media industry. Likewise, *Greed* (2019) was a dark comedy that served as a critique of the fashion industry. The film used flashbacks to depict the life of Sir Richard "Greedy" McCreadie (Steve Coogan), a billionaire fashion mogul who is accused of financial and ethical wrongdoing. McCreadie's company is ruthlessly exploiting sweatshop workers in Southeast Asia while engaging in tax avoidance, asset stripping, and embezzlement of company funds. At a public hearing, the character is admonished by a government official, "You've been described as the unacceptable face of capitalism ... you've been described as Sir Greedy, Sir Shifty, Greedy McCreadie." The film highlighted the plight of Syrian refugees against the backdrop of McCreadie's extravagant 60th birthday party on the Greek Island of Mykonos. The film's postscript delivers a powerful message about exploitation in fast fashion, migrants, and global wealth inequality.

The Enron scandal was depicted in the made-for-television movie, *The Crooked E: The Unshredded Truth about Enron* (2003). The film aired on CBS and was based on a book written by former Enron employee Brian Cruver. Although the key players in the scandal are depicted, both owner Kenneth Lay (Mike Ferrell) and CEO Jeffery Skilling (Jon Ted Wynne) play secondary roles. Instead, the scandal is told through the recent hire, Brian Cruver (Christian Kane). The wide-eyed Cruver is hired into his dream job, working for a world-class corporation. He is mesmerized by the glitz, glamor of the corporate world, where the top brass appears to be industry leaders and icons to the young Cruver. The film attempted to capture the excesses and debauchery of the corporate executives, with their propensity to hire ex-strippers and throw wild parties. Enron went bankrupt after it was revealed that it was engaged in accounting fraud that vastly inflated its revenues while minimizing its debt. The telefilm features a fictional Enron executive, Mr. Blue (Brian Dennehy), who commiserates with Brian, explaining the scheme.

> The system was corrupt, almost from the very beginning. It was designed to make people rich. Certain people rich. Based on the price of the stock. Any actual earnings, any real profits for the company that was a secondary consideration. Just, just keep the stock price going up. Co-opt the auditors, pay-off the sleazeball politicians, and dazzle the media and Wall Street, keep the lie going, just keep the lie going, and the bonuses, the stock options that keep coming ... there's hundreds of Enrons out there, thousand – cooking the books, inflating the earnings, hiding their debt, buying off the watchdogs.

In the end, the employees were terminated, but some of the top-level executives were paid handsome bonuses to stay on during the bankruptcy. At the end of the film, Brian quickly tells the viewer about the fallout, including the $40 billion that California paid in inflated energy costs, which ended in cuts to schools, hospitals, and daycare facilities.

The Enron saga inspired the comedy, *Fun with Dick and Jane* (2005), a remake of a 1977 film of the same title. The film depicts a well-off couple, Dick (Jim Carrey) and Jane (Tea Leoni), who turn to a life of crime after Dick loses his position as Vice President of Communication for Globodyne, a media conglomerate. The newly appointed VP is told to appear on the television program *Moneylife* to tout the quarterly profits of the company, where he is surprised to learn that the CEO of Globodyne, Jack McCallister (Alec Baldwin), made $400 million after he covertly sold 80 percent of his shares after he pilfered all the assets. Dick is confronted by Ralph Nader, who tells him, "I do not know how you sleep at night, sir. I believe that corporations like Globodyne pervert the American Dream. They leverage our futures, so the super-rich get richer. You are a disgrace." Dick and his wife, Jane, are unable to secure employment and comically turn to armed robbery. Meanwhile, McCallister gets away with the crime, as Dick and CFO Frank Bascombe (Richard Jenkins) take the blame for the fraud. Facing charges from the SEC, Dick tricks McCallister into transferring the $400 million into the Globodyne's defunct pension plan. The employees receive large cheques, while McCallister's worth drops to a meager $2,238.04. The ending credits roll, with special thanks given to Arthur Anderson, Enron, Adelphia, Cendant, HealthSouth, WorldCom, and their executives.

Corporate apologists contend that the vast corruption at Enron was an outlier. However, research has found that Fortune 500 companies with strong growth profiles are generally more likely to "cook the books" than smaller companies. The study found that larger corporations have a four times higher rate of securities fraud violations than smaller corporations. The bigger the corporation, the higher the likelihood of financial fraud (Schwartz et al., 2020). Essentially, many high-profile and seemingly "respectable" corporations engage in fraudulent accounting practices to deceive investors. The consequences can be very damaging, as regular folks lose their jobs and retirement savings, and the trust in the economy is eroded. The multinational food processing corporation Archer Daniels Midland (ADM) provides a case study in corporate corruption. Founded in 1902, ADM has been embroiled in many scandals. In 1920, the US Department of Justice charged that the company violated the Sherman Antitrust Act when it colluded to raise the price of linseed oil between 1916 and 1918, from 50 cents to $1.80 per gallon. In 2013, the SEC charged ADM for failing to prevent bribes paid by their foreign subsidiaries, violating the Foreign Corrupt Practices Act. The corporation also has an abysmal environmental record, paying millions in fines for violating federal and state clean-air regulations. Moreover, since 1980, it is estimated that ADM has cost the American economy billions of dollars with price gouging, government subsidies, and not paying their fair share of taxes. The CATO Institute estimates that at least 43 percent of ADM's annual profits are heavily subsidized – taxpayers pay $30 for every $1 profit that ADM reaps (Bovard, 1995). The *Washington Post* reported that in 2016, ADM sold property worth $5.5 million to incoming Secretary of Agriculture Sonny Perdue for only $250,000. Under Perdue's reign, ADM benefited from the loosening of regulations on pork production, fewer inspections, and not implementing a glyphosate ban (Butler, 2021).

However, ADM is most infamous for its role in a massive price-fixing scheme depicted in the highly entertaining film, *The Informant* (2009). Set in the 1990s, the film revealed how ADM colluded with other companies to inflate the price of lysine, a food additive used in commercial agriculture. The film starred Matt Damon as Mark Whitacre, a quirky executive who blew the whistle on the price-fixing scheme. Calling himself a "white hat," Whitacre assists the FBI in gathering video and audio evidence that led to senior ADM executives being charged and sent to federal prisons. The company was also fined over $100 million, which at the time was the largest antitrust fine in the United States. In a twist, while working for the FBI, Whitacre embezzled over $9 million from the company. Trying to mitigate the damages, Whitacre's lawyer Jim Epstein argued,

> C'mon, I'm not stupid. Mark committed a crime. He stole nine million dollars. That's indefensible. But these guys at ADM, they stole hundreds of millions of dollars … from innocent people all around the world. Mark showed you that four white guys in suits getting together in the middle of the day … That's not a business meeting. It's a crime scene.

148 *Harm to the Economy*

The increasingly delusional Whitacre continues to lie about everything, even claiming that the FBI coerced him and physically assaulted him. He was incarcerated for eight-and-a-half years in federal prison. In the concluding scene, the imprisoned Whitacre appeals for a pardon on video,

> I don't think what happened is fair ... when you look at me compared to Mick and Terry [ADM's top executives]. I mean, if you go and hold up your local grocery store ... you get maybe five years in prison. Mick and Terry held up every grocery store in the world, and they got three. So you tell me how it makes sense that I get nine.

At around the same time that Whitacre was whistleblowing against ADM, the Bre-X Mining scandal commenced. In March of 1993, Bre-X Minerals acquired the mining rights to a site in the province of East Kalimantan, Indonesia. In October 1995, the company reported that a large deposit of gold was uncovered, which resulted in a colossal surge in the company's stock, from 30 cents per share to more than $280. Touted as the richest gold deposit in history, the discovery turned out to be a fraud, and thousands of investors had lost their hard-earned savings. Moreover, the Canadian financial sector was disgraced, as billions of dollars were lost, including millions by three major public sector organizations. The Ontario Teachers' Pension Plan lost a staggering $100 million, the Quebec Public Sector Pension fund lost $70 million, and the Ontario Municipal Employees Retirement Board lost $45 million. The convoluted story involved fraudulent samples, international intrigue, corporate cover-ups, and a mysterious suicide. In the end, no one was held accountable for the massive fraud (Wilton, 2017). The Bre-X mining scandal inspired *Gold* (2016), which starred Matthew McConaughey as Kenny Wells, a down-on-his-luck owner of the Washoe prospecting company. After his girlfriend has a "dream," Kenny visits Indonesia, where he goes into business with geologist Michael Acosta (Edgar Ramirez) to pursue a gold prospect. Analogous to the actual story, Acosta "salts" the claim by planting gold in the samples, making it appear to be an extremely profitable venture. Later, Acosta's corpse is found in the jungle, with his hands and face chewed off by wild animals. It is assumed that he jumped (or fell) from the helicopter after being arrested by Indonesian authorities. The FBI told Kenny that Acosta had sold his stocks for $164 million before absconding. The FBI does not charge Wells, as he was not involved in Acosta's fraudulent activities. In the culminating scene, Kenny opens an envelope with a napkin that simply reads 50/50, the initial contract with Acosta. Under the napkin, there is a deposit slip for $82 million put in an international bank. The rags to riches story feature unethical business dealings, including corporate expropriation and monopolization, political interference, and huge profits based on fraud and insider trading.

Similarly, *Percy vs. Goliath* (2020) is also a loose adaptation of a true story. The film tells the story of elderly farmer Percy Schmeiser's (Christopher Walken) fight against corporate giant Monsanto. Set in 1998, in the Canadian town of Bruno, Saskatchewan, the film featured Schmeiser's legal fight against Monsanto, who alleged that Percy had infringed on Monsanto's patent on GMO seed, Roundup Ready Canola. He enlists the help of lawyer Jackson Weaver (Zach Braff), who advises him to settle with the giant conglomerate rather than fight a losing battle. However, Schmeiser stubbornly refuses, and the case goes to court, where Percy claims that he is a "seed saver" and that a windstorm blew the Monsanto seed from the neighboring farm, which resulted in cross-contamination. After losing the case, Percy faces seemingly insurmountable odds with few supporters, escalating debts and his reputation in tatters. However, an environmental activist, Rebecca Salcau (Christina Ricci), arrives in town and offers to help the beleaguered Percy. She convinces Percy to publicly speak out against Monsanto to gain public support and much-needed funds to fight the case in court. Initially hesitant, Percy becomes a vocal opponent of Monsanto greed and GMO seeds, starting a tour of 28 cities to spread his story. Despite his wife's reluctance, Percy attends a conference in India and learns firsthand how Monsanto exploits farmers in the poorest regions of the globe. Percy passionately tells the audience:

> Folks! Don't' fight! Don't do it. It's what they want … for us to fuss and argue, cause, while we fight, they take over. In this country, people die. They get into debt to Monsanto, they lose land. Sometimes, they end their life. For me, I understand that I might lose my farm. Now, if they take my farm, if they take my land, that is it. There's nothing left. So, I get it. No one's gonna help us but us. We gotta stop fighting. Do not give them what they want.

On return from India, Percy learns that he has lost a federal appeal and is on the verge of losing his farm. Against the advice of his lawyer, he and his wife decide to take the case to the Supreme Court of Canada. His lawyer dramatically resigns, but Percy crumples his letter and throws it in the trash. In the end, the Supreme Court ruled that the Schmeiser's can keep their farm but must return the seeds to Monsanto. In reality, in a 5–4 decision, the Supreme Court upheld the lower court's ruling that Percy had infringed on the patent. However, in the 9–0 decision, the court ruled that Schmeiser did not benefit from the seeds, and he did not have to pay damages to Monsanto. More importantly, his fight inspired thousands of wheat farmers to stop using Monsanto's genetically modified seeds. The ending intertitle reveals that since 1996, farmers have paid $85 million to $160 million in settlements to Monsanto and that GMO wheat has not entered the market. While *Percy vs. Goliath* takes ample amounts of creative license, features a predictable storyline, and oversimplifies the story, the film is a cautionary tale of corporate control and monopolization of the food industry (Allan, 2020). Essentially, the movie was an anti-corporate morality play that has the "little guy" standing up to corporate monopolies who utilize their unlimited resources, political power, and an army of legal experts to squash small independent business entrepreneurs.

The so-called "Panama Papers" scandal was depicted in Netflix's *The Laundromat* (2019). The film exposed the machinations of the law firm Mossack & Fonseca. In 2016, a whistleblower released over 11 million documents that detailed a shady world in which the rich use shell companies to avoid paying taxes. The film is narrated by founding partners Jürgen Mossack (Gary Oldman) and Ramón Fonseca (Antonio Banderas), who explain the shady manner in which shell companies and offshore accounts help corporations and the rich avoid taxes. Albeit a comedy, the film reveals how tax evasion, bribery, and greed are embedded in a corrupt global financial system. The film featured three fictional vignettes that highlighted corruption at the highest levels. The first vignette starred Meryl Streep as Ellen Martin, a grandmother who lost her husband in a tragic tourist boat accident. She cannot get compensation from the boating company, as the boat company owners are insured through a fraudulent shell company. She becomes obsessed with learning the truth, beginning an investigation into the United Reinsurance Group of Nevis, one of the thousands of shell companies that Mossack and Fonseca had formed. She becomes educated into the complex world of tax avoidance, shell companies, and the lack of accountability in the banking industry. The second vignette features an adulterous affair between Charles, an African billionaire and Astrid, the best friend of his daughter Simone. After Simone discovers the affair, Charles gives her a $20 million company to keep the secret but she soon discovers that the company is worthless, as it is also a shell company. The third and final vignette is a fictional retelling of the murder of Neil Heywood (given the name Maywood), a British businessman who serves as an intermediary for wealthy Chinese to hide their money in offshore accounts. The tale ends with the arrest of Gu Xilai and her husband Bo on charges of murder and corruption.

The film concludes with the Panama Papers being leaked by a whistleblower named "John Doe" to the press. While Mossack and Fonseca are briefly imprisoned, it is revealed that "John Doe" was Marla, an office worker at the law firm. In the last scene, Marla breaks the fourth wall, takes off her wardrobe, and the viewer discovers Meryl Streep playing a dual role in the film. Streep offers an impassioned soliloquy about global and political corruption involved in tax evasion. Streep laments that the checks and balances within democracy are failing, imploring viewers to ensure real action in upcoming elections, pithily stating that "reform of America's broken campaign finance system cannot wait." Just as the *Big Short*, the film used comedy to simplify the complex financial schemes. Unfortunately, the lighthearted nature of the film took away the gravity that the schemes wreak on the world economy. That said, the film should be commended as it exposed the vicious cycle of greed, in which the wealthy pay off politicians to protect their money in tax shelters. Hailed as a banking bombshell, the release of the Panama Papers did little to halt the practice of tax avoidance by the wealthy. The ending intertitle reads, that "In 2018, 60 of the largest companies in the USA paid no taxes on pre-tax income of 70 billion dollars."

The Oil-for-Food scandal was depicted in *Backstabbing for Beginners* (2018), adapted from Michael Soussan's memoir, *Backstabbing for Beginners: My Crash Course in International Diplomacy*. The book detailed the widespread corruption and financial fraud he discovered while working for the Oil-for-Food Program under the United Nations in Iraq. The film starred Theo James as

Michael Sullivan, an idealistic yet naïve 24-year-old who works under Costas "Pasha" Pasaris (Sir Ben Kingsley). Pasha was loosely based on Benon Sevan, the corrupt chief of the UN Oil for Food Programme. Initially, Per Fly sought to make a documentary about the geopolitical scandal but settled on a fictionalized story, employing real-life footage of events depicted in the film. The vision was to evoke a grey area around the Pasha character as a humanitarian and a grifter and mentor to Sullivan. In one scene, Pasha even tears up after seeing a young Iraqi girl needing serious medical care. The complicated plot involved politicians, bureaucrats, diplomats, and other nefarious characters. The level of corruption was horrifying in its magnitude. The money was intended to supply food and medicine to regular Iraqi citizens dually suffering under Saddam Hussein's regime and the international sanctions meant to cripple the country. Sullivan quickly learns that the program is corrupted, with supplies not being equally distributed and funds misallocated. With the help of his interpreter and love interest, Nashim (Belcim Bilgin), his suspicions of widespread corruption are confirmed. Although corporate wrongdoing was not the primary storyline, big businesses and banks were implicitly involved in the scheme, with a system of kickbacks, bribes, and oil vouchers that were dispersed to various stakeholders. In one pivotal scene, Pasha refuses to become an informant, telling the newly installed head of the Iraqi state that the conspirators are "protected by multinational companies who have governments who protect them." Shortly after, the new leader of Iraq is murdered in a car bomb. Sullivan is demoralized by the level of avarice and corruption, angrily claiming that the invasion of Iraq was just a "coalition of the fucking greedy, no one gives a shit about Iraq. Everyone just wants the money and the crude." In the end, Michael is transformed into a whistleblower, delivering evidence to the *Wall Street Journal*. The slow-moving film concludes with Michael telling the viewer that the corruption was so widespread that it involved "two-thousand companies and fifty-six countries." Unfortunately, like *The Laundromat*, *Backstabbing for Beginners* had a noble vision, but the execution was flawed, limiting the film's appeal to a broader audience.

Conversely, *Syriana* (2005) was a brilliantly scripted film that employed multiple, parallel storylines between Iran, Texas, Washington, DC, Switzerland, Spain, and Lebanon. The primary plot is corruption in the oil industry, interspersed with the dirty dealing of the CIA, Islamic militants, lobbyists, political maneuvering, high finance, lobbying, and revolution. The storyline centers around the dubious merger between Connex, a large oil company and Killen, a smaller oil company that inexplicably had been granted drilling rights in Kazakhstan. Connex has lost control of oil fields in a Persian Gulf Kingdom that the Al-Subaai family rules. The Emirate's foreign minister and eldest son, Prince Nasir (Alexander Siddig), granted natural gas drilling rights to a Chinese company. The decision angers both the US Oil Industry and the US government, propelling a CIA assassination of Nasir, which involves veteran CIA officer Bob Barnes (George Clooney). Meanwhile, the Department of Justice investigates the merger between Connex and Killen, and Connex hires the law firm Whiting Sloan to deflect allegations of corruption. The founder of the firm, Dean Whiting (Christopher Plummer) instructs lawyer, Bennett Holiday (Jeffrey Wright) to find out

> A very big company Connex, our client ... loses a huge natural-gas contract in the Persian Gulf ... to the Chinese. At the same time ... a smaller company Killen, somehow gets the rights to Kazakhstan ... one of the largest untapped oil fields in the world. The big company, our client, merges with Killen ... Justice wants to know how Killen got those rights. You've been scrutinizing exactly these types of deals ... so if there is something to find ... I expect you to get it before they do. And come straight to me.

Holiday's investigation reveals that a Killen associate Danny Dalton bribed Kazakh officials, securing the drilling rights. Dalton is irate when he learns that he is being charged with corruption,

> Corruption charges – corruption? Corruption is government intrusion into market efficiencies in the form of regulation. That's Milton Friedman. He got a Goddamn Nobel prize. We have laws against it precisely so we can get away with it. Corruption is our protection. Corruption keeps us safe and warm. Corruption is why you and I are prancing around in here instead of fighting over scraps of meat out on the street. Corruption is why we win.

Dalton is offered to the DOJ as the fall guy, but the US Attorney wants a more prominent figure to bring to justice. The CEO of Killen Oil, Jimmy Pope (Chris Cooper), suggests that a high-level partner at Whiting Sloan would be an appropriate choice. In the end, Holiday gives up his mentor Sydney Hewitt, a leading lawyer at Whiting Sloan, protecting both the corporation and the law firm, Holiday, telling Pope that "we are looking for the illusion of due diligence, Mr. Pope. Two criminal acts successfully prosecuted ... it gives us that illusion." True to real-life, corporations that are guilty of wrongdoing will deliver a scapegoat to minimize damages – "a page right out of the current real-life big firm playbook – plead the individual, save the corporation" (CCR, 2005).

Head Office (1985) was an unheralded comedy about corruption in the corporate world. The film opens as two corporate executives watch a corporate promotional video in the back of a limousine. The video features INC International CEO Peter "Pete" Helmes (Eddie Albert) touting his 10,000 products and claiming that "INC is the company that cares about people." Afterwards, the corporate executives discuss the co-option of a Senator for political favors:

CFO Scott Dantley: Mr. Helmes (CEO of INC International) wants Senator Issel's full cooperation when we make our Latin American move. What'd you get on him?
COO Bob Nixon: Yes, sir. He's Washington's strongest supporter of big business. That's his voting record. We contributed $150,000 to his last campaign and laundered it through our Mexican banks. These are the cancelled checks. His

wife's a heavy boozer. Those are copies of her liquor store bills. He's having an affair with a D.C. hooker named Kitten Davis. Those are the Polaroids. He's been bribed by all the major oil companies. These are the telephone transcripts and, of course, the standard men's room shots.
CFO Scott Dantley: Fine.
COO Bob Nixon: And his son's graduation is this month.

To curry favor with the Senator, the corporation hires the Senator's son, Jack Issel (Judge Reinhold), a slacker who recently graduated from business school. He is mentored by Max Landsberger (Richard Masur), who provides advice on how to move up the corporate ladder.

The film's primary plot involves INC relocating their Allenville plant to San Marcos, a fictional Latin American country, where workers' pay is 10 cents an hour. Helmes is planning to orchestrate a coup of San Marcos, claiming, "it's just a realignment of American interests abroad." He tells his young protégé,

> The Third World, Jack. The last frontier. That's where the Allenville plant is going. The corporation that controls the Third World in the next century, Jack, controls the globe. Think of that. One-world economy under INC. One corporation under God. One moral, spiritual, economic unity.

Jack is tasked with going to Allenville to conduct damage control, where he inadvertently gives an impromptu interview to local news media. To the chagrin of Max, Jack tells the reporter, "In business school, we learned that the main goal of corporations is to maximize profits and survive. So, uh, they act in their own self-interest … INC operates purely on a profit motive." Max scolds Jack, "Damn it, Jack. We went out there to tell them our side of the story. We didn't go out there to tell them the truth." In a typical 1980s formula, Jack falls in love with Rachel (Lori-Nan Engler), an activist who is protesting the closing of the plant, and the film concludes with an action scene, where Jack and Rachel are chased by INC security, escaping to inform the media about the company's nefarious plans. In a twist, it is revealed that Rachel is the radical left-wing daughter of Helmes. After her father is forced to resign, Rachel, now the majority stockholder, appoints Jack as the new CEO and reopens the Allenville plant. Certainly not a cinematic masterpiece, the film was one of the few satires about the ruthlessness of corporate culture.

Similarly, set in 1958, *The Hudsucker Proxy* (1994) is a comedy that features corporate shenanigans and deceits. The film opens with Waring Hudsucker, the CEO of Hudsucker Industrial, committing suicide by jumping out of a window on the 44th floor. The executives learn that the CEO's death triggers the shares to be publicly traded in one month. The stock price is too high, and the executives are unable to purchase a controlling interest. Sidney J. Mussberger (Paul Newman) schemes to depress the price of the stock, telling the executives, "what we need now is a new president who will inspire panic in the stockholder … some jerk, we can really push around." Meanwhile, Norville Barnes, a naïve business graduate from Muncie, Indiana is hired to work in the mailroom. Norville is to deliver Mussberger a "blue" letter but rather than delivering the letter, he pitches an idea to Mussberger – a drawing of a circle – which he describes as a "children's toy." Believing Barnes to be an idiot, Mussberger hires Norville as the new puppet CEO of Hudsucker Industries. The plan works, and the stock starts to plummet, even to the point where the executives sell their shares so that they can repurchase them at a much lower rate. In a clever twist, the circle drawing turns out to be a simple but brilliant design for the hula hoop, initially called the extruded plastic dingus. The failing company's stock surges, and Barnes becomes an uncaring tycoon, dismissing an elevator operator who invented the bendable straw. However, Barnes learns that he is just a "puppet" and will lose his position as CEO once the company is opened for public trading. In a fantastical ending, Barnes is chased to the top floor of the Hudsucker skyscraper, where he climbs out a window and accidentally falls, time is stopped, and Waring Hudsucker appears to Norville as an angel, instructing him to read the blue letter. The letter reveals that Waring's shares were to be transferred to his successor to avoid the company from being publicly traded. Ironically, Mussburger was the likely successor but had schemed to put Barnes in the position. In the end, Mussburger attempts suicide and is confined to a mental asylum, while Barnes comes up with another invention for kids, the frisbee.

Corporations without a Conscience: Lobbying

Corporations spend excessive amounts of money on public relations to portray themselves as an instrument of hope, prosperity, and opportunity. In reality, corporations hoard their wealth, avoid paying taxes, and wield undue influence over public policy (Burley & Hoedeman, 2021; Wall et al., 2019). An Oxfam report of 50 large corporations, including Pfizer, Goldman Sachs, Dow Chemical, Chevron, Walmart, IBM, and Procter & Gamble, revealed that these "American" corporations have stockpiled more than $1 trillion offshore and utilized upwards of 1,600 subsidiaries in tax havens to avoid paying taxes. The Oxfam report found that tax-dodging corporations cost US taxpayers approximately $100 billion each year. The average American taxpayer was forced to pay out an extra $760 year to recoup the lost taxes. The report also found that from 2008 to 2014, these companies amassed $11 trillion in federal loans, loan guarantees, and bailout assistance. The 50 corporations reaped $27 in loan aid for every $1 paid in federal taxes (Oxfam, 2021). The corporate tax rate has dramatically fallen, from a high of 52 percent in the 1950s to approximately 21 percent in 2019. Meanwhile, the proportion that the working poor pay in payroll taxes has risen (Hungerford, 2013).

Corporations also exert widespread and dangerous levels of influence over public policy. The Oxfam report found that for every $1 corporations spend on lobbying, they obtain $130 in tax breaks and even more than $4000 in federal loans, loan guarantees and bailouts. According to the Center for Responsive Politics, from 1998 to 2016, corporations spent hundreds of millions of dollars to have their interests met in Washington (Evers-Hillstrom, 2019). Both Democrat and Republican lawmakers adopt policies that make corporations and billionaires richer while harming American workers and consumers. Politicians who are bought and paid impose irresponsible tax cuts, rob governments of revenue for public goods and services, making communities and workplaces less safe through deregulation and assaults on unions. The crooked game of political lobbying and corporate welfare contributes to greater economic inequality and corporate impunity. In this way, corporate lobbyists are akin to "corruption consultants" that exploit and manipulate public policy to benefit the rich and powerful. Lobbying requires a combination of charm, relentless persistence, threats, and, most importantly, mountains of cash. Corporate lobbyists know how to effectively coax politicians to place business interests ahead of human rights, consumer health, workers' rights, and the environment.

The lobbyist is a central figure in films that depict politics and government. Several comedic films explore the role of lobbying in Washington, including *Duck Soup* (1933), *Mr. Smith Goes to Washington* (1939), *Dave* (1993), *Wag the Dog* (1997), *Primary Colors* (1998), and *Head of State* (2003). *The American President* (1995) features a romantic relationship between Democratic President Andrew Shepherd (Michael Douglas) and environmental lobbyist Sydney Ellen Wade (Annette Benning). The comedy depicted the "Capra-like" machinations of the political process with a melodramatic twist. After he betrays – and loses – his love interest, Shepherd surprisingly pushes forward controversial legislation to cut fossil fuels by 20 percent while withdrawing his support for an ineffective gun control bill. His romance with Sydney is rekindled, and once again, viewers experience a prototypical Hollywood happy ending. The shady business of lobbying is also a primary feature in the comedies, *Thank You for Smoking* (2005), *Casino Jack* (2010), *The Distinguished Gentlemen* (1992), and *Bulworth* (1998).

In film, the lobbyist is a charming figure who knows how to play the game, convincing politicians to "bend the knee" for the benefit of their clients. This is best exemplified by *Casino Jack* (2010), loosely based on Jack Abramoff (Kevin Spacey). Abramoff was convicted in a corruption scandal that also involved two White House officials, nine lobbyists, and congressional staffers. Abramoff was sentenced to six years for fraud, conspiracy, and tax evasion after it was revealed that he traded expensive gifts, meals, and sports trips in exchange for political favors. The fictionalized true story highlights corruption in politics, lobbying, and among big business. The story itself focused on Abramoff and Michael Scanlon's (Barry Pepper) lobbying for Native American casino gambling. The lobbyists overcharged the tribes, covertly splitting the multi-million-dollar profits and illegally giving gifts and making campaign donations to Republican Congressmen. The film focused on the fraudulent lobbying efforts activities within casino gambling, not corporate lobbyists. However, the film itself was a good illustration of the power the lobbyists hold over the political sphere, illustrated by the opening narration by Abramoff about lobbying,

> Next to God, faith and country, nothing is more important than influence. Political influence. Influence with the powerful is like influence with God.

Without it, there is only eternal hellfire damnation and congressional logjam. Here the influence we wield is more important than the air you breathe. As a licensed lobbyist, I am legally allowed to accept money from special interests in order to influence Congress on their behalf. I'm essentially a conduit to motivating sleepy lawmakers into getting bills passed and legislation done. The reality is without lobbyists, the wheels in Washington would come to a grinding halt. Why? Because the most powerful members of Congress rely on lobbyists like me for information to guide them on how to vote and how they vote sometimes requires taking them on fact-finding missions. Like house majority leader, Tom DeLay we brought to the Northern Mariana Islands in the South Pacific, a U.S territory where my textile clients produce American-made designer clothes without having to pay minimum wage. For example, your top of line stonewash jeans can stay on sale for $19.95 simply because labor costs in the Mariana's remain low. Lobbying is nothing more than American style democracy in action, and the more influence that we have, the bigger the smiles on our kid's faces.

Thank You for Smoking (2005) was a black comedy that depicted tobacco lobbyist Nick Naylor (Aaron Eckhart). The film satirized lobbyists, with Nick commiserating with other lobbyists, an informal club euphonically called the Merchants of Death or MOD squad. The club also includes Polly Bailey (Maria Bello), a spokesperson for the alcohol industry and Bobby Jay Bills (David Koechner), who represents S.A.F.E.T.Y. (Society for the Advancement of Firearms and Effective Training for Youth). The trio meets over drinks, comparing strategies to mitigate the harms inflicted by their various industries. In one scene, they argue about the deadliness of their industries:

Polly: Listen, we're all going to need bodyguards soon enough. Did you see the coverage the fetal alcohol people got themselves over this weekend? They made it seem like we were encouraging pregnant women to drink. I am surprised I didn't get kidnapped on my way to work this morning.
Nick: I don't think people from the alcohol beverage industry need to worry about being kidnapped just yet.
Polly: Pardon me?
Nick: Look, I mean nothing personal, but tobacco generates a little more heat than alcohol.
Polly: Oh, this is news.
Nick: My product puts away 475,000 a year.
Polly: Oh, okay, now 475 is a legit number.
Nick: Okay, 435,000. That's 1,200 a day. How many alcohol-related deaths a year?
Polly: Well, does that …
Nick: 100,000 tops? That's what 270 a day? Wow, Wee 270 people, a tragedy. Excuse me if I don't exactly see terrorists getting excited about kidnapping anyone from the alcohol industry.

Polly: Well, you haven't even taken into account the number of deaths
Bobby Jay: Okay, lets just …
Nick: How many gun deaths in the US?
Bobby Jay: 11,000
Nick: 11,000 are you kidding me? 30 a day. That's less than passenger car mortalities. No terrorist would bother with either of you. [pauses to reflect on hurting his friend's feelings] Okay, look … stupid argument.
Polly: I'll say.
Nick: I'm sure both of you warrant vigilante justice.
Polly: Thank you.

The merchants of death represented a stinging satire of lobbyists. However, the reality is much more sinister. Corporate lobbyists are in the business of deceit and denial, pushing fake science, absurd theories, and hackneyed philosophies to the American public while also "paying off" politicians.

A political satire, *Bulworth* (1998) starred Warren Beatty as Jay Bulworth, a Democratic US Senator from California. Initially liberal, Bulworth has grown increasingly conservative, accepting donations from large corporations and various lobbyists. Once idealistic, Bulworth has become disillusioned with his seemingly "happy" life, mired in a loveless marriage, and cynical about corruption in politics. He meets with a lobbyist for the American Insurance Federation, who requests that the Senator quash a bill requiring insurance companies to sell policies to the lower class, specifically poor African Americans. Bulworth agrees on the condition that he is given a $10 million life insurance policy. Afterwards, he arranges to have a contract killer assassinate him in two days, which will allow his daughter to collect the insurance money. After not sleeping for days, he speaks openly and honestly at a South Central Los Angeles church.

Audience member: We can't get health insurance, fire insurance, life insurance. Why haven't you come out for Senate Bill 2720?
Bulworth: Well, because you haven't contributed any money to my campaign. Have you? [audience boos] You have any idea how much these insurance companies come up with? They pretty much depend on me to get a bill like that and bottle it up in a committee during an election … and then in that way, we can kill it when you're not looking.

He starts a relationship with Nina (Halle Berry), a young African American woman whose brother is targeted by a notorious drug dealer. He begins a clunky rap about corruption in politics, banking, oil industry, warmongering, health care, insurance companies, and even advocates for Socialism while rapping at the fundraising event.

> You know, it ain't that funny, you contribute all my money. You make your contribution, then you get your solution. As long as you can pay, I am going

to do it all your way. Yes, money talks and the people walk. Yeah, now let me hear ya say it, big money. Big money, big money, big money ... Yo, over here, we've got our friends from oil. They don't give a shit how much wilderness is spoiled. They tell us that they're careful. We know that it's a lie. As long as we keep drivin' cars, they let the planet die

His stale campaign and popularity are invigorated as he begins to spew harsh and unvarnished truths about corporate control of politics. His motivation for living is restored, and he attempts to cancel the contract on his life, which he refers to as the "weekend research project." In a twist, it is revealed that Nina is the would-be assassin, but she decides to let him live. Bulworth wins the primary in a landslide, and his supporters want him to run for presidency. In the concluding scene, he is shot by Graham Crockett, who is afraid that he will support socialized health care. The fate of Bulworth is unresolved, the movie ending with a homeless black man telling the viewer, "You got to be a spirit. You can't be no ghost." The film was praised for exploring race, poverty, lack of health care, and corporate control of the political system.

More dramatic, *Power* (1986) starred Richard Gere as Pete St. John, a political consultant who utilizes slick marketing techniques to elect politicians to office. St. John is very successful, managing several campaigns regardless of political leanings. The film features several campaigns across the country, but the primary storyline showcased the Ohio Senatorial campaign of Jerome Cade (J.T. Walsh). A novice politician, Cade is a prominent businessman running for the seat vacated by St. John's former client and friend Sam Hastings (E.G. Marshall). Senator Hastings was a big proponent of solar energy, while his potential replacement Cade's anti-solar power stance will benefit Big Oil. Cade is being controlled by Andrew Billings (Denzel Washington), a lobbyist who runs a "public relations firm" in Washington. Billings works for Big Oil, as represented by a short scene involving Billings meeting with an Arab Sheik in the back of a limo,

> These have been difficult years for us. Prices keep falling. Populists like Cepeda keep nationalizing their oil and entering the market. Here we have Senators and Congressmen talking of solar generation and electrical wind generators and other such impractical ideas. Your upcoming elections are important to us, Mr. Billings.

Despite the reluctance of Billings, the Arab Consortium urges Billings to hire St. John as the campaign consultant for the novice politician. Although not political, St. John discovers that lobbyist Arnold Billings (Denzel Washington) secretly blackmailed Hastings's wife, Claire (Beatrice Straight), forcing Hastings to retire from Senate. This leads St. John to quit the campaign and provide free advice to an independent candidate, Phillip Aarons, a young professor running on an environmental platform. Aaron's idealistic campaign consultant is Wilfred Buckley (Gene Hackman), St. John's friend and former employee. In the end, Aarons surprisingly comes into second place, with Jerome Cade placing a distant third.

Aaron gives a speech supporting the notion of honesty in politics, telling his supporters that "something human came into this race. Some straight talk. Some honest feeling. Something that wasn't slick and prepackaged, that wasn't engineered by these media wizards." Although not entirely effective, *Power* critiqued the slick and artificial marketing campaigns often utilized in politics. Unfortunately, the big lobby angle was underdeveloped, lost in the convoluted and overly busy plotline.

The comedy, *A Distinguished Gentlemen* (1992) highlighted the political maneuverings of Washington, DC, where powerful lobby groups throw money at politicians. Eddie Murphy starred as Thomas Jefferson Johnson, a con artist elected to Congress after incumbent Jeff Johnson (James Garner) died before an election. Realizing an opportunity, Thomas shortens his middle name. He appears on the ballot as "Jeff Johnson," believing that name recognition may get him elected to Washington, where the "streets are paved with gold." He tells his con-artist partners,

> Washington, DC. That's where the money is, listen I have been doing some research. I have been to the library [his gang laughs]. Listen up, what you laughing at? Congressmen, when they get elected, they get $130,000 a year, that is their base salary. Then they have these things called PACs, the political action committees, right. Then they have these lobbyists. Their whole point in life is to buy you off, they just buy you off, and it's totally legal. It's the con of a lifetime!

He narrowly wins the election and arrives in Washington, where he discovers greed and corruption are more rampant than he ever imagined. At a gala dinner, veteran Congressmen Dick Dodge (Lane Smith) welcomes the new congresspersons,

> Welcome the new members of Washington. We haven't had a freshmen class this big in a long time. Well, Congress needs your new blood, and you, in turn, are going to need new friends. That is why tonight – we unite the two great pillars of our system – Political and financial.

Johnson schemes to get appointed to the Power and Industry committee, termed "the honeypot," as "every cash-rich trade group in town is constantly lobbying each member." Johnson begins to enrich himself until he learns that corrupt practices are harming citizens, highlighted by a young girl that developed cancer due to power lines installed by Gulf Coast Power. Developing a conscience, Johnson decides to help his constituents but is thwarted by Dodge, who refuses to inquire into the power lines' dangerousness. Using his skills as a con artist, Johnson exposes Dodge as corrupt and outs the nefarious activities of Gulf Coast Power and their powerful lobbyists. Despite the overwhelmingly negative critical reviews, the film was a brilliant satire of the inner workings of lobbyists and the greed of the political process.

Corporate Conspiracy-Thriller

The corporate thriller is a specific type of film heavily influenced by the political thriller popularized in the 1990s. These films feature plenty of deception with suspense, mystery, violence, and action scenes. The corporation is depicted as the foil to the protagonist, engaged in nefarious behavior that is immoral and criminal. There is no grey area regarding the corporations' actions or behaviors. The corporate conspiracy-thriller can be challenging to categorize, as the corporate wrongdoing is often overshadowed by the suspense or action integral to the storyline. The crimes are often shrouded in mystery and obscured by shoot-outs, car chases, skullduggery, and plot twists. These films are often offshoots of political thrillers, with corporations replacing the corrupt politicians as the primary villains. Essentially, the plotlines revolve around corporations' control over the political process and, ultimately, the economy.

In the 1970s, Alan J. Pakula directed the "Paranoia Trilogy," a trio of films that focused on the erosion of America's trust in its institutions. Capturing the cynicism of the times, *Klute* (1971), *The Parallax View* (1974), and *All the Presidents Men* (1976) mirrored a broadly held mistrust of government and big business, spinning memorable tales of avarice, corruption, and murder. Alongside films such as *The Conversation* (1974), *Chinatown* (1974), and *Three Days of Condor* (1975), Pakula set the standard for a barrage of political conspiracy-thrillers that appeared in the 1990s and beyond. In *Rollover* (1981), Pakula depicts a doomsday scenario, in which the entire global financial system collapses after the Saudis haul all their money out of US and European banks. To place into context, the 1973 Arab Oil Embargo and the Energy Crisis endangered the global economy and revealed the United States declining hegemony. During the 1970s and 1980s, the "Arabs" were painted as "villains" in many films. However, in *Rollover*, the banking industry was co-conspirators in the illegal activities, complicit in the collapse of the global economy. The film starred Jane Fonda as Lee Winters, a former actress-turned socialite who takes control of her murdered husband's company, Winterchem Enterprises. Lee becomes involved financially and romantically with Hubbel Smith (Kris Kristofferson), a no-nonsense banker in charge of the recently bailed out Borough National Bank. Together the pair discover the nefarious plot involving First New York Bank chairman Maxwell Emery (Hume Cronyn) and the Saudis, in which billions of dollars are siphoned into secret accounts across American and European banks. In the end, the Arabs decide to "rollover" their vast sums in the bank, which precipitates the global economy's collapse. The final scenes of the movie feature plenty of chaos, with empty trading floors and citizens rioting in the streets. Despite Pakula's pedigree, the film was poorly contrived, with melodramatic contraptions and a melange of financial jargon that confused even the most attentive viewers.

The Formula (1980) was a corporate thriller set in Los Angeles. It starred George C Scott as Lt. Barney Caine, a detective assigned to solve the murder of his former boss, friend, and disgraced cop, Tom Neeley. During the investigation, Caine discovers an evil plot orchestrated by the corporate tycoon Adam Steiffel

(Marlon Brando), which revolves around "Genesis," a synthetic fuel formula invented by the Nazis. The onset of Genesis would wreak havoc on the oil-based economy, and a cartel of influential corporations and businessmen used their wealth and political connections to keep the formula secret. The formulation uses anthracite or hard-based coal as the raw material that transforms into synthetic fuel. Consequently, Steiffel and his cartel partners attempt to monopolize the coal market before the formula is released. The vast international conspiracy involved murder, deception, and double-crossing. In the end, Steiffel reveals the cartel's plan to keep the formula secret, using Caine to help find the remaining members of those who knew about Genesis so that they could be assassinated. However, Caine reveals that he has already disclosed the formula to a Swiss Energy company. Steiffel negotiates with the Swiss CEO giving him 30 percent of his anthracite holdings for not using the formula for ten years. The film highlighted the greed of the oil industry and cartels, as vividly depicted in an exchange between Caine and Steiffel:

Barney Caine: You trade lives and human dignity for profit.
Adam Steiffel: "Money, not morality, is the principle commerce of civilized nations." Thomas Jefferson, 200 years ago. That is the philosophy that built this nation.
Barney Caine: What do you know about this nation. When did you ever give a second thought to American citizens? You're the reason their money is worthless. You're the reason old people are eating out of garbage cans, and kids get killed in bullshit wars. You're not in the oil business, you're in the oil shortage business. You're an ivory tower hoodlum, a common street killer.

Albeit fictional, the film delivers a thought-provoking glimpse at the extent that Big Oil could resort to maintaining its position of power in the world economy.

In the 1990s, political-conspiracy films became popular with the emergence of several films, including *Absolute Power* (1997), *Murder at 1600* (1997), *Enemy of the State* (1998), and *Snake Eyes* (1998). The movies were box office successes, action-oriented, and suspenseful. Generally, these films engage in standard generic formulas with hollow stereotypes and are devoid of social relevance. The corporate-conspiracy thriller was also seen in notable films such as *The Pelican Brief* (1993) and *The Firm* (1993). Based on a John Grisham novel, *The Firm* featured Bendini, Lambert & Locke (BL&L). The corporate law firm was complicit in their client's tax evasion and money-laundering schemes. The boutique law firm's head of security, Bill DeVasher (Wilford Brimley), also doubled as a firm's hired assassin, arranging murders to silence potential whistleblowers. The film starred Tom Cruise as Mitch McDeere, a newly hired attorney with BL&L that gets caught up in the firm's corruption. Aside from murders, the film illustrates corporate culture with strict loyalty, confidentiality, and a willingness to bend the rules and ethics. Also based on a Grisham novel, *The Pelican Brief* was a legal thriller that featured the murder of Supreme Court Judges. Although opposed to most issues, the justices were strong advocates of the environment.

162   Harm to the Economy

The assassinations were carried out on behalf of oil tycoon Victor Mattiece, who plans to drill oil in Louisiana marshlands, the habitat for an endangered subspecies of brown pelicans. The impending court case is expected to reach the Supreme Court. Mattiece believes his generous campaign contributions will persuade the President (Robert Culp) to appoint justices that favor big business over environmental concerns. The film's protagonist, law student Darby Shaw (Julia Roberts), uncovers the plot and teams with investigative reporter Gary Grantham (Denzel Washington) to expose the truth about the murders.

In a similar vein, *Edge of Darkness* (2010) was a conspiracy action film that starred Mel Gibson as Detective Thomas Craven of the Boston Police Department. At the film's beginning, Craven's sick daughter Emma is gunned down outside the family home, dying in her father's arms. Craven begins an informal investigation that reveals that Emma was a whistleblower about to expose Northmoor, a research and development corporation under contract to the US government. Craven is mysteriously visited by Darius Jedburgh (Ray Winstone), a private security operative tasked with covering up the murder of Emma and stopping her father's investigation. However, Darius likes Craven, revealing information about the murder, including that his daughter was an "activist." Craven discovers a tape, in which Emma gives a statement:

> Northmoor is breaking the law. They are making nuclear weapons. But these are not American nuclear weapons. They are weapons designed to foreign specifications ... and built with foreign materials. So, obviously, if these bombs were ever to be used ... they would be traced directly back to another country and not the United States. I've stolen documents, images, blueprints ... but we need proof of the weapons themselves. So I'm showing a team of people ... how to get into the Northmoor facility to video the evidence. I'm recording all this because I'm very scared. I'm under constant surveillance. My phone is tapped, and I'm being followed. So chances are that if you're watching this, I'll already be dead. I love you, Dad.

In a typical Hollywood action film, the protagonist metes out justice, killing Northmoor's CEO Jack Bennett (Danny Huston) and the agents that killed his daughter. Meanwhile, Jedburgh, suffering from a terminal disease, goes rogue and kills Senator Jim Pine, who was complicit in Emma's murder.

The International (2009) was loosely based on the Bank of Credit and Commerce International (BCCI) scandal in the 1980s. The film follows Interpol agent Louis Salinger (Clive Owen) and Eleanor Whitman (Naomi Watts), an Assistant District Attorney from Manhattan. The pair investigated corruption with the International Bank of Business and Credit (IBBC), a fictional bank based in Luxembourg. The bank conspires with organized crime groups, arms dealers, drug cartels, corrupt governments, and large multinational corporations. They engage in money laundering and utilize murder to meet their economic and political agenda. The pair are stonewalled in their efforts, as the IBBC has prominent connections in politics and law enforcement. They traverse the globe searching for an assassin, trying to connect him to the murders ordered by the bank. True to the genre, the film featured several action sequences, chases, and shootouts. In the end, the CEO is killed, but the bank continues its nefarious practices, too powerful to face justice.

A romantic comedy, *Duplicity* (2009) features corporate subterfuge between cosmetic industry rivals Burkett & Randle and Equikrom. Howard Tully, the CEO of Burkett & Randle, hires former CIA agent Claire Stenwick (Julia Roberts) to coordinate counterintelligence within the corporation. However, he discovers that Claire is covertly working for Ray Koval (Clive Owen), a former M-16 agent working as an intelligence expert at Equikrom. Rather than terminate Claire, Tully provides false information about a new "game-changing" product that they are about to put on the market. Claire provides a copy of Tully's speech to Dick Garsik (Paul Giamatti), the CEO of Equikrom. Garsik orders his intelligence team to steal the formula, which turns out to be a cure for baldness. Secret lovers Ray and Claire abscond with the formula, intending to sell it to a Swiss company for $35 million. However, their scheme backfires, as the formula is fake, just a generic lotion. The pair received a thank-you bottle of champagne from Tully.

Big Brother Is Watching: Big Tech Thrillers

Several corporate conspiracies films involve fictional big tech companies. *The Net* (1995) was a thriller that starred Sandra Bullock as Angela Bennett, a computer systems analyst discovering a nefarious plot involving Gregg Microsystems, a software company. The CEO, Jeff Gregg, developed "Gatekeeper," a computer security system that has a glitch that permits the corporation to hack into sensitive files. In a Kafkaesque-like scenario, Angela's identity is stolen, and she spends the remainder of the film evading a corporate assassin and the police. Employing her superior computer skills, Angela gets her identity back while alerting the FBI to the corporate plot to hack into sensitive government computer files. The hyper-glossy *Hackers* (1995) follows a group of high school hackers that uncover an extortion scheme involving the Ellingson Mineral Company. The cartoonish villains are Eugene "The Plague" Belford (Fisher Stevens) and his corporate boss, Margo Wallace (Lorraine Bracco), who plan to embezzle $25 million from Ellingson Mineral Company by funneling small amounts of money into a secret bank account. A former hacker, "The Plague," frames the hackers with a virus that threatens to capsize several oil tankers, creating an ecological disaster. Although superficial, the film garnered a cult following and was noted as the first depiction of the subculture of hackers. That said, their crimes were occupational, not technically corporate crimes.

Conversely, *Anti-Trust* (2001) features Tim Robbins as Gary Winston, the CEO of NURV, a technology company. The corporation is racing to develop "synapse," a digital communication tool that will transform the internet. NURV engages in monopolistic practices to stifle the competition and recruits top computer programmers in the country. NURV hires the film protagonist, Milo Huffman (Ryan Phillippe), to help complete synapse and meet a tight three-month deadline. After his best friend, Teddy Chin (Yee Jee Tso), is murdered, Milo uncovers the sinister truth behind NURV's operations. The tech company employs a surveillance system to observe and steal code, murdering the programmers to maintain their secret. Even Milo's girlfriend, Alice (Claire Forlani), is a plant, an ex-con that the corporation pays to spy and manipulate Milo. He enlists Lisa Calighan (Rachael Leigh Cook), an employee at NURV who appears to be under surveillance by the corporation. However, Lisa is Winston's accomplice and double-crosses Milo, who is now targeted for assassination. With the help of his old start-up friends and Alice, who had a change of heart, Milo exposes the corporation's sinister practices, monopolization, and murders. The synapse program is released as an open-source through Skullbocks, the start-up company that Milo and his friends initially founded. The film was an indisputable critique of Microsoft's monopolistic practices, with Tim Robbins a thinly disguised Bill Gates. Roger Ebert (2001) claimed that he was "surprised the [the writers] didn't protect against libel by having the villain wear name tag saying, "Hi! I'm not Bill!".

The theme of big-tech and surveillance was also featured in *The Circle* (2017), which starred Tom Hanks as Eamon Bailey, the CEO of the Circle, a tech and social media company. The company is about to launch SeeChange, a program that utilizes small cameras placed all over the globe to provide real-time, high-quality video. Bailey touts the new tech, telling his employees, "We will hear and see everything." The corporation's CFO, Tom Stenton (Patton Oswalt), defends the company against antitrust violations while arguing that more accountability and transparency should be in politics. Tom introduces Olivia Santos, a congressperson who agrees to allow the public to have open – and real-time – access to meetings, phone calls, and emails. The corporation is also planning to tie True You – a social media account that parallels Facebook – to voter registration, paying taxes, and parking tickets. Simply, a unified account will take over all government functions, making it convenient for citizens and saving the government billions of dollars. Meanwhile, Mae Holland (Emma Watson) is hired by the corporation to work in customer relations. She becomes immersed in the company's culture, where the "community" of employees socialize, keep open social media accounts, and know everything about each other's lives – even monitoring participation within the "communities" weekend "optional" events. At a company party, she meets a cynical employee, who turns out to be Ty Lafitte (John Boyega), the inventor of True You and the company's founding partner. Lafitte is "off the grid," keeping a low profile and not infringing his privacy. He warns Mae about the Circle's true intentions.

> The plan is everything recorded, seen, broadcast, stored, analyzed, available to the Circle in any way ... They can use it however they see fit. We're being studied. Everyone's data in the Circle is being studied, monetized .... Proud of what? The disregard for privacy, the use of personal data for the accumulation of wealth and control? I'm not proud. This is not what I created.

After being rescued in a Kayak accident, Mae becomes a social media celebrity after being covertly filmed on SeeChange. She agrees to wear a tiny camera becoming a "helper" that displays her life to a global audience with every moment captured on high-definition video. Mae is transformed into a full-fledged disciple of the corporation, even suggesting that the voting public should be required to have a Circle account. On "Dream Friday," a weekly company assembly, Mae promotes Soul Search, a revolutionary program that can find any human on the planet in 10 minutes. After demonstrating its effectiveness with capturing a wanted felon, the audience urges her to find her estranged friend, Mercer, a vocal opponent of social media. The Circle users descend on his cabin, forcing him to flee in his truck, where he dies in a tragic accident. In the concluding scene, Mae appears on stage with Eamon and Tom at the Dream Friday assembly. She requests that Eamon and Tom join her in becoming transparent to the public, giving up their privacy and life "above the cloud." She cleverly tells the audience that

> Ty Lafitte has helped us make every document in the company's history public. Every message, every plan including … And this is my favorite part, every email from Tom and Eamon's accounts, and their private accounts … and their secondary confidential accounts. And even their super-secret scrambled code accounts that nobody, not even their assistants or wives, knew existed. Until now. It's all been sent to you already.

Whereas, Eamon whispers to Tom, "we are so fucked." While Mae continues to tell the audience that "There are no more secrets. Privacy was a temporary thing. And now it is over." The film was a timely critique of social media, a cautionary tale about social media harassment, privacy breaches, and corporate control over societal institutions. It was a thinly veiled attack on corporate tech companies such as Facebook and YouTube.

Paranoia (2013) was a tech-thriller that starred Liam Hemsworth as Adam Cassidy, a lowly "cubicle drone" at Wyatt Corp, "one of the top tech companies on the planet." Cassidy highlights the film's premise in the opening narration, "We belong to a generation that watched our future get stolen out from under us. The American Dream, our parents knew has been hijacked by men who are willing to lie, cheat and steal to protect their wealth." Cassidy and his colleagues are summarily fired after pitching a new idea to CEO Nicolas Wyatt (Gary Oldman). Adam foolishly uses the company credit for an extravagant night, $16,000 at a local club. Wyatt seizes the opportunity to blackmail Adam into becoming a corporate spy, threatening to have him arrested for using the discretionary fund. Adam is trained by Judith Bolton (Embeth Davidtz) to infiltrate Eikon, a tech company controlled by Wyatt's former mentor, Jack Goddard (Harrison Ford). After securing employment at Eikon, Adam steals the designs for Occura, a revolutionary cellphone. The cellphone has a sinister purpose, the capability to invade personal privacy, Goddard telling Adam, "It'll know where you've been, who've you been with. It'll track your priorities, expenditures, your health, calendar. It will know who you are, and it's all ours." Adam becomes romantically involved with Emma Jennings, a high-level employee at Eikon, covertly using her thumbprint to access the corporate vault to steal the prototype. He is confronted by Goddard, who tells him that he has recorded evidence, texts, and conversations, which prove that Wyatt was criminally responsible for the attempted theft. He plans to use the incriminating evidence to force Wyatt to sell his company to Eikon. The viewer learns that Bolton was serving as a "double-agent," a corporate spy for Goddard. In the concluding scene, Adam covertly tapes a conversation between Wyatt and Goddard, where both men openly discuss their crimes. Goddard is charged with industrial espionage, obstruction of justice, and insider trading. Adam narrates, "I handed the feds, Wyatt and Goddard. They won't be seeing light for a very long time." Of course, a happy Hollywood ending obscures the reality that CEOs who are found guilty of crimes rarely do lengthy time in prison.

Captains of Industry: The Robber Baron on Film

From the silent era to the present day, the capitalist class's greed has also been depicted in historical films that feature "robber barons" or "fat cats." Several early silent films depicted the "robber baron" as a sinister and callous capitalist, characterized by a well-dressed, cigar-puffing, and money-obsessed antagonist. During the roaring 20s, portrayals of the robber baron largely disappeared but were restored during the Great Depression. The 1930s featured several films that were fictionalized biographies of tycoons, including *The Conquerors* (1932), *Come and Get It* (1936), and *The Power and the Glory* (1933). For instance, *The Power and Glory* starred Spencer Tracy as Tom Garner, a railway worker transformed into a railway magnate. Garner is both heroic and flawed, as he is increasingly ruthless and cold, eventually dying alone and unloved. A handful of comedies satirized the tycoon, including *Paddy O'Day* (1936), a spoof of Henry Ford, the richest man in America. Similarly, *Soak the Rich* (1936) was a screwball comedy that featured a stereotypical tycoon, Humphrey Craig. After endowing a University, Craig has a radical professor fired after teaching the merits of the so-called "soak-the-rich tax bill." However, complications arise when Craig's daughter falls in love with a radical college student protesting the firing of the progressive professor. According to Wilt and Shull (2004:299), "these films don't openly criticize the American free enterprise system, instead choosing to suggest that as people become more rich and powerful, they become removed from the emotions, desires and pleasures of everyday people – in essence, less human." During World War II, industrialists were celebrated as essential to the war effort, with films such as *Pittsburgh* (1942). For instance, in *An American Romance* (1944), an immigrant ironworker becomes an auto magnate, returning to lend his managerial expertise to manufacture planes for the war effort. The negative caricature of the "fat cat" robber baron persisted in *It's a Wonderful Life* (1946) and later in *Bright Leaf* (1950), where Gary Cooper is transformed into a greedy miser. In the 1950s, McCarthyism dominated the Hollywood landscape, so attacks on capitalism were virtually non-existent.

However, corporate culture started to appear in films such as *Executive Suite* (1954), *Patterns* (1956), and *The Man in the Gray Flannel Suit* (1956).

The Western genre has featured several films in which farmers or settlers were victims of Cattle Barons and unscrupulous land developers who wanted to monopolize the land. The rugged individualism of the American Western was at odds with business monopolization. Certainly, not anti-capitalist, the American Western painted an ugly picture of the so-called robber barons, industrialists that attempted to control the land and resources of the American West. There are numerous examples where cattle barons, railway barons, and mine owners are depicted as villains. An enduring example of the genre is the threat to the homestead in an economic system rigged for the wealthy and powerful. These powerful businessmen attempted to kill the American entrepreneurial spirit by creating cartels or displacing farmers or homesteaders. This is a common theme in American cinema, the rooting of the underdog against the rich and powerful. One such example is the film *Shane* (1953), in which a gunslinger arrives to help a group of settlers being terrorized by a cattle baron. There are several others, including the B-western *Barricade* (1950), in which a gold mine owner "Boss" Kruger (Raymond Massey) brutally mistreats his workers with a tyrannical and sadistic style of management. The model continued into the 1960s, with more famous films, such as Sergio Leone's *Once Upon a Time in the West* (1968), in which a railroad baron uses hired assassins to murder anyone who stands in his way. In *Silverado* (1985) and *Open Range* (2003), a land baron attempts to maintain an open range, driving lawful claimants off the land. A rip-off of Shane, *Pale Rider* (1985) featured an industrialist utilizing hydraulic mining and ravaging the landscape in their wanton search for gold.

Of note, *Walker* (1987) was a historical fiction that satirized mercenary William Walker's (Ed Harris) invasion of Nicaragua in 1853, which was financially backed by a robber baron, Cornelius Vanderbilt (Peter Boyle). After Walker appointed himself as president, he antagonized Vanderbilt by revoking his overland trade route. Vanderbilt promptly began to finance rebel forces to overthrow the increasingly delusional Walker. *There Will Be Blood* (2007) was loosely based on Oil, an Upton Sinclair novel. The film was primarily a character study of an oilman, Daniel Plainview (Daniel Day-Lewis), overcome with avarice and lust for wealth and power. Plainview was the epitome of the American Dream, working hard to achieve his wealth and status. However, he meets his goal at the expense of others and is transformed into a broken, hateful, and bitter man with little joy in life. Even the most recent iteration of *The Lone Ranger* (2013) highlighted a railroad tycoon as the primary villain. Likewise, several action-thriller films feature industrialists or tycoons that attempt to exploit the natural resources of less developed countries. *The Dogs of War* (1980) follows mercenaries that a British tycoon hires to depose the president of a fictional African country. The tycoon wants to enrich his corporation by gaining unlimited access to a platinum deposit. Similarly, *A Dark Truth* (2012) featured the exploitation of an unnamed Central American country. The Clearbec corporation has a monopoly on the water, caused a typhus outbreak, and was complicit in genocide.

Although well over 100 years separate the likes of Rockefeller, Gould and Carnegie from the Gates, Zuckerbergs and Bezos of these times, the link between robber barons of the past and the modern-day oligarchs can help inform society and the immense power that their corporations have in shaping society, culture, politics, and the economy (Naughton, 2012). Hollywood has produced several biopics that celebrate business giants, such as Bill Gates and Steve Jobs (*Pirates of Silicon Valley,* 1999); Howard Hughes (*The Carpetbaggers,* 1964; *The Amazing Howard Hughes,* 1977; *Hughes and Harlow: Angels in Hell* (1978); *Melvin and Howard,* 1980; *The Aviator,* 2004; *Rules Don't Apply,* 2014); Steve Jobs (*Jobs,* 2013; *Steve Jobs,* 2015); Mark Zuckerberg (*The Social Network,* 2010); and Ray Kroc (*The Founder,* 2016). Hollywood even produced *Joy* (2015), a film about Joy Mangano, an entrepreneur who invented the self-pressing mop. Although the films are not entirely flattering, the current billionaire class generally receives more positive depictions in film, especially when compared to the robber barons of the past. Billionaires such as Jeff Bezos jet off to "outer space" while workers are toiling at non-unionized Amazon facilities, experiencing low pay, poor working conditions, arbitrary discipline, and the exploitation of "gig" labor. For instance, Jessica Bruder's 2017 book *Nomadland: Surviving America* in the twenty-first century was a blistering critique of Amazon, while the film version, *Nomadland* (2020), was more ambivalent, some would argue inherently positive in its depiction of Amazon (Chan, 2021).

Concluding Thoughts

The corporation is all-powerful – an institution that values profit over humanity. Corporations control the world's economy, where their sole objective is to generate profit. According to Joel Bakan (2012), the corporation is a pathological institution that operates on its own economic self-interest, impervious to the harms that it produces. Corporations enjoy the benefits of monopolization, generous tax breaks, increasingly lax regulations, excessive political influence, and when things go awry, even taxpayer bailouts. Filmmakers have not ignored this reality. Several movies depict the Great Recession, while even more films feature narratives that condemn the greed of big business. The Robber Baron has been largely vilified in film, personified as paternalistic and uncaring. The conspiracy thriller is rooted in paranoia about undue corporate control, with antagonists that embody a lack of humanity, morality, and ethics. Moreover, several films play on fears that technology could be used as a tool of domination and repression. Of course, this fear is not unfounded. Big tech use algorithms to track and manipulate social media users, breach privacy, and influence elections (Foer, 2017). That said, most Hollywood films celebrate wealth and glorify the American Dream, an ethos in which success is measured by affluence and status rather than humane values.

Note

1 The Trump presidency rolled back several banking regulations, which appeased many corporate apologists and supporters (Levintova, 2020).

Reference List

Allan, B. (2020). New movie about Sask. Farmer who went up against Monsanto dredges up old fight over accuracy of his story. *CBC News*. https://www.cbc.ca/news/canada/saskatchewan/percy-movie-farmers-1.5748575

Bakan, J. (2012). *The corporation: The pathological pursuit of profit and power*. Hachette UK.

Blodget, H. (2013, July 31). This one tweet reveals what's wrong with American business culture and the economy. *Insider*. https://www.businessinsider.com/business-and-the-economy-2013-7

Bovard, J. (1995, September 26). Archer Daniels Midland: A case study in corporate welfare. Cato Institute. https://www.cato.org/policy-analysis/archer-daniels-midland-case-study-corporate-welfare

Bruder, J. (2017). *Nomadland: Surviving America in the twenty-first century*. WW Norton and Company.

Burley, H., & Hoedeman (2021). The 10 worst corporate Lobbyists: It's big business to promote, defend big business interests. The Monitor: Canadian Centre for Policy Alternatives. https://www.policyalternatives.ca/publications/monitor/10-worst-corporate-lobbyists

Butler, D. (2021, June 29). The land was worth millions. A Big Ag Corporation sold it to Sonny Perdue's company for $250,000. *The Washington Post*. https://www.washingtonpost.com/climate-environment/interactive/2021/sonny-perdue-adm-land-deal/

Chan, W. (2021, February 22). What Nomadland gets wrong about gig labor. *Vulture*. https://www.vulture.com/article/nomadland-amazon-warehouse-chloe-zhao.html

CCR. (2005, December 9). Syriana, corporate lawyers, and the illusion of due diligence. *Corporate Crime Reporter*, *48*(3). https://www.corporatecrimereporter.com/syriana120905.htm

Ebert, R. (2001, January 12). Antitrust. https://www.rogerebert.com/reviews/antitrust-2001

Ebert, R. (2011, October 19). Long night's journey into collapse. https://www.rogerebert.com/reviews/margin-call-2011

Evers-Hillstrom, K. (2019, January 25). Lobbying spending reaches $3.4 billion in 2018, highest in 8 years. *Open Secrets*. https://www.opensecrets.org/news/2019/01/lobbying-spending-reaches-3-4-billion-in-18/

Foer, F. (2017). *World without mind: The existential threat of Big Tech*. Random House.

Hubbard, S. (2021). *Monopolies suck: 7 ways big corporations rule your life and how to take back control*. Simon and Schuster.

Hungerford, T.L. (2013, June 4). Corporate tax rates and economic growth since 1947. Economic Policy Institute. https://www.epi.org/publication/ib364-corporate-tax-rates-and-economic-growth/

Levintona, H. (2020, June 25). Trump regulators just rolled back a major Obama-era bank reform. [Blog Post]. *Mother Jones*. https://www.motherjones.com/politics/2020/06/trump-regulators-just-rolled-back-a-major-obama-era-bank-reform/

Naughton, J. (2012, July 1). New-tech moguls: The modern robber barons? *The Guardian*. https://www.theguardian.com/technology/2012/jul/01/new-tech-moguls-robber-barons

Oxfam. (2021). Inequality and poverty: The hidden costs of tax dodging. Oxfam International. https://www.oxfam.org/en/inequality-and-poverty-hidden-costs-tax-dodging

Oxfam. (2021). 5 shocking facts about extreme global inequality and how to even it up. Oxfam International. https://www.oxfam.org/en/5-shocking-facts-about-extreme-global-inequality-and-how-even-it

Rebovich, D.J., & Kane, J.L. (2002). An eye for an eye in the electronic age: Gauging public attitudes toward white-collar crime and punishment. *Journal of Economic Crime Management*, *1*(2), 1–19.

Reich, R. (2008). Supercapitalism. The transformation of business, democracy and everyday life. *Society and Business Review*, *3*(3) 256–258. doi:10.1108/sbr.2008.3.3.256.1

Schurenberg, E. (2011, May 25). Wall Street 2: Shorting the financial crisis on the big screen. [Blog]. *Huffington Post*. https://www.huffpost.com/entry/wall-street-2-gekko-garbl_b_737300

Schwartz, J., Steffensmeier, D., Moser, W.J., & Beltz, L. (2020). Financial prominence and financial conditions: Risk factors for 21st century corporate financial securities fraud in the United States. *Justice Quarterly*, Vol. Ahead of Print, 1–29. https://doi.org/10.1080/07418825.2020.1853799

Speri. (2019). Corporate power & the global economy. [Blog Post]. Sheffield Political Economy Research Institute. http://speri.dept.shef.ac.uk/2019/01/03/corporate-power-the-global-economy/

Tombs, S., & Whyte, D. (2020). The shifting imaginaries of corporate crime. *Journal of white collar and corporate crime*, *1*(1), 16–23.

Wall, M., Root, D., & Schwartz, A. (2019, July 22). *Corruption consultants: Conservative special interests and corporations hurt state economies and democratic processes*. Center for American Progress. https://www.americanprogress.org/issues/democracy/reports/2019/07/22/472363/corruption-consultants/

Wilt, D.E., & Shull, M. (2004). Robber Barons, media Moguls, and power elites. In P.C. Rollins (Ed.), *The Columbia companion to American history on film: How the movies have portrayed the American past*. Columbia University Press.

Wilton, S. (2017, Jan 27). Bre-X: The real story and scandal that inspired the movie Gold. *Calgary Herald*. https://calgaryherald.com/news/local-news/bre-x-the-real-story-and-scandal-that-inspired-the-movie-gold

7 The Social Construction of Corporate Harms

> *The truth, oh. Oh. I thought we were talking about a court of law. Come on. You've been around long enough to know that a courtroom isn't a place to look for the truth. You're lucky to find anything here that in any way resembles the truth ... You want to know when this case stopped being about dead children? The minute you filed the complaint, the minute it entered the justice system.*
>
> Jerry Facher (Robert Duvall) Attorney for
> Beatrice Foods, *A Civil Action* (1998)

In truth, the corporation inflicts enormous harm on workers, consumers, the environment, and the economy. That said, the mainstream media ignore most corporate harms, especially compared to overwhelming coverage of street and public order crimes. When reported, corporate wrongdoing is generally depicted as isolated events rather than systemic failures of economic and geopolitical systems. This is not surprising as the mainstream media – corporations themselves — create narratives and meanings attached to corporate harm. This pro-capitalist and, by extension, pro-corporate ethos permeates popular cultural narratives, allowing the wrongdoings of corporations to go unchecked and unabated. In Hollywood film, narratives are focused on individual heroes and villains, with very few films that engage in social critique or call for social justice. Films that depict corporate wrongdoing are a rarity but not completely absent.

In this way, social construction theory is beneficial to understanding the portrayal of corporate harm in film. The theory suggests that social reality is manufactured and based on the "active" construction of information, including media portrayals. The media is active in the construction or manufacturing of information. The media frame, modify, and edit claims while attaching meaning to various social issues or events (Loseke, 2003). As such, the media serves the role of "claimsmaker," actively constructing narratives to help the public attach meaning to several issues and concerns. This is especially true for knowledge about crime and justice, as the media is the primary source of information for most people (Dowler et al., 2006; Surette, 2014). Popular culture narratives can impact viewers' perception of victims, criminals, and criminal justice officials (Dowler, 2003). That said, it is necessary to recognize that claims or narratives presented by the media are often

DOI: 10.4324/9781003163855-7

skewed. Claimsmakers construct narratives that appeal to the public through exaggeration, the distortion of facts, and sensationalism. Many "crime" narratives are one-dimensional and simplistic and easily translated to entertainment-motivated audiences. Essentially, crime narratives serve to reinforce common stereotypes about criminality while also expounding the danger of lower-class or street crime.

As such, the identification of narratives is a critical element in social construction theory. Narratives are defined as "less encompassing, pre-established mini-social constructions found throughout crime and justice media" (Surette 2014, p.41). Popular criminal justice narratives include the victim and the "innately evil predatory criminal." Victim narratives center around innocence and helplessness (Altheide et al., 2001; Loseke, 2003). Dependent on their blameworthiness, victims are judged as either deserving or non-deserving, allowing audiences to assign a moral hierarchy to the victim. The evil predatory criminal is a popular narrative found within the media and serves multiple purposes. First, the evil predator conjures fear among viewers, allowing for more entertainment value. Second, constructing criminals as violent and evil is a "socially palatable explanation of crime" (Surette, 2014, p.55). This oversimplification focuses on individual explanations of crime rather than social factors. Generally, the entertainment media employs frames and narratives with easily identifiable narratives. However, it is challenging for filmmakers to replicate common crime and justice narratives in films that depict corporate wrongdoing. Corporate wrongdoing is more complex than street crime, with less identifiable victims and perpetrators. That said, this chapter will identify the overarching narratives that embody corporate wrongdoing in Hollywood films. Specifically, narratives surrounding the protagonist, antagonist, and victim will be discussed.

The Protagonist

The protagonist is an essential character that serves as the focal point of the narrative. As the primary character, the protagonist drives the plot and provides direction for the goal or purpose of the story. In films that feature corporate harm, protagonists are generally depicted as noble characters attempting to gain justice for victims of corporate harm. That said, there is a subset of films in which the protagonists are not seeking justice but serve to move the story forward as insiders to the corporate wrongdoing (*Margin Call, The Big Short, The Crooked E*) or being caught up in the tragic events of the story (*Deepwater Horizon, The 33*). Conversely, they can also be anti-heroes in which the audience has "rooting" interest or morbid fascination (*Barbarians at the Gate, Thank you For Smoking, The East*). That said, the leading narratives include: (1) The Whistleblower, (2) The Crusader, (3) The Rabble-Rouser, and (4) The Activist.

The Whistleblower

In the corporate wrongdoing film, the most common type of protagonist is the whistleblower. The whistleblower is often depicted as an outspoken informer or critic of harmful practices perpetrated by big business. Some of the most notable films include *The China Syndrome, North Country, Silkwood, Concussion, The Informant, The Insider,* and *Quiz Show*. However, the whistleblower has also been prominently featured in less acclaimed and popular films such as *Backstabbing for Beginners, The Laundromat, Anti-Trust, Consumed,* and *The Circle*. In most films, the whistleblower is a courageous character that exposes unsafe working conditions, environmental pollutants, cheating and stealing, and other nefarious behavior perpetrated by multinational corporations. Arguably, the most significant depiction of a whistleblower was based on the real-life story of Jeffrey Wigand, a Big Tobacco executive. *The Insider* offers a riveting depiction of Wigand's journey, highlighted by a re-enactment of the infamous *60 Minutes* interview with Mike Wallace, which served as a damning indictment of the Tobacco industry:

Jeffery Wigand: We are in the nicotine delivery business.
Mike Wallace: And that is what cigarettes are for.
Jeffrey Wigand: Delivery device for nicotine.
Mike Wallace: A delivery device for nicotine. Put it in your mouth, light it up, and you're going to get your fix.
Jeffrey Wigand: You're gonna get your fix.
Mike Wallace: You're saying that Brown & Williamson manipulates and adjusts the nicotine fix not by artificially adding nicotine but by enhancing the effect of nicotine through the use of chemical elements such as ammonia.
Jeffery Wigand: The process is known as impact boosting. While not spiking nicotine, they clearly manipulate it. There is extensive use of this technology, known as ammonia chemistry. It allows for the nicotine to be more rapidly absorbed in the lung and therefore affect the brain and central nervous system. The straw that broke the camel's back for me and really put me in trouble with Sandefur (CEO) was a compound called "coumarin." When I came on board at B&W, they had tried to transition from coumarin to a similar flavor that would give the same taste and had been unsuccessful. I wanted it out immediately. I was told that it would affect sales, so I should mind my own business. I constructed a memo to Mr. Sandefur indicating I could not in conscience continue with coumarin in a product that we now knew we had documentation was similar to coumadin, a lung-specific carcinogen.
Mike Wallace: And you sent the document forward to Sandefur?
Jeffrey Wigand: I sent the document forward to Sandefur. I was told that we would continue to work on a substitute. We weren't going to remove it as it would impact sales, and that that was his decision.
Mike Wallace: In other words, you were charging Sandefur and Brown & Williamson with ignoring health considerations consciously?
Jeffrey Wigand: Most certainly.
Mike Wallace: And on March 24th, Thomas Sandefur, CEO of Brown & Williamson, had you fired. And the reason he gave you?
Jeffrey Wigand: Poor communication skills.

Mike Wallace: And you wish you hadn't come forward? You wish you hadn't blown the whistle?

Jeffrey Wigand: Yeah, there are times I wish I hadn't done it. There are times I feel compelled to do it. If you'd asked me, would I do it again, do I think it's worth it? Yeah, I think it's worth it.

Moreover, many films highlight the transformation of the protagonist into a whistleblower. For instance, several films depict a pro-corporate protagonist morphing into a whistleblower. In *Promised Land*, Steve Butler is disillusioned after realizing that his company is engaged in manipulation and deception to meet their goal of acquiring fracking mining rights. Butler decides to tell the townsfolk the truth, which costs him his position with the corporation. In *The East*, an undercover operative is enlightened after learning about the enormous harms that corporations inflict on society and decides to become a whistleblower. *The China Syndrome's* supervisor Jack Godell is the ultimate "company man," defending the nuclear plant's safety. However, he dramatically resorts to hijacking the control room to inform the public about the potential for a nuclear meltdown. Finally, *The Informant's*, Mark Whitacre, becomes a whistleblower while defrauding the Archer Daniels Midland out of millions of dollars.

The Legal Crusader

In corporate wrongdoing films, the protagonist is often depicted as a "legal crusader," a character that uses the law to remedy corporate harms. The legal crusader is a conduit for justice and has appeared in several films, including *A Civil Action*, *Dark Waters*, *The Verdict*, *The Rainmaker*, *Class Action*, and *The Good Fight*. The crusading attorney often overcomes personal and professional challenges, characterized as the "against the odds narrative." The characters are usually depicted as exhibiting a dogged determination, a persistence that enables the character to tirelessly struggle for justice at any personal and financial costs. The crusader is also depicted as fighting "the good fight" against an unfeeling and powerful corporation with an overwhelming advantage in the court proceedings. In *Class Action*, attorney Jedediah Tucker Ward is portrayed as the prototypical champion of the little guy, a charismatic personality that spews memorable dialogue,

> These bastards they just think they can do anything they want. Lie, kill, destroy whatever they touch and get away with it. Let me tell you something, Steven [plaintiff]. They don't always get away with it. Once in a while, people like us. This law firm, we stop them. This is going to be one of those times.

Ward refers to corporations as "vermin," telling his colleague that the "firm was built on David and Goliath cases, they're just not around anymore. You got all these fascist Reagan justices. They hear you're after a big corporation, and they throw your ass right out of court."

Although more subdued, *Dark Waters'*, Robert Bilott is determined to get justice for his clients but is initially unwilling to go to court, telling his client, "Earl, these companies, they have all the money, all the time, and they'll use it. Trust me, I know I was one of them." Bilott secures a reasonable settlement for his client but convinces his boss, Tom Terp (Tim Robbins), to engage in a class-action suit that includes medical monitoring of victims of DuPont's poisoning of waters. A junior partner questions Bilott, arguing that "what he's proposing here is nothing less than a shakedown of an iconic American company," decrying that their corporate reputation will be tarnished, and they will be known as "ambulance chasers." In a surprising response, at least for a corporate attorney, Terp passionately responds,

> Has anyone even read the evidence this man collected? The willful negligence? The corruption? Read it. And then tell me we should be sitting on our asses. That's the reason why American's hate lawyers. This is the crap that fuels the Ralph Naders of the world. We should want to nail DuPont.

In a similar vein, the preservation and passion of the protagonist were vividly depicted in *The Rainmaker*, *The Verdict*, *A Civil Action*, and *The Good Fight*. In *The Good Fight* and *Civil Action*, the protagonist's dedication to the case resulted in the bankruptcy of their respective firms, demonstrating that their virtuous actions circumvented monetary considerations. *The Verdict* features Frank Galvin, an "ambulance chasing" attorney that is transformed after visiting his client, a comatose young woman. Rather than take a quick and easy payout, Frank decides to try the case, telling the opposing attorneys,

> That, that poor girl put her trust into the … into the hands of two men who took her life. She's in a coma. Her life is gone. She has no home, no family. She's tied to a machine. She has no friends. And the people who should care for her – her doctors … and you and me – have been bought off to look the other way. We've been paid to look the other way. I came here to take your money. I brought snapshots to show you so I could get your money. I can't do it; I can't take it. Cause if I take the money, I'm lost. I'll just be a … rich ambulance chaser. I can't do it. I can't take it.

A paralegal, Erin Brockovich is one of the most famous legal crusaders in the history of film. Brockovich fought tirelessly against Pacific Gas & Electric (PG&E), a California power company that polluted the city's water supply. A single mother, Brockovich's working-class background brought a sense of naivety to complex legal proceedings, adding elements of levity to heavy drama. Although compassionate, Erin has a very tough exterior and no filter when speaking her mind, which became an endearing quality for viewers. Dismissed as a "bimbo" who dresses provocatively, she tenaciously gathers evidence that proves that PG&E knowingly poisoned the water supply. Her boss, Ed Masry, provides a realistic appraisal of the legal challenge,

Ed Masry: Something like this, Erin ... It could take forever. They're a huge corporation. They could bury us in paperwork for the next 15 years. I'm just a guy with a small, private firm!
Erin Brockovich: Who happens to know they poisoned people and lied about it.

Later in the film, Erin eviscerates an uptight female lawyer that questions "holes in her research," with Erin telling the young lawyer, "Don't talk to me like I'm an idiot, okay? I may not have a law degree, but I've spent 18 months on this case, and I know more about these plaintiffs than you ever will." Erin recites details about the plaintiffs, showing that she is more than competent and also dedicated to the victims.

Rabble-Rouser

The "rabble-rouser" or troublemaker is also a prominent type of protagonist in corporate wrongdoing films. These characters generally advocate on behalf of workers whom corporations are exploiting. Most often, the rabble-rouser pushes back against corporate tyranny by organizing labor. The most prominent films include *Norma Rae* and *Matawan*. The iconic Norma Rae symbolizes this narrative as an agitator with a sarcastic personality and witty dialogue. She is a "firebrand" that refuses to be intimidated by company goons. In a climactic scene, Norma is surrounded by intimidating company supervisors and fired by the manager. She defiantly tells the security officer, "Forget it! I'm stayin' right where I am. It's gonna take you and the police department and the fire department and the National Guard to get me outta here!" Norma's sidekick is union activist, Reuben Warshowsky who also delivers memorable dialogue and is relentless in pursuing workers' rights. Less memorable, *Harlan County War* also features a coal miner wife that becomes a union activist with the help of a union representative, Warren Jakopovich. Further, the union activist is prominently featured in *Bread and Roses, In Dubious Battle, Cesar Chavez, 10,000 Black Men Named George*, and *The Killing Floor*.

The rabble-rouser can also include characters not involved in organizing labor, such as journalists and vigilantes. Surprisingly, the journalist has been featured in only a handful of films, including *Minimata, The Pelican Brief, Bhopal: A Prayer for Rain, The China Syndrome*, and *The Insider*. *Minimata* depicts photojournalist Eugene Smith as a flawed character that is an alcoholic and failed husband and father. He is a tortured soul that has nightmares from his experiences as a war photographer. Smith's redemption arrives in his photography, which vividly and grimly documents the devastating effects of mercury poisoning. *The Insider* features Al Pacino in a memorable performance as *60 Minute* producer, Lowell Bergman who is enraged after CBS cut the interview with Big Tobacco whistleblower, Jeffrey Wigand

> And he's only the key witness in the biggest public health reform issue, maybe the biggest, most expensive corporate malfeasance case in US history. And

Jeffery Wigand, who's put out on a limb, does he go on television and tell the truth? Yes. Is it newsworthy? Yes. Are we gonna air it? Of course not. Why? Because he's not telling the truth? No. Because he is telling the truth. That's why we're not gonna air it. And the more truth he tells, the worse it gets.

Some films also feature a vigilante character that metes out retributive justice against corporate transgressors. The vigilante includes law enforcement figures that fit the prototypical action narrative. The lone-wolf cop fights institutional bureaucracy and corruption to achieve justice. The *Edge of Darkness* best exemplifies this narrative. However, persistent investigations blended with action are also evident in films such as *The Formula* and *The International*. In a handful of action-based films, the protagonists utilize martial arts to battle corporate thugs (*The Fire Down Below, On Deadly Ground, Taffin*, and *Sweet Girl*). Finally, eco-terrorists offered vigilante justice in films such as *The East* and *Night Moves*.

The "Activist"

Aside from union organizers, activists are rarely depicted in film, and when so, they are secondary characters grounded in familiar tropes. However, there are a handful of films that depict the work of activists. Shown as an "ordinary" housewife, Lois Gibbs was transformed into an important grassroots activist within the environmental movement in the television film about the Love Canal tragedy. Similarly, *Bitter Harvest* featured a fictional farmer that worked tirelessly to educate his neighbors and community about the contamination of livestock feed in Michigan. In *Promised Land*, Hal Halbrook gives a powerful yet subdued performance as a local high school teacher that highlights the harm of fracking, illustrating how grassroots activism works. Likewise, in the *Milagro Beanfield War*, Sonya Brago delivers an impressive performance as Ruby Archuleta, an activist organizing grassroots resistance to land development in a poor Hispanic community. Rachel Weisz was nominated for dupont an Oscar for the best-supporting actress as Tessa Abbott-Quayle, an Amnesty International Activist that uncovered Big Pharma exploitation of African HIV patients in *The Constant Gardener*. One of the vignettes of *Fast-Food Nation* featured university student activists that protested a large meatpacking plant in a failed attempt to expose animal cruelty in factory farming. Finally, *Minimata* provides an excellent portrayal of grassroots activists – including family members of victims – that forced the Chisso corporation and the Japanese government to be held s*omewhat* accountable for Mercury poisoning.

Interestingly, Hollywood has not been so kind to climate activists. Many are subjected to misleading and unimaginative tropes, such as being naïve, manipulative, mentally unstable, or violent. Film producers resort to tired typecasts that paint environmentalists as non-conforming "weirdos" who have free sex, live on communes, and even resort to eco-terrorism to meet their goals. Hollywood reinforces conservative talking points that environmentalists want to restrict lifestyles and preach "climate alarmism" (Buckley, 2019; Bunch, 2019). Although thought-provoking, *The East*, *Night Moves*, and *First Reformed* depict environmentalists as eco-terrorists that resort to extreme measures to highlight pollution and the climate crises. In *The Edge of Darkness*, the protagonist brutally beats up an environmentalist that betrayed his daughter, which led to her death at the hands of a corporation. In *Salt and Fire*, a CEO kidnaps and strands a scientist in a barren region to highlight the decaying global climate. Environmentalists are depicted as political opportunists in *Percy vs. Goliath*. Finally, *Fast Food Nation* and *The Nice Guys* portray environmentalists as naïve and ineffectual.

The Antagonist

Serving as the foil to the protagonist, the antagonist plays a vital role in Hollywood films. In films that depict corporate harms, the antagonist is generally depicted as a proxy or representative of the corporation. This can include CEOs, lawyers, thugs, assassins, or corporate lackeys. It is very challenging for filmmakers to depict the reality of corporate wrongdoing, as it is multi-faceted, complex, and involves multiple transgressors. Hollywood tends to simplify the narratives, ensuring that audiences can quickly identify the wrongdoing, the harm, and the culpability. The primary narratives generally include: (1) The Mustache Twirler, (2) Deception and Denial, (3) Dirty Tactics, and (4) Greed.

The Mustache Twirler

In Hollywood vernacular, a "mustache twirler" refers to an antagonist that embodies villainy, evilness, and immorality. The mustache twirler utilizes predictable and clichéd dialogue, which undoubtedly reveals their malevolent nature. There are several prominent examples of mustache twirlers in corporate harm films, including some cartoonishly villainous characters, such as Michael Caine in *On Deadly Ground*, Alfred Molina in *The Devil Has a Name*, and Marlon Brando in *The Formula*. Bruce Willis makes a memorable cameo in *Fast Food Nation* as a brutish, misogynistic executive VP with Mickey's Burgers. He appears in only one scene, where he minimizes contaminated food:

> You want to be safe, huh? Perfectly safe? Well, forget about it. That's not gonna happen, okay? Everybody just needs to get that through their heads. Just cook the meat, and you'll be fine … 40,000 people die in automobile accidents every year. Does that mean Detroit should stop making cars?

He ends his rant, claiming that "the truth is we all have to eat a little shit from time to time." The character symbolizes the problem with free-market capitalism, a system in which greed trumps compassion, ethics, and morality.

Several films feature prominent villains that represent evil within big business. In *Deepwater Horizon*, John Malkovich depicts BP executive Donald Vidrine, who urged the crew to continue despite safety concerns. Vidrine serves to infuriate the audience by highlighting a culture in which profit is prioritized over safety.

In *Cesar Chavez*, Malkovich also plays the villain, depicting a grower that suppresses farm workers' unionization. He tells other growers,

> We don't have to negotiate. We have to dictate terms ... But you don't negotiate with children. You don't give children every piece of candy in the store. With children, you set the rules, and you make sure they obey.

Similarly, *In Dubious Battle* features Robert Duvall as a paternalistic landowner who disingenuously tells his workers that it "pains" him to cut their wages due to a "bad market." This element of paternalism is also featured in *Bhopal: A Prayer for Rain*. Warren Anderson believes that the Union Carbide plant provides a better quality of life for residents in one of the poorest regions in India. He tells a reporter, "It (Bhopal) stinks okay. We are not making perfume here, but this factory feeds this town." He claims that he is "just a hardworking yank that is trying to make weed-killer" and that "you know we all want a better world. Someone has to break ground to build it." Ultimately, Anderson refuses to be held accountable for the worst chemical poisoning in human history. Despite authorizing dangerous alterations to the plant, Anderson tells an executive, "Well, these people failed us, Shane. We did everything for them, and they let us down. They have no one to blame but themselves now."

Many films in the conspiracy genre feature corporations that hire assassins to carry out murders to meet their goals, including *The Constant Gardener*, *Michael Clayton*, *Rollover*, *The Formula*, *The Pelican Brief*, *Edge of Darkness*, and *The Firm*. The murder-for-hire narrative is classic Hollywood, incorporating suspense and action to corporate wrongdoing narratives. The reality is lacking, as corporations do not have a stable of assassins that carry out contract murders on their behalf. In the current economic and political system, corporations do not have to hire assassins. They already control and pay off politicians, have vast legal teams, and face few domestic and global sanctions. However, there is little doubt that corporations' actions kill, through pollution, unsafe work conditions, harmful drugs, and dangerous products. Corporate malfeasance is often too complex for Hollywood, with layers of transgressors covering up, defending, and rationalizing harmful actions.

Deceit and Denial

A hallmark of corporate wrongdoing is utilizing deceit and denial to minimize or repudiate harm to the public. There are several examples of corporations burying evidence of harm in film and refusing to be held accountable for their actions. Erin Brockovich delivers a memorable line, telling a water board employee, "Hey, Scott, tell me something. Does PG&E pay you to cover their ass ... or do you just do it out of the kindness of your heart?" *The Insider* provides an excellent illustration of how big tobacco lied about their culpability in their product's enormous toll on human health. The viewer is introduced to corporate deniability, with Mike Stern (Robert Harper) colorfully telling the meaning:

> What that is, is tobaccos standard defense. It's the "we don't know" litany. Addiction? We believe not. Disease? We don't know. We take a bunch of leaves, we roll them together, you smoke 'em. After that, you're on your own. We don't know.

Stern further adds that the stratagem is working as they never get sued.

> They don't need the right. They got the money. The unlimited checkbook. That's how Big Tobacco wins every time on everything. They spend you to death. $600 million a year in outside legal. Chadbourne & Parke, Ken Starr's firm, Kirkland and Ellis. Listen, GM and Ford, they got nailed after 11 or 12 pickups blow up, right? These clowns have never ever … Not even once. Not even with hundreds of thousands dying each year from illness related to their product have ever lost a personal injury lawsuit.

Also based on a true story, *Dark Waters* offers one of the best illustrations of deceit and denial. The film tells the story of DuPont chemicals coverup of the harmful effects that Teflon had on consumers. The film also revealed how DuPont poisoned water and lied about it, even sending fraudulent letters to residents claiming it was safe for human consumption. In a poignant scene, Rob Bilott informed his client about the corporate dumping of toxic waste:

> DuPont knew everything. They knew that the C-8 they put into the air and buried into the ground for decades was causing cancers. They knew that their own workers were getting these cancers. They knew that the consumers, too, were being exposed. And not just in Teflon. In paints, in fabrics, in, uh, raincoats, boots.

Similarly, *A Civil Action* illustrates a legal strategy that corporations employ to deny culpability by suggesting that cause of illness is unknowable. After a deposition, WR Grace attorney William Chessman has a conversation with Al Love (James Gandolfini), a receiving clerk at a polluting factory.

Chessman: Al, that water hasn't made anybody sick.
Love: How do you know?
Chessman: I just do
Love: There's a lot of people in my neighborhood that are dead or dyin' Mr. Chessman, from somethin'.
Chessman: Look if I, Uh – If I took a hundred pennies and threw them 'em up in the air, about half of 'em would land heads and the other half tails, right? Now, if I looked around closely, I'd probably find some heads grouped together in a cluster. What does that mean? Does that mean anything? See, no one knows what causes leukemia, Al. No one knows what caused that cluster.
Love: I know what happened. And I know who did it.

Essentially, deceit and denial obscure corporate liability. Corporate proxies take advantage of legal loopholes, plausible deniability, and a lack of stiff or enforceable regulations. The public coverup is aided by massive spending on public relations, corporate law firms, dubious scientific experts, and lobbyists.

Dirty Tactics

Aside from deceit and denial, the corporation will also engage in "dirty tactics" to win legal challenges or cover up wrongdoings. In film, fighting dirty is a standard narrative in the portrayal of corporate harm. This narrative is popular as it also serves to drive the "against the odds" narrative, in which the protagonist faces a seemingly unwinnable battle against a powerful corporation. The "against the odds" narrative is ubiquitous with legal dramas, where corporate law firms employ underhanded tactics to gain an advantage over the protagonist. The corporation will use its vast financial resources to outspend and outmaneuver the plaintiffs' attorneys. Typically, these films feature corporate law firms burying their adversaries with a blizzard of paperwork and files. In a poignant scene, Rob Bilott sits in a room surrounded by mountains of files, slowly and methodically organizing years of documents. Moreover, in almost every legal drama, the plaintiff lawyer is vastly outnumbered by high-paid corporate lawyers. In the aptly titled *Percy vs. Goliath*, a seemingly "out of his element" lawyer battles against Monsanto on behalf of his client. In a particularly comedic scene, Percy's lawyer Jackson Weaver looks toward the ever-growing team of Monsanto lawyers, sarcastically quipping, "looks like they are multiplying." Later in the film, Weaver angrily defends himself after being accused of giving poor legal advice to Percy.

> Are you kidding me? I've been doing everything I possibly can for the last two years, up against a behemoth with … with infinite financial and legal resources. And I'm completely on my own. I've been putting my professional reputation, my career, on the line.

In *The Rainmaker*, Rudy Baylor is fresh out of college and inexperienced. His paralegal, Deck Shifflet (Danny Devito), has failed the bar multiple times. Baylor quips, "there's gotta be a hundred years of law experience sitting at this very table. My staff has flunked the bar exam six times." Conversely, *The Verdict* and *Class Action* feature more experienced lawyers, but they undergo the dirty tactics of high-priced corporate law firms. In *The Verdict*, a corporate lawyer plants a mole to spy on Frank's legal strategy and also deters potential expert witnesses from testifying. In *Class Action*, lawyers commit perjury, conceal witnesses, and destroy evidence of corporate negligence.

Although not unique to the corporate harm genre, lawyers are often depicted as sleazy characters who lack ethics, morality, and, most importantly, compassion. Several films underscore the ruthless nature of corporate lawyers, highlighted by scenes in which a corporate attorney coldheartedly grill and humiliate a witness during a deposition. In *The Good Fight*, a smug lawyer for Big Tobacco mercilessly attacks a cancer patients' father, bringing up an extramarital affair and implying that poor diet led to a cancer diagnosis. Shaken by the attack, the witness refers to the lawyer as a "filth eating jackal." In *Class Action*, corporate attorney Maggie Ward callously discredits a plaintiff by blaming his "slow driving" for an accident that killed his wife and child, even confronting the wheelchair-bound father with graphic pictures of the crash. Another "dirty tactic" is when corporations hire private investigators to harass, follow, and spy on the protagonist. The objective is to "dig up dirt" on their adversaries to discredit or intimidate them. Several films feature this element, including *Erin Brockovich*, *Minimata*, *The Devil Has a Name*, *The China Syndrome*, *Consumed*, and *The Insider*. These threats enhance suspense within the narrative and reveal the insidious nature of the corporation. Erin Brockovich receives a threatening phone call from a "heavy-breathing sicko," Karen Silkwood is mysteriously followed, and Jeffrey Wigand is targeted with threatening phone calls and emails. In *Percy vs. Goliath*, Monsanto hires "seed police" to snoop around properties, while the fictional Clonestra corporation harasses an organic farmer in *Consumed*. In *Dark Waters*, DuPont used political clout to manipulate reports suggesting that substandard farming practices – not toxic dumping— led to the illnesses of the victim's livestock.

The struggle of labor also draws attention to the dirty tactics used by big businesses. The strategies include bribery, utilizing spies, dividing workers, and using goons or thugs to intimidate workers and their allies. Vocal supporters of unionization are offered promotions – less work and higher pay – to cease their union activities. Although the protagonists are approached, they never take the "bait" and remain steadfast in their ideals. However, several films (*In Dubious Battle*, *Bread and Roses*, *Harlan County War*) feature supporting characters that betray the union, working as scabs, spies, or informants. Moreover, the division of workers is a common tactic that companies use to dissuade unionization. The company will use economic uncertainty to divide workers. The French-language film *Germinal* vividly illustrated this realization. There is an extremely poignant scene in which a group of mothers beg for bread – for their starving children – leading to the death of a greedy and unfeeling local merchant. The scene illustrates the sheer desperation of hunger, which capitalists exploit, breaking the spirit of striking workers and their families. Similarly, companies use racial and ethnic division to divide workers, shown in *Matewan*, *The Killing Floor*, and *Norma Rae*. In *Norma Rae*, Reuben Warshowsky speaks to workers about the benefits of a union:

> When they spoke, they spoke in one voice, and they were heard. And they were black, and they were white. They were Irish, and they were Polish. They were Catholic, and they were Jews. And they were one. That's what the union is, one.

In *Matewan*, labor organizer Joe Kenehan arrives in a coal town, imploring the coal miners to allow African American and Italian immigrants into the union:

You think this man is your enemy? Huh? This is a worker! Any union keeps this man out ain't a union, it's a goddamn club! They got you fightin' white against colored, native against foreign, hauler against hauler, when you know there ain't but two sides in this world – them that work and them that don't. You work. They don't. That's all you got to know about the enemy.

Similarly, Mexicans and Filipinos joined together to fight oppression in Cesar Chavez's biopic, while white immigrants and African Americans team up to organize meatpackers in *The Killing Floor*.

Finally, several films feature goons or gun thugs that intimidate union activists and their allies. In *Matewan*, the Baldwin-Felts men begin a campaign of terror against striking coal miners. N*orma Rae* features a group of burly and intimidating supervisors, while *In Dubious Battle* and *Harlan County War* feature characters that use violence to break the resolve of striking workers. In *Cesar Chavez,* a group of thugs attempt to prevent a union protest on a highway, telling the protestors, "We don't need you. We want you out of our country. We want you back to Mexico. Get the hell out of our country", ending with Chavez being stricken with the butt of a rifle, which is ignored by local police. Likewise, in several films, law enforcement is used as an instrument to suppress unionization and workers' rights.

Greed

A good story delivers an explanation for the actions of both the antagonist and the protagonist. In corporate wrongdoing films, protagonists are often driven by noble pursuits, while the antagonist motivations are almost always rooted in greed or the pursuit of profit. The concept of greed is easy for audiences to grasp, and the motives that drive the villain's action or behavior. Greed is even celebrated in some films, with protagonists cheered or idolized by audiences, including films such as *Wall Street* and *The Wolf of Wall Street*, both of which glamorized the criminal activities of the wealthy and the materialistic. In this way, greed is celebrated as a part of the entrepreneurial spirit, in which the American Dream is achieved. Even in films such as *The Big Short*, the audience cheers for venture capitalists to profit from the housing collapse. Ben Rickert (Brad Pitt) laments the predicament:

> You just bet against the American economy … Which means if we're right, people lose homes. People lose jobs! People lose retirement savings. People lose pensions. You know what I hate about fucking banking? It reduces people to numbers. Here's the number, every 1% unemployment goes up, 40,000 people die. Did you know that?

That said, in most corporate wrongdoing films, the concept of greed is tied to a plethora of harmful consequences, usually in the form of illness, injury, or death. This profit at any cost narrative is illustrated in several films, *Deepwater Horizon* provides an excellent illustration, as the oil rig workers sarcastically sing *For the Love of Money*, "Money, Money, Money ... Money!", to explain the lack of safety testing on new cement drilling foundation. The greedy BP executives were concerned that delays hurt the bottom line. *Greed* concludes with the ABBA song, *Money, Money, Money* playing as postscripts detail the exploitation of garment workers and global wealth inequality. Similarly, Conservation officer Dan Lawn (*Dead Ahead*) fittingly sums up the oil industry's response to the Exxon Valdez spill, claiming "all they care about is getting back to shipping oil from that pipeline at 400,000 thousand dollars an hour." Later in the film, he dejectedly pronounces, "what kind of world is it, when the stock market and the bottom line is more important than the land and the sea." In *Fast Food Nation*, an elderly rancher tells the protagonist,

> This isn't about good people versus bad people. It's about the machine that's taking over this country. It's like something out of science fiction. The land, the cattle, human beings. This machine don't give a shit. Pennies a pound, pennies a pound. That's all it cares about. A few more pennies a pound.

While Rob Bilott confronts DuPont's attorney, angrily telling him that:

> You [DuPont] were making too much money. $1 billion a year, just in profit, just in Teflon. And so you pumped millions more pounds of toxic C-8 into the air, into the water, so much so you could actually see it foam.

Although greed is the ultimate motivation, film narratives surrounding antagonists also encompass elements of bullying combined with a pro-capitalist ethos, which paints collective action as socialistic or communistic. For instance, the floor managers in *Norma Rae* and *Silkwood* are on power trips intimidating their workers to ensure the company increases production and profits. That said, the typical Hollywood film – with a focus on individual action to solve problems – allows capitalism's ethos to thrive, as there are very few heroic depictions of collective action and grassroots activism.

The Victim

In Hollywood, crime victims are rarely the focal point of a narrative. There are only a few films that focus exclusively on victims. Mirroring the crime genre, corporate wrongdoing films often neglect victims of crime. Generally, victims are secondary characters that are helpless pawns of large corporations. In this way, victims are used to move the story forward, allowing the audience to feel outraged toward the harms perpetrated by the corporation. Victims garner sympathy and serve as a call to action by the protagonist to achieve justice. However, the true costs of corporate harm are often obscured in Hollywood narratives. That said, the primary narratives within film include (1) Sickness and Disease and (2) Exploitation and Oppression.

Sickness and Disease

The hallmark of corporate harm is sickness, disease, and ultimately death. In film, victims of corporate crime are rarely the primary characters. However, the victim serves as a sympathetic character that compels the protagonist to action. They help thrust the justice narrative to ensure that corporations or their proxies wear the proverbial "black hat" while the protagonist dons the "white hat." Some of the most prominent films depict the devastating impact of toxic dumping on communities, including *Erin Brockovich, A Civil Action, Dark Waters,* and *Minimata.* Erin Brockovich meets with several victims, vividly establishing the harms of PG&E. As such, the story is more than a legal drama, as it shows the real consequences of corporate wrongdoing – cancer, miscarriages, and a variety of severe health issues. In a memorable scene, Erin meets with the Daniels family, whose child has cancer. The sick child serves as a lightning rod for Brockovich to start a crusade against PG&E. Similarly, In *The Distinguished Gentlemen,* an encounter with a young girl with cancer transforms the protagonist from a grifting politician into a crusader that fights a large power company. *A Civil Action* features several children that died from leukemia after corporations poisoned the water. Anne Anderson (Kathleen Quinlan) is the mother of one of the children and steadfastly seeks an apology from the guilty parties. She enlists Jan Schlictman, who is initially reluctant to take the case, telling his partners,

> I mean, I can appreciate the theatrical value of several dead kids. I mean, I like that. Obviously, that's good. But that's all this case has going for it. That's not enough.

Anne plays a supporting yet important role in the film by highlighting the unthinkable grief and horror of the death of a child. In a memorable exchange with the protagonist, she objects to a low settlement of $375,000 per death:

Ann Anderson: When you first came out here, Mr. Schlichtmann, When we first spoke, I told you I wasn't interested in money. What I wanted was an apology from someone for what they did to my son. And you said, "money is the apology." That's how they apologize, with their checkbooks. Would you call this an apology?
Jan: No. The only meaningful apology you're going to get is from me. I'm sorry.
Ann: I'm afraid that isn't meaningful.
Gordon: Mrs. Anderson, You're looking at four guys who are broke. We lost everything in this case.
Ann: How can you even begin to compare what you've lost to what we've lost?

In real life, Anderson, along with grassroots activists and a local newspaper reporter, played a prominent role in uncovering the cancer cluster in Woburn. They educated the residents about toxic dumping, propelled the creation of new laws, and forced companies and politicians to be more accountable for their actions (Kennedy, 1998).

Like *A Civil Action*, *Dark Waters* was a lawyer's story, the victims playing a secondary role in the story. That said, farmer Wilbur Tennant (Bill Camp) plays an essential role as the whistleblower, providing evidence of the harmful effects of toxic dumping on his livestock. In a memorable scene, Bilott confirms that DuPont dumped toxins into the water.

Tennant: Put 'em behind bars. Whole damn lot of 'em, rot in jail.
Bilott: I understand, believe me, but this is a civil case. The most that we could hope for is damages.
Tennant: Don't want no money! Whole damn world need [violently coughing] needs to see what they done.
Bilott: You're right. They should. And it kills me that they won't. But that would mean going to trial and proving that C-8 killed your cows. And every scientist who knows anything about any of this already works for these chemical companies. That's not an accident, Earl. Earl, these companies they have all the money, all the time, and they'll use it. Trust me, I know I was one of them.
Tennant: You're still one of 'em.
Bilott: You can't be serious. You know what I put on the line here?
Tennant: You want a prize? Some medal, cause for once in your life, you took the side of the little guy? Sorry, no prize. All you get is your share of this blood money. And you sleep real good tonight.

Finally, *Minimata* delivers one of the most impactful depictions of the harms of environmental pollution. The film is overflowing with heart-wrenching scenes of victims of mercury poisoning. Coupled with a melodramatic soundtrack, the viewer becomes visually immersed in the tragic consequences. The most compelling moment was a mother lovingly feeding her severely deformed and disabled daughter. Later in the film, the mother and daughter pose for *Tomoko in her Bath*, which is considered one of the most important images in the history of photojournalism. In the end, the filmmakers dedicate the film to "the people of Minimata and the countless victims of industrial pollution around the world and those that stand with them."

To a lesser extent, sickness and disease also appear in films that feature harm to workers and consumers. Although brief, black lung disease has been depicted in several films that feature the struggles of coal miners. In *Harlan County War*, viewers are exposed to the incessant coughing and wheezing of the protagonist's father, who tragically succumbs to the disease. Similarly, *Radium Girls* and *Silkwood* highlight the harmful effects of radiation poisoning, while *Concussion* depicts the harmful effects of brain injuries on athletes. *Fast Food Nation* briefly discussed contaminated food, while *The Good Fight* depicted a young man dying of cancer from the adverse effects of chewing tobacco. *A Private Matter* and *Side Effects* depicted the harmful impacts of pharmaceutical drugs and *Consumed* suggested a link between children's allergies and GMO seeds.

Exploitation and Oppression

In film, corporate exploitation and oppression are visible, generally delivered in highly emotional and poignant scenes. Although rare, some films feature the exploitation of the environment. In *Dead Ahead*, there are haunting images of wildlife struggling to survive after the Exxon oil spill. At the same time, impacts on farm animals are strikingly depicted in *Dark Waters* and *Bitter Harvest*. That said, most portrayals of exploitation and oppression involve workers. History has shown that without pushback from unions, corporations will squeeze their workers by lowering wages, increasing hours, reducing benefits, and minimizing the rights to a safe work environment. In Hollywood, several films highlight poor and dangerous working conditions. In *Norma Rae*, the constant and pounding noise of the textile machines overwhelm the factory floor. The viewer is left to ponder how the characters can function in such a miserable environment. Later in the film, Norma's dad collapses and dies on the line after a heartless supervisor refuses to allow him to take a "break." To organize the workers, Warshowsky delivers a memorable speech,

> Ladies and gentlemen, the textile industry, in which you are spending your lives, and in which your children and their children will spend their lives, is the only industry in these United States that is not unionized. They are free to exploit you and to take away what is rightfully yours. Your health, a decent wage, a fit place to work.

In *Silkwood*, workers exposed to radiation are forced to strip, shower, and undergo invasive medical procedures. The company paid doctor – who was trained as a vet – lied to workers about the actual danger of the contamination. Similarly, the workers in *Radium Girls* are falsely told that their poisoning resulted from a venereal disease, not radium.

The exploitation and oppression of immigrants, migrant workers, and people in less developed countries are major themes in corporate wrongdoing films. *Bread and Roses* provides an intense depiction of primarily immigrant janitorial staff, whose rights are seemingly non-existent. One janitor fittingly tells the protagonist about his theory about uniforms, telling her that they "make us invisible." One of the most powerful scenes is the firing of an elderly cleaner who was late for work.

Mr. Perez: Bullshit, your bus was late. Everybody else was on time. What happened? You know what? You lose a shift.
Teresa: I sorry, sir.
Mr. Perez: Ok, and don't come back here without your glasses. You can't see.
Teresa: I forget in my ...
Mr. Perez: The fuck is goin' on?
Teresa: I'm sorry!
Mr. Perez: Fuckin' elderly and fuckin' blind. You know what? Get some crippled people, some fuckin' lepers. This is a fuckin' business we're running, not a fuckin' camp for spastics. Jesus Christ.

Teresa: I sorry I ...
Mr. Perez: Do yourself a favor, don't come back!
Teresa: Tomorrow ...
Mr. Perez: There is no tomorrow.
Teresa: Sir, please.
Mr. Perez: Don't come back.
Teresa: I need my work.
Mr. Perez: You can never finish on time.
Teresa: I need it ...
Mr. Perez: I don't wanna hear it. You're fired. Get outta here.
Teresa: I need my work.
Mr. Perez: You can't finish on time anyways. Do somethin' else.
Teresa: I need ... I need work. [sobs]

The exploitation of migrant workers is featured in *Syrania* and *Greed*, while *Backstabbing for Beginners* and *The Whistleblower* expose corruption in United Nations, implicitly fueled by corporate greed. *The Constant Gardener* features the exploitation of African HIV patients, illustrating the so-called throwaway victims, whom big pharma use as guinea pigs in a voracious desire for profit. A supporting character, Dr. Lorber (Pete Postlewaite), describes the throwaway victim:

> Free medicines, Mr. Black. Most of them well beyond their sell-by date. The drug companies donate them. It's a tax break for them. Disposable drugs for disposable patients. Out here, they have absolutely no shelf life. Safest thing to do is to incinerate them [throws pills into a burn barrel]. Big pharmaceuticals are right up there with arms dealers. This is how the world fucks Africa, Mr. Black.

Another prominent narrative is economic dependence, in which the corporation controls the economic viability of the area, which allows companies to oppress workers and pollute the environment. The communities rely on these large corporations to provide jobs, even if they are low-paying, unsafe, and harmful to the environment. Corporations attempt to take advantage of economically depressed regions in *Main Street* and *Promised Land*, while *Bhopal: Prayer for Rain* and *Greed* illustrates global economic inequality. Dependency is highlighted in *Dark Waters*, where Parkersburg, West Virginia residents were beholden to DuPont. As the protagonist drives through the community, he sees a DuPont-sponsored community center and sports fields. The viewer is made aware of the immense power that the corporation holds over the residents' day-to-day lives. In *Silkwood*, the characters are fully aware that their economic prospects are limited, forcing them to work in an unsafe nuclear facility. Winston (Craig T. Nelson), a co-worker who serves at that behest of management, explains the mentality:

> It doesn't matter whether you work in plutonium or dog food because they ain't gonna give you a thing, there's nowhere left to go! You close this plant

down, and then what? You're gonna be up in Washington, but we're gonna be down here outta work! Your cancer's a maybe. That's all it is, a maybe.

Essentially, corporate control over the community propels against the odds narrative, in which protagonists also must face a skeptical community that relies on the corporation for economic viability.

Concluding Thoughts

As evident by this book, corporate wrongdoing is not entirely ignored in Hollywood. Some very compelling and informative depictions periodically appear in theatres and on television. That said, depictions of corporate wrongdoing are very rare – just a drop in the proverbial bucket – compared to other portrayals of crime. A perusal of the box office confirms this reality, as only a few films that were discussed in this book enjoy successful runs in theatres. For example, only a handful of films finished in the top 50 at the box office in their release year, including *Erin Brockovich*, *The China Syndrome*, *Norma Rae*, *Silkwood*, and *Civil Action*. *Dark Waters* was one of the most intelligent and entertaining depictions of corporate wrongdoing. However, it finished at #116, earning just over $11 million (Box Office Mojo, 2021). The public is more interested in spending their dollars gazing at superheroes than being exposed to narratives about corporate harm.

However, corporations are not immune from public criticism or shaming. Surveys have shown that Americans are increasingly skeptical about corporations' nefarious actions and detrimental impact (Edelman, 2020; Pirson et al., 2019). In response to the growing public distrust and possible government intervention, corporations endorse the idea of fair, honest, and ethical corporate social responsibility (CSR). The corporate public relations machine argues that big business can be a constructive force in social action and justice. That said, this faux corporate citizenship is not sincere, nor does it realistically address the harms that corporations perpetrate. Corporations are only responsible for their shareholders, using CSR to squeeze out more profits through positive public relations. Corporations will spin their own narrative to dismantle the truth, dismissing facts and concealing evidence to suit their goal of profit maximization. Labeling it a "con," Robert Reich (2021) argues that corporate social responsibility can only be achieved through increasing corporate taxes, breaking up monopolies and creating laws that allow workers input on corporate decision-making.

Moreover, a small but important step is to change the narrative about corporate wrongdoing. The news and entertainment media can challenge existing narratives that depict corporations that engage in wrongdoing as bad apples. Unfortunately, corporate wrongdoing has become normalized as a standard business practice that suffers little to no consequences. In this way, Hollywood can transform audience perceptions and reactions to the growing power of corporations. A compelling film with strong characters, dialogue, and acting can strike an emotional chord with the audience and resonate well past the viewing. Furthermore, a compelling film can highlight corporate harms and serve as a call to action, even being fodder for change. Both *The China Syndrome* and *Silkwood* called attention to safety issues within the nuclear industry. *The China Syndrome* debuted just weeks before the infamous meltdown on Three Mile Island, while Karen Silkwood became a martyr for whistleblowers and anti-nuclear activists. However, her detractors insinuated that she was a disgruntled and drug-addled employee that smeared plutonium in her house to gain sympathy for her plight. Calling it the "Erin Brockovich effect," Sedina Banks (2002) argues that the film could have the same impact as Rachel Carson's *Silent Spring* and Love Canal. Banks claimed that the film brought awareness to water quality, the toxicity of chromium 6, and the health effects. The film has its critics, primarily from industry advocates who claim that adverse health effects were exaggerated. These corporate apologists also claim that, although innocent, PG&E settled through arbitration because they feared jury bias and the power of the attorneys representing the plaintiffs. Of course, the public should be skeptical of claims made by corporate shills, including scientists who are paid handsomely by corporations. After the release of *Brockovich*, the potential health risks of chromium 6 and groundwater contamination were highlighted in the news media, including major newspapers and television shows. The PR team at PG&E downplayed the film, claiming "our general response with respect to the movie is just that we recognize it's a dramatization. It's an entertainment vehicle." They even crafted an internal memo that read, "based on a true story doesn't mean that everything in the story is true." Interestingly, Rachel Carson experienced the same skepticism after the publication of *Silent Spring*. At the same time, Lois Gibbs and Anne Anderson were dismissed as hysterical mothers after calling attention to Love Canal and Woburn, respectively.

Similarly, the PR team at DuPont claimed that "Hollywood is in the business of telling stories. While seeking to thrill and entertain, these stories often stretch facts." They further argue that *Dark Waters* "grossly misrepresented things that happened years ago, including our history, our values, and science." While promoting the film, the real-life Rob Bilott suggested that *Dark Waters*

> is going to really help. I think, with the education process for people that are learning about the chemical in their water ... I think they'll see that it tells us these are things we need to be concerned about and to take action on now.

The film was produced by actor Mark Ruffalo, an ardent environmental activist. Against his Hollywood instincts, Ruffalo claimed that

> to play against the heroism took a lot of discipline for me. I've spoken at these rallies. I've been a rabble-rouser. I've been righteous. But that wasn't the nature of this. So I always had to pull back into thoughtfulness and modesty.
> (Kaufman, 2019)

As such, the protagonist narrative in *Dark Waters* was undoubtedly different from films such as *Erin Brockovich*, *Class Action*, and *A Civil Action*, which depicted charismatic and quick-witted leads.

A cynic may suggest that the repercussions from film are limited, other than bad press and PR headaches. The public image of the corporation initially hurt, but their business practices and profits remain unchanged. Undeniably, the production of film is highly corporatized, and major studios are generally unwilling to produce films that critique big business or be harbingers of social justice. Corporate Hollywood sticks to standard tropes that individualize social problems and solutions. The depictions of corporate wrongdoing serve as "less urgent calls to action than reminders of the long, hard slog required to hold big business accountable" (Vasquez, 2019). That said, it is entirely plausible that a truthful and entertaining depiction of corporate harm can inspire grassroots activists. At the very least, these films may inspire audiences to demand that politicians at every level of government address corporate harms. In this way, corporate wrongdoing can be embedded within the collective consciousness. As it is told, a picture is worth 1000 words.

Reference List

Altheide, D.L., Gray, B., Janisch, R., Korbin, L., Maratea, R., Neill, D., & Van Deman, F. (2001). News constructions of fear and victim: An exploration through triangulated qualitative document analysis. *Qualitative Inquiry, 7*(3), 304–322.

Banks, S. (2002). The Erin Brockovich effect: How media shapes toxics policy. *Environs: Environmental Law and Policy Journal, 26,* 219.

Box Office Mojo. (2021). https://www.boxofficemojo.com/

Buckley, C. (2019, August 14). Why is hollywood so scared of climate change? *The New York Times.* https://www.nytimes.com/2019/08/14/movies/hollywood-climate-change.html

Bunch, S. (2019, January 3). Environmentalists make good movie villains because they want to make your life worse. *The Washington Post.* https://www.washingtonpost.com/opinions/2019/01/03/environmentalists-make-good-movie-villains-because-they-want-make-your-real-life-worse/

Dowler, K. (2003). Media consumption and public attitudes toward crime and justice: The relationship between fear of crime, punitive attitudes and perceived police effectiveness. *Journal of Criminal Justice and Popular Culture, 10*(2), 109–126.

Dowler, K., Fleming, T., & Muzzatti, S.L. (2006). Constructing crime: Media, crime, and popular culture. *Canadian Journal of Criminology and Criminal Justice, 48*(6), 837–850.

Edelman. (2020, January 19). 2020 Edelman trust barometer. https://www.edelman.com/trust/2020-trust-barometer

Kaufman, A. (2019, November 29). How Mark Ruffalo found an outlet for his political passions in 'Dark Waters.' *The Los Angeles Times.* https://www.latimes.com/entertainment-arts/movies/story/2019-11-29/mark-ruffalo-rob-bilott-dark-waters-dupont

Kennedy, D. (1998, December 18). 'A Civil Action': The real story. [Blog Post] *Media Nation.* https://dankennedy.net/woburn-files/a-civil-action-the-real-story/

Loseke, D.R. (2003). *Thinking about social problems: An introduction to constructionist perspectives* (2nd ed.). Transaction Publishers.

Pirson, M., Martin, K., & Parmar, B. (2019). Public trust in business and its determinants. *Business & Society, 58*(1), 132–166

Reich, R. (2021, September 26). Why corporate social responsibility is BS. *The Guardian*. https://www.theguardian.com/commentisfree/2021/sep/26/why-corporate-social-responsibility-is-bs

Surette, R. (2014). *Media, crime, and criminal justice*. Cengage Learning.

Vasquez, Z. (2019, November 25). Can a movie bring about major corporate change? *The Guardian*. https://www.theguardian.com/film/2019/nov/25/dark-waters-movie-dupont-company-toxic-chemicals

Index

A Civil Action 22, 65, 174–175, 180, 185–186, 190
A Corner in Wheat 13
A Dark Truth 167
A Day Without a Mexican 92
A Family Man 104
A Private Matter 115, 186
abuse 87, 100, 143; culture of 100; employment 99; occupational safety 2; of patients 7; patent 3; of power 103; social 11; substance 100
abusive: labor practices 99; language 87; verbally 94
accountability 164; corporate 47; lack of 108, 150
accounting: fraud 4, 146–147; illegal 138
Act of Vengeance 90
activist 64–65, 86, 107, 153, 162, 177; Amnesty International 112, 177; anti-nuclear 190; black power 50; citizen 47; climate 177; consumer 47; environmental 68, 70–71, 79, 149, 190; grassroots 177, 185, 191; labor 16, 46, 94; underground 69; union 176, 183; university student 177; young 117
ageism 104
Alambrista! 92
All the President's Men 160
Allan, A. 18
Allan, B. 149
Allen, B.L. 61
Altheide, D.L. 172
AMA 106
American Bar Association 48
American Civil Rights movement 95
American Dream 7
American Federation of Labor (AFL) 5, 16–17
American President, The 155

American Sociological Association 2–3
An American in the Making 13
An Inconvenient Truth 7
animal rights 7
Anti-Trust 163, 173
anxiety 103; social 18
Any Given Sunday 88
Apartment, The 47
Arab Oil Embargo (1973) 160
Associated Press 114
Association for Motion Picture Producers 41
Atomic Twister 75
auto industry 47–48, 68–69, 100, 107, 117–121
automation 18, 27, 43, 128, 133
Avatar 78

Backstabbing for Beginners 150–151, 173, 188
Bakan, J. 168
Banks, S. 190
Barbarians at the Gate 143, 145, 172
Barricade 167
Beggars in Ermine 26
behavior: aggressive 114; conditions 126; corporate 4, 160; criminal 2–3, 139; driver 117; environmental 78; hostile 87; illegal 6; immoral 47; nefarious 139, 160, 173; restrictions on 23; suicidal 114; unethical 2–3; violent 114
Best Years of Our Lives, The 39
Betsy, The 118
Bhopal: A Prayer for Rain 65–176, 179, 188
Big Pharma 107, 111–115, 177
Big Short, The 22, 139–141, 172, 183
Bilott, R. 66, 175, 180–181, 184, 186, 190
Bitter Harvest 62, 64, 126, 177, 187

Black Fury 31–32, 88
Blacklist, The 8
Blodget, H. 137
Blood of Children, The 11
Blue Collar 54
Bollier, D. 48
Bonger, W. 2
Boomtown 35–36
Bovard, J. 147
Box, S. 6
Box Office Mojo 189
Braithwaite, J. 2–4
Bread and Roses 92, 176, 182, 187
Breast Men 115
bribery 2, 79, 107, 111, 113, 130, 138, 150, 182
Bright Leaf 128, 166
British Academy of Film and Television Arts (BAFTA) 78
Brownlow, K. 8–11, 14
Bruder, J. 168
Buckley, C. 77–78, 177
Bulworth 155, 157–158
Bunch, S. 177
Bureau of Motion Picture Affairs 34
bureaucracy 73, 114, 151; government 64, 98; incompetent 48; inflexible 75; institutional 177; machinations 52; medical 117; office 101; power structure 51; unsympathetic 98
Burley, H. 154
Bush, G.W. 49
business: benefits 19; corrupt 22, 44; crimes of 3; dealings 44, 56; elite 41, 71; ethics 26, 43, 47, 117–118; ethos 4; exploitation 92; fraudulent 48; interests 5, 51, 55, 94, 116, 135, 155; model 6; monopolization 167; power of 18; predatory 143; rivals 24; undervalued 19; unethical practices 2, 27, 127, 148; world 20, 25, 43, 47; wrongdoings 2, 4, 8, 13, 33
Butler, D. 147

Cabin in the Cotton 31
capitalism 2, 22, 24, 26, 29, 36, 40–41, 78, 104, 138–139, 142, 145, 166, 184; consequences of 9; critique of 92; evils of 10; exploitative 2, 31; free-market 178; global 57; greed of 50; ills of 10; industrial 18, 40; laissez-faire 35; machinations of 18; modern 38; speculative 26; survival-era 26; uber- 20, 143; unrestrained 47; venture 19; vulture 98, 145

Carson, R. 7, 59, 190
Carter, J. 64
Cash McCall 47
Casino Jack 155
CCR 108, 152
Center for Responsive Politics 154
Center for the Study of Responsive Law 48
Center for Western Priorities (CWP) 72
Centers for Disease Control (CDC) 106, 127, 135
Cesar Chavez 94, 179, 183
Chan, W. 168
Chaplin, C. 10, 27, 30
cheating 90, 103, 120, 131–132, 143, 173
Chernobyl Nuclear Power Plant 76
Chernobyl: The Final Warning 76
Chicago Race Riot (1919) 95
child labor 2, 8–11, 14, 84
Children Who Labor 11
China Syndrome, The 22, 48, 57, 74, 173–174, 176, 182, 189–190
Chinatown 52–53, 160
Circle, The 164–165, 173
Citizen Kane 38
City Lights 27
Clarion, The 15
class: bourgeoisie 2; business 41; capitalist 9, 24, 29, 31; dismantling of 46; divisions 18; higher 2, 6; laboring 18; landowning 36; lower 3, 8, 92, 157, 172; situation 31; struggles 17–18; under- 6, 13; upper 8, 27, 31, 40; working 2, 8, 15–17, 27, 29–30, 54, 64, 84, 92, 175; world- 146
Class Action 22, 120–121, 174, 181–182, 190
Clean Air Act 48
climate change 70, 76–78, 80, 106; causing 78; consequences of 61; existence of 77; fueling 72
Clinard, M.B. 3–4
Cold War 74
collateralized debt obligation (CDO) 142
collectivization 30
Columbia 23, 57, 135
Coma, The 52
Commoner, B. 59
communism 18, 27–28, 31, 41
Company Men, The 101
compensation 83–84, 86, 108, 150
Comprehensive Environmental Response, Compensation and Liability Act (CERCLA) (1980) 64
Concussion 87–88, 173, 186

Conscious Club 126
conservatism 61
Constant Gardener, The 111, 113, 115, 179, 188
Consumed 123–124, 173, 182, 186
Consumer Product Safety Commission (CPSC) 48
consumerism 61, 78
Contrast, The 17
Conversation, The 51, 160
Cook, D.A. 50
cooperative communes 30
Corner, The 13
corporate: cruelty 43; culture 41, 43, 47, 100, 103–104, 117, 139, 153, 161, 167; downsizing 100–101; mentality 83, 103; welfare 48, 137, 155; wrongdoing 1, 3–8, 19–20, 22, 43–44, 54–55, 57, 65, 69–70, 85–86, 128, 131, 138, 151, 160, 171–172, 174, 176, 178–179, 183–185, 187, 189, 191
corruption 2, 9, 18–19, 22, 29, 44, 47, 49–50, 52, 54, 66, 79, 84–85, 90, 113, 124, 143, 145, 147, 150–152, 159–162, 175, 177, 188; consultants 155; corporate 49, 147; economic 52; global 150; government 48; ingrained 53; political 8, 52, 150, 155, 157; scandal 155; union 45, 54
Country 98–99
crime: corporate 2–6, 20, 22, 138, 163, 185; environmental 70; financial 138; occupational 4, 20, 103; organized 54, 84, 162; of passion 25; public order 171; street 2, 4, 6, 172; study of 3; violent 4, 6; white-collar 1–4, 19–20, 139
Crime of Carelessness, The 12
criminal negligence 92, 119
criminality 1, 4, 6, 19, 23, 142, 172
Croall, H. 106, 122
Croce, N. 23–24, 27, 33, 39, 41, 49, 54, 57
Crooked E: The Unshredded Truth about Enron, The 145, 172
Crowd, The 29
Cry of Children, The 11
Cullen, F. 5
Curry, C. 71

Dallas Buyers Club, The 114
Dark Waters 22, 66, 174, 180, 182, 185–190
Day After, The 74
Day After Tomorrow, The 77

Dead Ahead: The Exxon Valdez Disaster 72, 184, 187
deceit 104, 119, 122, 153, 157, 179–181
Deepwater Horizon 22, 73, 178, 183–184
dehumanization 56, 103
denial 59–60, 157, 179–181
Desk Set 43, 46
Devil Has a Name, The 66, 121, 178
Dickens, C. 40
discrimination 84, 118; racial 85
dishonesty 29, 35, 52, 121, 143
dissatisfaction 103
Distinguished Gentlemen, The 185
divisions 18, 95; ethnic 89
Doctor, The 111
documentary 1, 7, 17, 71, 74, 89, 123, 151
Dogs of War, The 167
Doherty, T. 23–24
Dow Jones 139
Dowler, K. 171
Downsizing 78
drug addiction 27
Duplicity 163
Dusk to Dawn 16

Earth Day 59
East, The 69, 172, 174, 177–178
Ebert, R. 141, 164
ecological: balance 56; concerns 61, 72; disaster 72, 79, 163; responsibility 76; system 59–60
economic: benefits 71, 84; climate 102; collapse 140; consequences 73; corruption 52; costs 122; crises 30, 102; damage 4; decline 69; dependence 188; depression 188; deprivation 77; devastation 140; disaster 92; downturn 99; front 57; growth 137; hardship 36; inequality 137, 155, 188; interest 73; issue 76; justice 22; laissez-faire 29; life 1; policy 31; recovery 31; self-interest 168; structure 23; survival 44; systemic failure 171; theories 30; uncertainty 182; unity 153; viability 188–189
eco-warriors 61
Edelman 189
Edge of Darkness 162, 177–179
Ehrenreich, B. 19
Eller, C. 48
Emerald Forest, The 78
empathy 101, 103, 111
Empire Zinc strike (1951) 46
Employee's Entrance 25
End Poverty in California (EPIC) 30

Index

Energy Crisis (1973) 160
enterprise 24; capitalistic 6, 22, 84; free 29, 166; vigor of 59
entrepreneurial spirit 29, 34, 138, 167, 183
environmental: activist 68, 71, 79, 149, 190; apocalypse 77; behavior 78; concerns 71–72, 162; costs 122; crimes 70; destruction 79; disasters 59; groups 72; harm 60–61; impact 80; issues 59, 61; justice 64; law 65; messages 72, 77; movement 59–60, 71, 177; neglect 18; organization 69; platform 158; pollution 69, 71, 126, 173, 186; problems 62; racism 64; record 147; regulations 59–60, 77; sustainability 78; themes 60; toll 73; violations 72; wrongdoing 60–61
Environmental Protection Agency (EPA) 48, 59–60, 62, 65, 67
environmentalism 59, 61, 72
Epic of the Wheat, The 13
Erin Brockovich 22, 65, 175–176, 179, 182, 185, 189–190
ethics 24, 43–44, 115, 161, 178; business 26, 43, 47, 117–118; corporate 47; lack of 120, 122, 168, 181
Evers-Hillstrom, K. 154
Executive Suite 41–43, 46, 103, 167
exploitation 18, 52, 92–96, 146, 167–168, 177, 187; of animals 125; business 92; corporate 187; culture of 100; of the environment 187; industry 44; of labor 11, 84, 104; of land 45; sexual 10; of workers 7, 46, 84, 92–93, 96, 100, 105, 124–125, 184, 187–188
Exxon Valdez 72, 184

F.I.S.T. 54
Falling Down 133
false advertising 3, 15, 131
False Claims Act 107
Farm Aid 98–99
Fast-Food Nation 177
Federal Film Corporation (FFC) 17
Federal Trade Commission (FTC) 48, 132
Filler, L. 2
film noir 41, 52
financial crash 138–139, 141
Fire Down Below, The 67, 177
Fire in the Amazon 7–79
Fire Next Time, The 77
Fires of Youth 12
Firm, The 161, 179
First Reformed 70–71, 178
Flash of Genius 121

Foer, F. 168
food: adulterated 107, 122, 135; chain 63, 126; communal supply 18; contaminated 5, 63, 123, 178, 186; crime 122; fast 104, 124–126, 132–133; forest 76; genetically modified 19, 123–124; healthy 122; high cost of 14; industry 106, 108, 122–125, 149; intellectual 9; lack of 77; natural 18; organic 122, 124; poisoning 122; preparation 133; prices 14; production 99, 106; rationing 91; rations 18; riots 14; science 124–125; sugary 122; supply 13, 62; tainted 107; unhealthy 106, 122, 132; unsafe 106; workers 124
Food Gamblers, The 14
For His Son 15
Ford Motor Company 5
Foreign Corrupt Practices Act 147
Formula, The 160, 177–179
fossil fuels 72, 77–78, 155
Founder, The 133, 168
Fox Warner Brothers 23
fracking 71, 174; anti- 7; global 71; harm of 177; hydraulic 71; pro- 71
fraud 3, 25, 34, 85, 115, 122, 138, 143, 146, 148, 155; accounting 146; consumer 128; corporate 4, 138–139; criminal 19; documentation 143; financial 25–26, 147, 150; history of 107; purveyors of 53; serious 138; stock 25, 103, 119; violations 147
Free Willy 2: The Adventure Home 73
Freedom of Information Act 48
Friedrichs, D.O. 2
Fugitive, The 113, 115
Fuller, J.G. 74
Fun with Dick and Jane 146

gangster 1, 10, 19, 23, 25–26
Gasland 7, 71
Gates, B. 49, 164, 168
Geis, G. 2–3
General Electric 62
General Motors 48, 62, 117
genocide 7, 167
geopolitical: scandal 151; systems 171
Geostorm 78
Germinal 88, 182
Gerson, J. 60
gig economy 104
Gillam, C. 107
Glengarry Glen Ross 103
global warming 7, 61, 76–78, 80

globalization 83, 122
Gold Is Where You Find It 60
Good Burger 126
Good Fight, The 128, 134, 174–178, 181, 186
Gore, A. 49
government 50–52, 73–74, 113, 122, 138, 140, 151, 155, 163, 191; accountability 47; agencies 2; approval 64; bailouts 137; bureaucrats 64, 98; commission 51; committee 51; conservative 57; contracts 44, 137; corruption 48, 162; cover-ups 111; failure 138; federal 33–34, 44, 72, 107, 117, 139; functions 164: inaction 77; intervention 2, 5, 23, 189; intrusion 152; leaders 76; local 66; mistrust of 160; official 112, 145; oversight 66, 142; policy 7, 71; power 127; quasi 78; response 140; subsidies 147; support 138
Grapes of Wrath, The 96
Gray, A. 106, 122
Great Depression 23, 27–28, 96–98, 118, 166
Great Recession (2007-2008) 100, 102, 138–140, 143, 168
greed 2, 11, 18–19, 26, 29, 32, 34, 40, 52, 57, 103–104, 109, 113, 115, 117–118, 128, 143, 145, 149–150, 159, 161, 166, 168, 178, 183–184; apparent 145; of capitalism 50; celebration of 142; concept of 183; corporate 22, 44–45, 66, 74, 114, 143, 188; culture of 20, 140; excessive 20
Greed 145, 184, 188
Green A. 83
greenhouse: effect 18, 77; gas emissions 62, 76, 80, 106
gun control 7, 155
Gung Ho 101

Hackers 163
Hamilton, M. 25, 48
Harlan County War 89–90, 176, 182–183, 186
Head Office 152
health and safety 5, 84–85, 107
Hearst, W.R. 38–39
heatwave 76–77
Hebberecht, P. 2
Heroes for Sale 27
homelessness 36
homophobia 7
Hospital, The 108

House of Un-American Activities Committee (HUAC) 41, 45–46
How Green Was My Valley 32, 37, 88
How to Succeed in Business Without Really Trying 47
Hubbard, S. 138
Hudsucker Proxy, The 103, 153
Hughes, H. 49, 168
humanity 5, 15, 36, 44, 76, 78, 107, 168
Hungerford, T.L. 154
Hurst, R.M. 23

immigration 8, 92
immorality 5, 23, 30, 178
In Dubious Battle 97, 176, 179, 182–183
Industrial Revolution 62
Informant, The 22, 126, 147, 173–174
Insider, The 22, 128, 130, 173, 176, 179, 182
Inside Job 7
insider trading 19, 44, 103, 138, 148, 166
Intergovernmental Panel on Climate change (IPCC) 76
International Union of Mine, Mill and Smelter Workers 46
International, The 162, 177
It's a Wonderful Life 39–41, 166

Jacobs, L. 10
Jacobson, R. 115
Jobs, S. 49, 168
John Q 117
Johnson & Johnson 5
Joy 97, 168
Jungle, The 9

Kaltenbach, C. 77
Kantor, J. 100
Kaufman, A. 190
Kazan, E. 45
Keefe, P.R. 7
Kennedy, D. 186
Kenney, K. 53
kickbacks 2, 55, 93, 151
Killing Floor, The 95, 176, 182–183
Kindling 10
Koppes, C.R. 34

labor: abusive practices 99; activists 16, 46, 94; agitators 16; anti- 15–16; cheap 133; collusion 54; contract 83; dispute 92; disturbances 15; domestic 83, 104; exploitable 83, 104–105; injustice of 9; laws 86, 96; leaders 2; legislation

33; migrant 92; movement 15–18, 31, 53–54, 96; organized 38; pro- 31–32; protections 100; protest 53; regulations 83; -saving device 28; spy 53; standards 100; strife 38, 46; strikes 97; support of 16; ticket 16; troubles 31, 34; unfair practices 54, 85; union 33, 83, 85, 105; unrest 10, 33, 39; wage 36; wars 53; *see also* child labor
Labor's Reward 17
Last Days of the Lehman Brothers, The 139
Laundromat, The 149, 151, 173
legal: action 121; advice 181; battle 66; challenges 85, 175, 181; crusader 174–175; definition 122; drama 116, 181, 185; experts 149; fight 128, 148; immigrants 93; inexperience 121; loopholes 181; obligations 119; proceedings 175; resources 121, 181; rights 33; sanctions 6; skills 120; strategy 180–181; teams 179; trickery 121; wrangling 66
Lens, S. 15
Little Accidents 91
Llamas, M. 114
lobbying 20, 106–107, 124, 131, 138, 151, 154–156, 159
Locked Door, The 12
Lois Gibbs: The Love Canal Story 64, 177, 190
Lone Ranger, The 167
Looker 19
Lorence, J.J. 46
Loseke, D.R. 171–172
Louisiana Story 60

Main Street 69, 188
Malaspina, A. 127
Man in the Gray Flannel Suit, The 41, 43, 167
Manchurian Candidate, The 19
Margin Call 139, 141, 172
Match King, The 25
Matewan 88–89, 182–183
Mattera, P. 133
Mayer, L.B. 35
McCarthyism 10, 41, 84, 166
Meat Inspection Act 2
medical: benefits 90; bureaucracy 117; care 151; errors 107–108, 111; establishment 52, 108; expert 111; industry 108, 111; litigation 108; malfeasance 109; malpractice 111;

monitoring 175; negligence 109, 111; procedures 187; profession 110; professionals 107–108; studies 116; system 108; team 76; treatment 110
Medicine Man 78
Men of Steel 16
Merchant Mayor, The 14
Metropolis 18
Michael Clayton 67, 69, 126, 179
Milagro Beanfield War, The 94, 177
Mills, C.W. 5
Milov, S. 127–128
Minimata 176–177, 182, 185–186
Mishel, L. 83
Modern Times 27
Mokhiber, R. 4
Molly Maguires, The 15, 53, 88
Money 9
Moneychangers, The 9
money-chase 143
monopolies 13, 124, 138, 149, 189
monopolization 13, 33, 35, 40, 57, 126, 128, 138, 148–149, 164, 167–168
Moore, K. 7, 86
morality 2, 23, 50, 78, 143, 145, 149, 161, 168, 178, 181
mortgage 139–140, 142; -backed securities 141–142; crisis 142; defaults 142; industry 142; loans 139; practices 141; predatory 138; risky 140; securities 142; subprime 139–140; unconventional 139
Mother and the Law, The 17
Motion Picture Alliance for the Preservation of American Ideals 30
Motion Picture Production Code (Hays Code) 23
Mr Mom 100
Mulvey, L. 39
Munby, J. 23

Nader, R. 4–5, 47–49, 107, 116–119, 146, 175
National Association of Manufacturers 13
National Child Labor Committee 11
Naughton, J. 168
Navasky, V.S. 45
Net, The 163
Network 55, 57
Neve, B. 30
New Disciple, The 17
Newman, R.S. 64
Nice Guys, The 68–69, 178
Nichols, B. 7
99 Homes 143

Night Moves 69–70, 177–178
Noakes, J.A. 41
Norma Rae 22, 48, 57, 85, 176, 182–184, 187, 189
North Country 87, 173
North Dallas Forty 88
nuclear 69; accident 20, 61, 74–76, 86; anti- 74, 190; attack 74; disarmament 74; energy 48, 74–75; facility 75, 188; industry 22, 74, 76, 190; meltdown 74, 76, 174; plant 75, 174; power 74–75; testing 74; war 74; warheads 19; weapons 59, 74, 162

occupational diseases 5
Occupational Safety and Health Administration (OSHA) 48
Office Space 101
Oil for the Lamps of China 41–42
oil spill 20, 61, 69, 72–73, 187
Omen 2, The 19
On Deadly Ground 72, 177–178
On the Waterfront 45
Once Upon a Time in the West 167
Our Daily Bread 29–30, 33
Out of Darkness 15
overpopulation 77–78
Owen, N. 40
Oxfam 137, 154

Pajama Game, The 45–46
Pale Rider 167
Parallax View, The 51, 160
Paramount 23, 39, 135
paranoia 50–52, 168
Paranoia 160, 165
Partnoy, F. 25
Pasquale, F. 100
Passaic Textile Strike (1926) 17
Passaic Textile Strike, The 17
patent abuse 3
patriotism 34, 39, 51, 96
Patterns 41, 43–44, 46, 103, 167
Pelican Brief, The 161, 176, 179
pensions 48, 183
Percy vs. Goliath 126, 148, 178, 181–182
Pierce, D. 8
Pirson, M. 189
Pittsburgh 34–36, 166
Places in the Heart 98
Planet Placement Initiative 78
poisoning the public 61
police: authorities 18; brutality 7, 27; procedural 1

pollution 7, 50, 61–62, 67, 69, 77, 118, 178–179; air 61–62, 106; corporate 67, 80–81; environmental 69, 71, 126, 189; human 76; ill effects of 61; industrial 62, 186; industry-driven 80; oil 72; repression of controls 69; toxic 64; water 48, 61, 106
poor working conditions 8–11, 13, 16–17, 22, 85, 89, 94, 99, 125, 133, 168
Pootie Tang 132
Popovich, N. 60
poverty 3, 8, 10, 27, 77, 158; abolishing 95; bleakness of 11; blinding 36; Depression-era 36; extreme 36; -level wages 83, 104; row 23, 25–26, 30; staggering 18; -stricken 27; tenants' 32
Power 158–159
Power of Labor, The 15
price fixing 3, 13, 122–124, 126, 147
Production Code Administration (PCA) 24
profits 16, 33, 38, 42–43, 52, 83, 88, 102, 105, 108, 112–113, 119, 122, 137, 146, 148, 153, 155, 184, 189, 191; annual 147; enormous 19, 48, 62; higher 59; large 19; massive 122, 137; real 146; record 27; short-term 137; substantial 5
Promised Land 71, 174, 177, 188
propaganda 7, 11, 34–35, 40, 60, 77
Public Be Damned, The 14, 25
Public Citizen 107, 114, 116
public relations 38, 55, 71, 75, 87, 106–107, 127, 154, 158, 181, 189
Pure Food and Drug Act (1906) 2, 48
Putney Swope 49, 131

Quiz Show 131–132, 173

rabble-rouser 89, 172, 176, 190
Rabin-Havt, A. 127, 131
racial: discrimination 85; divisions 89, 182; identities 30; minorities 92; rift 95; tensions 95
racism 7, 46, 49, 67, 92, 94, 96, 98; environmental 64; unrelenting 94; virulent 95
Radium Girls 86, 186–187
Rainbow Warrior, The 74
Rainmaker, The 116, 174–175, 181
Reagan, R. 57, 60, 174
Rebovich, D.J. 138
Red Alert 75
Reich, R. 137, 189
River, The 98–99
RKO 23, 39

robber barons 52, 166–168
Robinson, D. 10
Rollerball 18
Rollover 160, 179
Ross, E.A. 2
Rowell, A. 135
Ruffalo, M. 66, 190
Runner, The 73

Safe Drinking Water Act 48
safety: abuses 2; automobile 48, 119; commission 45; concerns 71, 88, 91, 178; conditions 12; consumer 117; device 13, 34; equipment 13, 55, 72, 97; features 55; guarantee of 128; inspection 75; issues 54–55, 84, 190; lack of 90; measures 11–12, 76, 86; occupational 48; patient 108; precautions 12; protocols 85, 92, 96; public 74; records 47, 86, 118; reform 12; regulations 64; report 120–121; research 117; right to 107; shafts 34; standards 66, 86, 89; testing 184; vehicle 48; worker 90; workplace 4
Sainato, M. 84
Saks, M.J. 107–108
Salt and Fire 79, 178
Salt of the Earth, The 46, 92
Schatz, T. 39
Schindler, C. 26, 33
Schurenberg, E. 140
Schwartz, J. 147
Service Employees International Union (SEIU) 93
sexism 7
sexual: advances 100; assault 89; depravity 118; exploitation 10, 94; harassment 25, 85, 87; homo- 118; immorality 30; innuendo 23; relationship 94; shenanigans 118; suggestive 23
Shane 167
shareholders 1, 4–5, 42–44, 83, 86, 102, 137, 140, 189
Shor, F. 49
Side Effects 114–115, 186
Silkwood 22, 85–86, 173, 184, 186–190
Skyscraper Souls 24
Snowpiercer 77–78
Soak the Rich 166
social: abuses 11; anti- 2; anxiety 18; causes 7; change 7; commentary 10, 13, 18, 27, 61; conflict 33; conscience 65; consciousness 7, 27, 41, 124; construction theory 171–172; contexts 1; crises 30; critique 8, 24, 61, 171; disaster 92; drama 33; factors 172; ills 8; inequality 18, 27; injustices 7; issues 7–8, 48, 57, 76, 171; justice 6–7, 10, 22, 118, 171, 189, 191; landscape 47; life 1; meaning 54; media 69, 71, 124, 135, 164–165, 168; messages 37, 61; misfits 70; questions 118; reality 171; reform 8; relevance 161; responsibility 189; sanctions 6; sentiment 10; standing 34; statement 73; status 3; unrest 28
socialism 10, 84, 157
Sokol, K.C. 127
Solid Gold Cadillac 44, 46
Soylent Green 18, 77
Speri 138
Steigerwald, B. 91
Stein, L. 96
stock fraud 25, 103, 119
stolen valor 27–28
Strike at Coaldale, The 16
strikes 10, 15–17, 27, 33, 38, 46, 88–90, 93–94, 97, 99; -breakers 15–16, 33, 54, 89; vocal 89; workers' 8, 16
Struggle, The 16
Surette, R. 171–172
Sutherland, E.H. 2–3, 118
Svoboda, M. 77
Sweet Girl 113, 177

Taffin 67, 177
Take Shelter 78
Taubes, G. 106
Taxi Driver 50, 71
Thalidomide 115
Thank You for Smoking 130, 134, 155–156, 172
Thatcher, M. 57
The 33 91, 172
theft 138–139; attempted 166; corporate 138; wage 84, 99
theory 51, 87, 187; differential association 3; murder 86; *see also* social
There Will Be Blood 167
Thomson, D. 53
10,000 Black Men Named George 94, 176
Threads 74
Thunder Bay 60
Titicut Follies 7
Tlis, F. 76
tobacco industry 127–130, 134–135, 173
Tombs, S. 139
Too Big to Fail 139–140

toxic 86; assets 138, 140; chemicals 4, 63–65, 70; contamination 62; corporate culture 100, 103; dumping 64, 66, 69, 72, 182, 185–186; dump site 70; gases 62; levels 66; poisoning 64; pollution 64; salt flat 79; sludge 66; substance 86, 126–127; waste 61, 64, 66–67, 69–70, 180
Triangle Factory Fire Scandal, The 96
Tucker: The Man and His Dream 119
20th Century Fox 37, 57

unemployment 27, 30, 183; chronic 69; mass 118
unethical business practices 2, 27, 127
unionism 84, 95
United Artists 23, 30, 57
United Farm Workers (UFW) 94
United Mine Workers of America (UMW) 89–91
United Nations (UN) 76, 79–80, 87, 150–151, 188
Universal Pictures 23, 135
unsafe products 13, 107, 135
Up in the Air 101
US Environmental Protection Agency (EPA) 48, 59–60, 62, 65, 67
US Food and Drugs Administration (FDA) 114, 116

Vasquez, Z. 191
Verdict, The 111, 174–175, 181
vertical integration 33
Vice 77
vigilante 1, 157, 176–177
violence 4, 6, 16, 45, 49, 54, 88, 95, 97, 113, 160, 183; depictions of 23; excessive 72; gang 107–108; graphic 23; gun 7

Wages of Fear 44
Wagner Act 97
Waldorf Declaration 41
Walker 167
Wall, M. 154
Wall Street 9, 49, 83, 138, 140, 142, 146; Banking 100; Crash (1929) 27
Wall Street 19, 103, 183

Wall Street: Money Never Sleeps 140
WALL-E 61
Walton, B. 64
wartime trade violations 3
Watergate 50–51
Waterworld 77
Weapons of Mass Distraction 145
Welles, O. 38–39
Wheels 117
Which Way Is Up? 53
whistleblower 22, 50–51, 75, 85–87, 114, 124–126, 128, 132, 149–151, 161–162, 172–174, 176, 186, 190
Whistleblower, The 87
White Mile 103
White Terror, The 14
white-collar workers 43, 85, 100
Why? 9
Wild Boys of the Road 27
Wilson, W. 2, 11
Wilt, D.E. 166
Wilton, S. 148
Wind Against the Everglades 61
Wizard of Lies, The 19–20
Wolf of Wall Street, The 19–20, 103, 183
Woman that God Sent, The 11
Woman's World 43
Women Strike For Peace 74
workers' rights 49, 84, 96, 105, 155, 176, 183
working conditions 16, 93, 95, 105, 118–119; better 15; dangerous 12, 38, 46, 53, 84–85, 89, 187; hazardous 12, 92; honorable 95; horrible 9; poor 8–11, 13, 16–17, 22, 83, 85, 89, 94, 99, 125, 133, 168; sweatshop-type 84; unfair 54, 96, 173; unsafe 91
work–life balance 104
Workman's Lesson, The 13
World Gone Mad, The 25
World Health Organization (WHO) 106, 135
World War I 95, 98
World War II 33–34, 39, 59, 62, 84, 166
wrongful conviction 7

Zinn, H. 16

Printed in the United States
by Baker & Taylor Publisher Services